EMERGENT VOICES OF SOUTHEAST ASIAN WOMEN NOVELISTS

EMERGENT VOICES OF SOUTHEAST ASIAN WOMEN NOVELISTS

BN Joshi

MD PUBLICATIONS PVT LTD
NEW DELHI
www.mdppl.com

Published by:

MD Publications Pvt Ltd
"MD House", 11, Darya Ganj,
New Delhi - 110 002
Phone : +91-11-45355555
E-mail : contact@mdppl.com
website : www.mdppl.com

ISBN: 978-81-7533-308-6

Published and Printed by Mr. Pranav Gupta on behalf of **MD Publications Pvt Ltd** at JJ offset Printers, Delhi.

Preface

Although not as well known as many Western female authors, South Asia women writers have produced an incredible collection of writings, many done under extreme and potentially dangerous circumstances. Early South Asian literature has been dominated largely by male writers people like R.K. Narayan, Mulk Raj Anand, Nirad Chaudhuri and, more recently, V.S. Naipaul and Salman Rushdie. Early women writers include Anita Desai, Nayantara Sahgal, Attia Hosain, and the emigré, Ruth Prawar Jhabvala. Since the 1980s a number of new writers have come up, who are often included, for example, in publications like the New Yorker special issue or in Rushdie's recent anthology.

More recent women writers from South Asia have been put into two kinds of "camps," if one can call it that: one, "indigenous" writers from India, Pakistan, Sri Lanka, and two, South Asian-American writers, immigrant writers, of whom Bharati Mukherjee and Chitra Divakaruni, who has published a collection of stories called Arranged Marriage, are the best known. Of course, currently the best-known Indian woman writer is Arundhati Roy, whose book The God of Small Things received the Booker Prize in 1997. There are also, of course, many second - and third-generation South Asian women writers from Britain such as Meera Syal. So what we have is not only a national phenomenon, but also a diasporic phenomenon. What comes out of all this, then, is a combination of concerns that have to do with post-colonialism and the history of colonisation, but also its consequences, migration and diaspora.

We can talk about gender with regard to male writers, too, most certainly, but with women writers, a whole different set of concerns emerges. With regard to feminism and nationalism, one of the classic problems is that for women writers, and for feminists as well, if you criticize traditional forms of cultural practice, including patriarchal societies, or religious and ethnic groupings, you are often attacked for not fitting into the colonial nationalist project. This is something Arundhati Roy takes up in her book. But the whole question of setting up a gender critique of patriarchal systems is something that becomes very problematic for women writers, particularly when they are seen as allying themselves with so-called white feminism.

Recently, in the work of post-colonial critics like Lata Mani and Rajeswari Sunder Rajan, a new or at least a slightly different issue that comes up is the question of colonial legacies for women in post-colonial national discourse. The diasporic writers we're looking at often describe very new problems and circumstances. They often talk about how enabling it can be for women to be in a different kind of community.

I am very grateful to Mr. Pranav Gupta, Director of MD Publications Pvt Ltd, New Delhi, for his kind cooperation and support for this book.

BN Joshi

CONTENTS

	Preface	*v*
1.	Women Novelists in Modern Malay Literature	1
2.	Novels in English by Singaporean Women	57
3.	Filipino Women Novelists and their Novels	107
4.	Novels by Indonesian Women	153
5.	Emergence of Women Writers in Thailand	185
6.	Novels by Vietnamese Women	229
	Bibliography	273
	Index	277

1

Women Novelists in Modern Malay Literature

FEMINIST CRITIQUE OF THE SEXUAL DISCOURSE OF THE MODERN MALAY NOVEL

In order to problematize how use of language is at the center of the discussion on explicit sexuality in the modern Malay novel, here it will depart from Orwell's (1945) point that the decay of language marks the decay of civilization and explicate the role of language in debates on political correctness as presented by Deborah Cameron (1995b). The relationship between language and civilization has been discussed at length by George Orwell in his essay Politics and the English Language (1945). Orwell argues that the decay of a civilization and the decay of its language are related, and that furthermore, the decay of a language can be traced to political and economic influences.

Whilst it is clear that modern Malay literature has evidently been influenced by the political and economic climate of the country, I propose that the explicit sexual discourse found in the works of Malay authors such as Shahnon Ahmad is not only politically incorrect, but needs to be interrogated for its potential conflict with definitions and ethics of Malay literature which carries the burden of being located within the larger Islamic literature.

POLITICAL CORRECTNESS AND LANGUAGE USE

How does the issue of political correctness fit into a discussion of what is literature? As a form of verbal hygiene, political correctness is a unique instance in sociolinguistics whereby prescriptivism triumphs over descriptivism. In other words, it is an example of society shaping language, instead of language shaping society. Before we look at how this can be applied to a discussion on definitions of literature, this chapter will begin with a critique of chapter four of Cameron's (1995) book Verbal Hygiene, titled "Civility and its Discontents: Language and 'Political Correctness'".

In the chapter, Cameron unpacks the term "political correctness" rigorously and explores the idea that "political correctness" is seen as a worrying manifestation of the 1990s zeitgeist (the spirit of the age). In doing so, she not only questions where the information or examples of "political correctness" are coming from, but also connects them to language use and raises the more important question of "why the illiberalism, extremism and general absurdity of radical projects should so frequently be evoked through stories about their verbal hygiene practices". In other words, why so much dispute over "mere words"?

What she is suggesting here is that although it is obvious that the "political correctness" debate is more than only about language, the conflicting views about language itself is a worthy area of investigation for understanding how language works and how it ought to work. Arguments about definitions of Malay (Islamic) literature, when juxtaposed against the bigger question of 'what is literature', can also be seen to contribute to the prescriptive versus descriptive debates on language. Is Malay literature by nature didactic and therefore prescriptive? If so, does it not limit what Malay literature is?

Literature can be seen as a form of resistance to such practices of verbal hygiene that of prescribing what should or should not be used in our language. Cameron perceives that the so-called "politically correct" are known for their insistence on replacing usage which they deem insulting and objectionable to various "minorities". Well-known examples are high school girls becoming "women", mankind becoming "humanity", disabled people becoming "physically challenged" and black people in the United States becoming "African-Americans".

This "war of words" has been going on for more than forty years or so, starting with feminists introducing new pronouns and titles such as "Ms. A, chairperson of B" (cited in Cameron 1995: 18) followed by other embattled groups such as ethnic and sexual minorities, older people, and people with disabilities opening or re-opening similar fronts. What Cameron further questions and then answers is why is there such resistance to this linguistic change. She also criticizes what she calls "simplistic statements by linguists" to explain this phenomenon.

This includes Crystal's (1984) assertion that the "feminist campaign against sexist language was among the most successful instances of prescriptivism in living memory" (cited in Cameron 1995: 18) and Cheshire (1984) putting the success of non-sexist language down to "natural linguistic evolution in the face of social change." Alternatively, Cameron argues that this kind of linguistic change should be of great interest to linguists due to the fact that although at one level anti- sexist and anti-racist verbal hygiene practices are obviously about non-linguistic matters of political belief or allegiance, they are also about the nature of language itself and about people's conceptualisations of language.

According to Cameron, this unfortunately tends to go undiscussed because of the over-simple assumption that 'language reflects society', and that movements for linguistic change are common-sensically represented as merely parasitic on movements for social change; at the same time they are felt to be a superfluous embarrassment to those movements, since any social change will 'naturally' produce linguistic change. (1995: 118) Here, again Cameron questions why so many people so deeply resent campaigns against sexist, racist, ageist and ableist language and suggests that objections to linguistic reform are rooted in the general illusion that language (English in this case) can be neutral, that a term like "chairman" is neutral.

An even more fundamental illusion according to Cameron is that speakers have total control over the meaning of their own discourse – that when we speak, we engage in individual acts of will whose outcome, ideally, is to communicate our own unique intentions. Yet another cherished illusion highlighted by Cameron (1995:120) is that "although my utterances express my own unique intentions, the linguistic code through which those intentions were 'put' into words is unproblematically shared by other speakers of my language". Thus, again, "this implies that someone who fails to recognise what I 'really mean', or who imputes to me intentions I do not in fact have, is not only in error but in breach of universally accepted rules".

These illusions are closely linked to the idea of language as a unifying thread in society, that ultimately there is a common language, a neutral and universal language and the emergence of so-called "political correctness" may, observes Cameron, be a challenge to this. "It pushes to the limit established beliefs about what a language is, or ideally should be and therefore it causes considerable anxiety". Thus, it is clear that the new politically motivated verbal hygiene practices assumes that language is not just a medium of ideas but a shaper of ideas; that it is always and inevitably political; and that the 'truth' someone speaks may be relative to the power they hold. And to Cameron, it is this set of assumptions, rather than the mere intention to substitute one set of terms for another, that makes the question of "politically correct" language so explosive.

DEFINITIONS OF MALAY LITERATURE

It is clear that the issue of political correctness is more than simply a matter of changing unacceptable terms to those more acceptable to society. To consider Malay literature in the light of verbal hygiene practices, such as one that is raised by the issue of political correctness. This leads to an examination of sexuality as represented in Malay literature as a potential area that resists definitions of political correctness and verbal hygiene practices. It is therefore pertinent, at this juncture, to explore the confusion demonstrated by Malay authors as they struggle to assert an Islamic identity in their writings, particularly exemplified by the works of one of its more prominent national laureates, Shahnon Ahmad.

This confusion can be seen in the tendency towards discomfiting descriptions of sexuality and sexual behaviour in the discourse of modern Malay literature, paradoxically while Islamic values is simultaneously being promoted and such explicit sexual expressions and sexist language can be defined as being politically incorrect in view of the premise that Malay/Islamic literature emphasizes "beautiful language and beneficial content". Ungku Maimunah (2003:54-55) explains that: in general sastera ("literature") is used to connote language that is beautiful and content that is good or beneficial. Notwithstanding the two aspects singled out, the emphasis on language, in particular beautiful language, seems to dominate Malay understanding of literature. Beautiful language is seen as an integral component whose presence gives validity to a text's claim to literariness.

This understanding of what is literature within Malay contexts helps to define Malay literature and continues to be used as a measurement of what should and should not be accepted within the Malay literary canon. Ungku Maimunah (2003:55) points to the emphasis on language, and not content, in the Malay understanding of literature as in Kamus Dewan, which defines literature as "language used in books, not colloquial or bazar language". This definition, she argues, "not only emphasizes language and its employment but also distinguishes language that is not beautiful as 'not literature'" (ibid.). Kamus Dewan however is clear that aesthetics refers to language or beautiful language, and is significantly silent on the question of content.

With regard to content, whilst concession for its presence is made, the elaboration is at best general and is content with the insistence that it should be "beneficial". However, of more importance is the glaring absence of a demand for a particular kind of content in a work before it can be designated as literature. The explicit references to sexual acts and sexuality in the modern Malay novel may thus be perceived as transgressing the definition of literature above by the use of language that disturbs the sensibilities of the Malay Muslim reader and which displays ambivalence in its moral content. Interestingly, it is Shahnon Ahmad himself, criticized for his works which have been claimed to border pornography, who postulates that – a legitimate literature is a moral literature, and who is the first critic of Malay literature who is responsible for the location of Malay literature within the larger Islamic literature and has since created continuous polemics on the matter, both through his critical and creative works.

SEXUALITY AND MALAY IDENTITY

Public concerns over the increasing preoccupation of the population, particularly in Malay society, with sex, can be seen to escalate with an increasing awareness of the way that sex is used especially to sell the news. The popular women's magazine Jelita in its August 2004 issue addresses the issue of detailed reports on sex related cases in the Malaysian media. News reports on high profile sex crimes such as the murder of Noritta Samsudin are sensationalised stories highly newsworthy in media practice. Norhaizan Ahmad questions the need for the description of every little detail of the case including the sexual act itself, without apology and without consideration of its effect on the mind of society. By such detailed and explicit description of the internal and external physical condition of the individual, Norhaizan argues that through such reporting, the media has indirectly become a legal source of pornographic material. Malay sexuality has often been assumed to be kept under wraps and talked about in "hushed tones".

In exploring the connection between Malay sexuality and identity, Tope (2004) finds that: ... there is relative silence on the invisible aspects such as sexuality. To begin with, sexuality has a confidential, secret nature that keeps it invisible. This invisibility is usually personal in nature. In traditional Malay societies, it is a topic generally avoided, elided, or often dismissed as a non-issue. Regarded as a taboo subject, or a necessary evil at best, sexuality seems to be regarded as a discomfiting, discomforting, do-we- have-to-talk-about-it topic meant for hushed whispers or instant dismissals. Tope further observes that this silence has influenced literature written by Malay writers (her research is limited to creative works in English) to the effect that, there seems to be among Malay writers a hesitation, refusal or inability to express the sexual self. I can only conjecture explanations for the silence.

Perhaps it is because of Islamic sanctions against the use of the human body for aesthetic purposes. Or perhaps Malay traditions impose strict cultural control on the sexual self. Whatever the reason, Malay sexuality may be invisible not only in the personal sense but also in the ethnic sense. The reticence creates a hushed air around this identity site, implying the hidden, buried nature of the Malay sexual self. Contrary to Tope's observation, scholars of Malay literature have asserted that far from being taboo, sexuality has unassumingly become an important ingredient in modern Malay literature, thus allowing modern Malay literature to become a space for the explicit expression of sexuality, revealing a tendency to cater for the prurience of the Malay reader. On this, Mohd Zariat Abdul Rani (2004: v), posits "manifestations of sex act as additional ingredients to spice up the text".

ISLAM AND MODERN MALAY LITERATURE

As a country geographically rooted firmly in the East, Malaysia finds itself still shaky in trying to define itself as a modern progressive nation, while retaining its Eastern identity, led by a government that operates within the framework of an "Islamic government". Islam is the official religion of Malaysia, meaning that its rituals are observed during state official functions. Within the majority Malay Muslim community in Malaysia, fears have arisen about the dilution of identity and consequently the loss of spirituality as Malays face the onslaught of rapid modernization.

The process of modernization has resulted in a dichotomous position for the Malays as they struggle for a balance in their spiritual (good) and material (evil) self. This dilemma can be seen in the Malay Muslims' tendency to Islamise practices they deem as non-Islamic or secular. Modern Malay literature can be seen to have undergone, or rather, is still undergoing, this process of Islamization whereby it locates itself within the bigger pool of modern Islamic literature.

Mohd. Affandi Hassan (1992:3), however, cautions against such a superficial Islamization of Malay literature, arguing that such superficial or artificial treatment may produce writers labelled as Islamic who produce works that are anti-Islamic or which have even inadvertently secularised Islam. Modern Malay literature exists within the context of modern-day Malaysia, an Islamic but multicultural country. Whilst labelling itself as an Islamic multicultural nation is not unproblematic in itself, Malaysia also struggles as a nation balancing its Islamic identity with the rapid material and social developments brought about by its pursuit of a "developed nation" status by the year 2020.

POLITICAL CORRECTNESS IN LITERATURE

Malay political correctness and language use have not been an issue that has received much attention from language scholars. While the issue of the derogatory term 'keling' in reference to the Indians in Malaysia, and which was included in the Kamus Dewan became an issue a couple of years ago, leading to Dewan Bahasa dan Pustaka being accused of promoting racist discourse, not much have been talked about it in relation to sexist language or sexuality. The opinion that the Malay language is not sexist is often explained away using the fact that the third person pronoun 'dia' in Malay does not indicate sex, leading to the simplistic conclusion that Malay language does not contain prejudicial elements or gender bias. I would propose here that political correctness in the Malay language should be a concern, especially when Malay language use itself reflects the Malays' insensitivity towards language use that can be seen as insulting or offensive. Thus, politically incorrect occurrences in Malay would be dependent on the contexts of use and generally not embedded within the system.

It is the stand of this chapter that sexually explicit language in modern Malay literature can be read as a form of political incorrectness. The use of overtly sexual language in modern Malay novels reveals a preoccupation with sex and sexuality within Malay society. As a literature that claims to continue in the tradition of Islamic literature, Malay literature that uses explicit language in its depiction of sex and sexuality reflects a confused identity paradoxically opposed to Islamic practice and Islamic literary traditions. In order to problematize how use of language is at the center of the discussion on explicit sexuality in the modern Malay novel, I will depart from Orwell's (1945) point that the decay of language marks the decay of civilization and explicate the role of language in debates on political correctness as presented by Deborah Cameron (1995b).

The relationship between language and civilization has been discussed at length by George Orwell in his essay Politics and the English Language (1945). Orwell argues that the decay of a civilization and the decay of its language are related, and that furthermore, the decay of a language can be traced to political and economic influences. Whilst it is clear that modern Malay literature has evidently been influenced by the political and economic climate of the country, I propose that the explicit sexual discourse found in the works of Malay authors such as Shahnon Ahmad is not only politically incorrect, but needs to be interrogated for its potential conflict with definitions and ethics of Malay literature which carries the burden of being located within the larger Islamic literature.

Perhaps, unfortunately for him, Shahnon Ahmad's most well known (and presumably most widely read) novel is his notorious Shit (1999). Written to express his disgust at the political scenario in Malaysia, Shahnon wrote to shock and successfully did so. The use of such openly taboo language in a creative work written by a national laureate helped sell the book; the Malaysian public was certainly fascinated, despite at the same time being repelled by it. The novel's title, Shit pukimak created a furore and shocked the sensibility of a nation undergoing what was seen as possibly the biggest political upheaval that Malaysia had ever experienced. This chapter looks at Shahnon's works that have clearly juxtaposed religiosity with sexuality, namely Tok Guru, Ummi & Abang Syeikhul and TIVI.

A feminist reading reveals a categorization of women and their sex and sexuality through consistent dehumanisation of the woman's body and the sexual act itself. Shahnon's works illustrate the trend in Malay literature in dealing with morality whereby the wakil rakyat ("parliamentarians/state councillors/people's representatives") were particularly targeted for their indulgence in illicit sex while religious leaders were depicted as hypocrites who used religion to further their own interests, namely their polygamous inclinations. In short, all figures of authority were similarly cast as negligent of their duty, selfish and corrupt, and held directly responsible for the plight of the poor Malay masses. Two main labels in the categorization in Shahnon's works are the categorization of women as soil that needs to be planted with seeds or land that needs to be farmed, and also as garments for men to wear. In Tok Guru, Shahnon depicts the Malays' desire to be close to God and to strengthen their piety.

The novel is told from the first-person perspective of the members of a family who seek the guidance of a pious person, Tok Guru, in practising their religion. As the story progresses, it is clear that the brand of religiosity taught by Tok Guru is one that centres on sex and sexuality through the abuse of the privilege of polygamy amongst men. In the novel, to have more than one wife is the measurement of religiosity, the more wives you have (maximum four), the more religious you are. And for women, their ultimate test of religiosity is in their involvement in helping their husbands find new wives. Early in the novel, as they adjust to a more religious lifestyle under the guidance of Tok Guru, Mami (the wife) is pressured with the task of finding Nana (the husband) a new wife.

The categorization of women's sexuality begins with Mami's question to Nana, "Nana nak cari yang jandakah atau anak dara?" The metaphor of the wife as soil in which seeds are planted continues throughout the novel, alongside the metaphor of husband and wife as garments for each other to wear. The second novel analyse is Ummi & Abang Syeikhul, which is clearly similar to Tok Guru in representing Shahnon's perception of the sexual exploits of a religious leader (albeit via the legal contract of marriage), and the excesses and corruption of polygamy as practised by the religious leader. "Strikingly, both Tok Guru and Ummi dan Abang Syeikhul are about false religious teachers with overwhelming sexual appetites". In the novel, a young woman finds that her desire to be close to God through her husband, the leader of a religious commune, means pandering to her husband's desires in the marital bedroom, be they of a violent and abusive nature.

Ummi, the protagonist, discovers her own sexuality and comes to the realisation that the role of a wife is mainly to cater to a husband's sexual desires, which in turn will make him a better 'man of God', enabling him to concentrate on his missionary work better outside of the marital bed. Ummi is content to serve her husband with her body because this will sooth his nafsu and he can become a better missionary; her service will ensure her of a secure position in heaven as his sexual partner there as well. Ummi's naivety in accepting her husband's teachings as she strives to be a pious woman creates the effect of foregrounding her husband's corruption and abuse of religion.

Again, as in Tok Guru, the metaphor of the woman as agricultural soil is used by Shahnon in explaining the sexual act between husband and wife. That sex with a religious man tends to be of a violent and abusive nature is repeatedly described in the novel by contrasting Abang Syeikhul's behaviour inside and outside of the marital bed. Such violent behaviour is depicted as the norm in such a marriage and is crucial for sexual gratification, and is a shadow of the gratification to be enjoyed in paradise in the Hereafter.

The repeated use of such well known metaphors by Shahnon Ahmad means that for the Malay reader, the sexual scenes become as explicit as if they are described literally, due to the metaphors being habitualized in the discourse. In Tivi (1995), Shahnon Ahmad admits that he at times crosses the border over to pornography. Different from Tok Guru and Ummi & Abang Syeikhul, Tivi tells the story of an ordinary family living in a rural village whose life is disrupted by modernization through the influence of the eldest daughter of the family, Chah, who works in a factory in a big town, Sungai Petani, and who buys a television for the family. In Tivi, the television set which represents the modernisation of the Malays easily brings about change in the lifestyle of the family, taking them further away from religion and God, leaving them obsessed with sex and sexual activities, and even leading to incestuous acts between the father and the two daughters.

The explicitness in the discourse of Tivi can be seen particularly in descriptions of the daughters' bodies as the characters' senses (particularly the father's) become increasingly heightened through much contact with pornographic material on the television, and through the eldest daughter Chah's provocative behaviour. The description becomes more explicit as Mat Isa becomes more aware of her daughter's body.

Tope (2004) explains such depictions (as illustrated by Shahnon's novels) as "clearly showing that Malay female identity is closely linked not only to the maternal or servile, but also to functions of the body that are in the purview of sexuality" and more importantly, that as prostitutes, midwives, abortionists, victimized wives, favored mistresses, etc., Malay female identity is sexually defined. Also, except for the femme fatale, the women in these portrayals are disempowered, something that Malay women share with other women in communities ruled by patriarchy.

DEFINITION OF MALAY ISLAMIC LITERATURE

Whilst the novels analysed in this chapter are those by Shahnon Ahmad, it is interesting to note that it was Shahnon who started spotlighting the need for Malay literature to realize its role as Islamic literature. He defines Islamic literature as literature produced in the name of Allah and for humankind. The two expressions, "in the name of Allah" and "for humankind", are closely interrelated, for when we produce literature in the name of Allah, we believe automatically, without any doubt, that everything which Allah commands of us (through the Quran and the Sunna) is for the well-being and happiness of human beings.

As such, we can conclude that Islamic Literature is literature in the name of Allah and for the good of all humankind. Ungku Maimunah traces Islamic influence on traditional Malay literature and explains that this is not something new, although the 'dakwah' movement of the 1960s and 1970s meant a revival of Islamic awareness in Malay literature. Literary writings of the early years mapped out a moral order that was unmistakably underpinned by Islam, thereby establishing in the clearest terms possible the Islamic component of Malay identity.

Added to this was the geographical boundary of the rural scene which became a pivot of the Malay world and from which it drew its strength, both religious and cultural. In articulating this world, the literature was informed at all times of the need to protect and preserve this world from the onslaught of the "West" and its decadent values. This was the cry of the Malay masses for which the literary expression was a legitimate platform. She explains further the aim of Sastera Islam (Islamic Literature), that by giving witness to God's oneness and truths as laid down in the Quran and the Traditions, Sastera Islam sought to invite its readers to "return" to Islam and to achieve Allah's grace.

With its clear moral orientation it lent support to a literary form which sanctioned the use of literature for social purposes, a tradition inherent in Malay literature which had unstintingly charted the ebb and flow of the country's history. This development in modern Malay literature led to stories which bore the imprint of Sastera Islam … thus highlighted instances of transgressions such as syirik ("attributing divine qualities to other than Allah"), illicit sex, corruption, dereliction of duty and the like, and the consequences of these lapses which included chaos, misfortunes, ignoble ending or such like catastrophes.

It is thus clear that defining Sastera Islam in terms of the larger Islamic tradition obviously serves the goal of establishing links with a heritage that has spanned centuries and transcended geographical boundaries. Such a definition of Malay literature is not without its problems. Mohd. Affandi Hassan worries over what he sees as a growing confusion or inability among writers and critics alike to differentiate between elements of Islam in literature (unsure Islam) and the more rigorous and demanding employment of Islamic literature as a formal discipline in creative writing and its attendant literary criticism.

This confusion in turn leads to what he sees as the adoption of the trappings of Islam such as the use of terminology associated with Islam, Quranic verses and references to the Traditions, all of which are grafted onto literary works to give them a superficial Islamic identity. They are then passed on or bandied about as sastera Islam or Islamic literature. According to MAH Mohd. Affandi Hassan, such works are not informed by clearly defined Islamic philosophical framework and do not demonstrate the necessary Islamic worldview and, as such, are a travesty of Islamic literature.

Politically Incorrect Literature

A Feminist Critique Shahnon, however, defends his style of writing what he calls Islamic literature, especially in the controversial Tivi, as representing society's reality. In claiming it to be within the genre of Islamic literature, Shahnon asserts that readers who criticizes Tivi as pornographic have missed the point. It is apparent that Shahnon Ahmad as the proponent of Islamic literature within the Malay literary tradition has paradoxically created ambiguities in the definition of what is literature, more specifically, what is Malay Islamic literature.

This state of affairs has led Aveling to conclude that it may be regretted that the task which Shahnon set himself, the creation of an authentic, moral and non-violent Islamic literature based on a recognition of all persons as the servants of God, remains as yet unfulfilled in Shahnon's writing.

This state of affairs certainly does not augur well for the state of modern Malay literature, since it appears to still be grappling with its identity, and still trying to prove its worth within the tradition of Islamic literature. A close reading of the above novels reveals the objectification of women whereby women are reduced to being body, thus still confirming a Western bias in the representation of Malay sexuality. Malay female sexuality is sensationalised and becomes the centre around which the narration of Malay sexuality revolves. In Tivi, it is done through Chah, who brings home a television set for her family and subsequently creates an atmosphere fraught with sexual tension, both through the vicarious television experience and also through her infectious wanton behaviour.

In Tok Guru and Ummi & Abang Syeikhul, Shahnon places the pious woman at the centre, struggling to come to terms with her sexual desires even as she seeks God's pleasure. Tope (2004) argues that there is a "strong moral component attached to Malay female sexuality. Sexuality, especially female sexuality, seems to be a nemesis of morality" and that such literary works "open the window slightly into that space of sexuality which defines ethnicity". It is not surprising then that sex and sexuality tend to be foregrounded in modern Malay literature albeit within "the acceptable notion of sex in Malay culture which is that it must be conjugal, procreative and heterosexual".

There is a strong interconnection between sexual/textual politics and creative writing. The interconnection can be seen in the explicit sexual themes addressed in the modern Malay novel and in the use of sexist discourse particularly in reference to women. While my framing of sexual and sexist discourse in Malay novels as a form of political incorrectness means that the definition of Malay literature is limited or narrowed, the justification for the use of politically correct language can be seen from the belief that its use fulfils the demands for politeness, accuracy and justice in Malay Islamic literature. These three aspects of politically correct language better suit the definition of Malay Islamic literature to be expressive of "beautiful language and beneficial content". A familiar criticism of political correctness is that it is actually only a form of euphemism going against the norm of plain language, and which "tells it like it is" or "calls a spade a spade".

Orwell (cited in Cameron) feels that this euphemism has a calming effect on the listener/reader "by wrapping unpleasant truths in a soft cloud of 'verbal cotton-wool'". Cameron, however, asserts that just because an expression is more polite than other expressions, does not necessarily make it a euphemism. Cameron compares politeness and euphemism, and differentiates the two; politeness shows awareness and sensitivity to others' feelings, while euphemism is avoidance of use of a word or an idea which if expressed openly is taboo. The definition of political correctness in this chapter has been expanded to include writings that use explicit sexual discourse. The use of such explicit sexual discourse is found to be in opposition to the ethics and politeness of the tradition of Malay Islamic literature and gives rise to the question about which literary tradition modern Malay novelists follow.

At the same time, such sexual discourse reveals a sexist approach to representation and categorization of women particularly apparent in the dehumanization of women characters. The application of political incorrectness to the use of sexual and sexist discourse in the modern Malay novel has opened up a space for a discussion of what is appropriate and what is not in discourses on sex and sexuality within Malay Islamic contexts. This discussion is important in order for Malay Muslim writers to resist uncontrolled sexual liberation and also the habitualization of sexually explicit discourse in Malay literature. Resistance this habitualization process can be seen as a positive move towards critical language awareness of literary texts via a defamiliarization of the term "political correctness" itself.

"It is totally unfair to draw the conclusion that the education of the Malays only come about after the coming of the British. Malay education before the advent of the West was in the form of religion. Much of the knowledge studied came from religion and the reading of the Quran. On the East Coast, Terengganu was best known for religious studies. Children who attended these schools were taught by Arab teachers well-versed in the Islamic law, all of which constituted a religious tradition already existing long before the coming of the West.

British colonial rule for a time was merely attracted to economic gain so the responsibility of giving education was apparently left to the Christian missionaries. The London Missionary Society had built Malay and a Chinese school in Malacca around the year 1815. In Penang the first Malay school was a branch of the Penang Free School established in 1812. Then between 1821 and 1839 other Malay school branches were set up in Glugor and Air Hitam. In 1878 a teachers' training college was set up in Singapore. For seventeen years this college produced the first Malay teachers.

Prof. Awang Had Salleh regards the efforts of the missionaries as the first stage in the development of Malay schools in the Straits Settlements. The second phase began with the transfer of the Straits Settlements to the administration of the District Office in 1867. The total number of Malay schools continued to increase. In the Federated Malay States in the years 1900-1920 there were in all 400 schools and an increase in the student population from 6,000 to 20, 319.

At a glance, this increase was indeed greatly encouraging. But what in actual fact was the objective in educating the indigenous people as seen by the British colonials? The report of a Director of Education in 1920 makes a rather interesting study:

The aim of the Government is not to turn out a few well educated youths, nor a number of less well-educated boys; rather it is to improve the bulk of the people, and to make the son of the fisherman or peasant a more intelligent fisherman or peasant than his father had been, and a man whose education will enable him to understand how his lot in life fits in with the scheme of life around him.

How far were the British colonials trustworthy in giving vernacular education is another question altogether. In the 1970s (sic; probably 1910s?) for instance, the subject of education was not given much attention at all. In 1914 expenditure for schools in the Federated Malay States amounted to $443, 209 and in the Straits Settlements $493, 447. This merely represents 4.8% of the total expenditure in the Federated Malay States.

How did the indigenous people react towards these developments in education? It was evident that this early formal education was received with great suspicion and scepticism. The same is true too of the schools run by the missionaries. Furthermore this sceptical and suspicious attitude dragged on for a long time especially over the education of girls.

What was felt to be of great significance in the development of education among the Malays was the establishment of the Malay College, Kuala Kangsar (MCKK) and the Sultan Idris Teacher's Training College, Tanjong Malim (MPSI). According to a researcher of the development in education, this college not only opened a social gap between the Western-educated Malay aristocrats and the other races similarly educated but it also created an aristocratic gap among the Malays themselves.

MPSI and MCKK presented different objectives and interests to quote Roff:

On the one hand, at Kuala Kangsar there were the sons of the traditional ruling class and the wealthy, undergoing training for entry into the English-speaking world of government and administration and occasionally the professions; on the other, at S.I.T.C. the sons of the peasantry and the poor, undergoing training for return to the Malay-speaking world of the rural village school. Yet there were equally striking resemblances between Malay College and S.I.T.C. as elite producing institutions of a special kind.

A matter of no less importance was the departure of the local youths to the Middle East countries to study. And they were wholly exposed to the development of new thinking in the Middle East and these revolutionary ideas were brought back to the motherland. The contribution of the group who were influenced by the reformist Islamic movement in the development of knowledge and thinking should not be disregarded.

So the early 20th century saw the development of knowledge among the indigenous -people as determined by their education. On the one hand there was the English-educated group, on the other, the Malay-educated group as well as those who received religious education in the Middle East. Despite it all, their contribution towards the development of thinking of the Malays is another question.

However what remains clear is that education became the main starting point to the change in thinking in Malay circles. Munshi Abdullah and his radical thoughts foundered because of a generally illiterate society. So it was with Abdullah's contemporary, Raja Ali Shah, who could not channel ideas to the masses because they were illiterate. However with the development in knowledge and the attitude shown by Malays towards knowledge, it was of great significance to the intellectual development of the Malays themselves.

Development in education is closely linked to the newspapers, and magazines are tools of great importance whatever the purpose or aim may be. Through this mass media we find evidence of the attitude, values and interests of the society which created them. Such is the important role of the mass media in the development of thinking of Malay society to the extent that nearly all their intellectual capabilities, be it from the literary or nationalism angle, are derived from it.

Modern Malay literature is not a form of expression which emerged all of a sudden but was more of a continuation of several forms of expression already existing in Malay society earlier on. So the birth of modern Malay literature was not altogether stimulated by the inclination to bring about reform in literary expression. It is also not a direct outcome of a sort of socio-cultural consciousness nor has it arisen from a new awareness regarding the process of composition.

What has actually taken place is an incidental but definite transition from the traditional literature of the feudal society or from the illiterate peasantry towards utterance of a different kind. Old Malay literature emanating from traditional Malay society throughout the history of its development had never been ruffled by any drastic digression. If at all, it probably pushed to the fore a new idea at the time of its emergence and even then, it was merely one episode which really did not affect the whole of its development.

The thinking advanced by Hamzah Fansuri as well as the polemics around it is one good example. It is a matter of regret that the differences seen in the works of Hamzah merely represent an isolated episode which does not bring about any change whatsoever to the pattern of the development of literature from the point of view of characteristics or its goal direction.

Hamzah Fansuri is more of a man who tries to bring about spiritual reforms, who invites us not just to follow what is already prescribed but to search for knowledge through understanding the soul, to love God and banish superstitious teachings. He seeks the power of the intellect in thinking and to him man is a noble being who should know himself before knowing his God.

Regrettably the reformed ideas which should run counter to the orthodox values could not be developed as well as they should because of the attacks from groups who were uneasy on their account. In the end, Hamzah sinks into the folds of history although in fact he was the pioneer of the new thinking such as that highlighted in the mystic poems so very highly acclaimed.

The question as to who is the pioneer of modern Malay literature has been posed time and again. Is it Hamzah Fansuri with his mystic poems within which an intellectual ability to challenge the ideology already in existence can be seen or is it Munshi Abdullah 19th century essayist whose individual works have almost amazed everyone? Munshi Abdullah produced works which originated from him.

He showed an individualistic quality which almost cannot be found in classical literary works except perhaps through implication. Hamzah emerges amidst the classic society on his own, without patronage and in isolation, unlike Abdullah who enjoyed the patronage of the British. It is not surprising that Hamzah's teaching was not widely spread to the extent that in *Hikayat Acheh,* which recorded contemporary events, there is no mention at all of Hamzah's name nor his contribution either.

The difference between him and Abdullah is that he i.e. Abdullah writes about the Malays at the time when the Malays themselves were totally illiterate and under the protection of the British. He was also fortunate to be free from the palace circle and feudal chains and thus was able to pass criticisms or hurl condemnations at the Malays. This piece of writing is not intended as a comparative discussion on Abdullah or Hamzah.

The question is not to determine who the pioneer of modern Malay literature is. Nor is it intended to make a comparison of the quality of contribution of their works. Both Hamzah and Abdullah, each has shown his own distinctive versatility. Each of these men became the proposer hurling new ideas and criticism which were suspect in their period.

The thinking from Hamzah's doctrine of existentialism became a victim of pressure from the orthodox group in Acheh in the 17th century, particularly from Sheikh Nuruddin al-Raniri. Meanwhile Abdullah did not leave any impression on the thinking of the Malay society of his period.

What is required to be brought to the fore here is the collective rising of the Malays. This took the form of a consciousness or an awareness radiating in the writings which depicted their genuine expression. This rising was also not merely a literary renaissance, but a resurgence of values and mentality, concept and ideology which involved the participation of society as a whole and at the same time gave an alternative to literary expression before that.

However it should be remembered this rising was not revolutionary in nature. It was the result of a change made possible by the encounter between values already existing and new values. The solid traditional society shackled for hundreds of years by feudal chains was all of a sudden confronted by new values which were probably frightening.

The changing situation in the early period of Western colonization in fact became the catalyst for the development of modern Malay literature which was more realistic, more individualistic, more commercial with a wider circulation and audience. It now became the media of expression of every member of society as long as they could read and for a long while it became the arena for the outpouring of feelings, the conflict of ideas as well as attacks and criticisms both daring and forthright.

Whether this is agreed upon or not, the emergence of the mass media in the form of newspapers and magazines at the end of the 19th century made possible by the printing press invented by the West, was the beginning or opening chapter in modern Malay literature in the real sense of the word. The tendencies shown as regards language as a tool of expression via a mass media was thought to be of increasing importance in an effort to highlight the beliefs, values and sentiments of contemporary society, all of which make up a part of the renaissance mentioned earlier.

A key feature of the development of Malay culture has been its exposure to and its assimilation of foreign elements. Malay society was rooted in ancestor worship and animism, before being exposed to the influence of Hinduism-Buddhism. But the hold of this culture waned after the adoption of Islam, the influence of which reached its zenith in the 16th and 17th centuries, as will be discussed later. Subsequently, in the 18th and 19th centuries, Malays had to contend with the arrival of

Western colonial powers whose priorities were initially economic in nature. Thus, though the Western powers were successful in monopolizing much of the economy, they could not deter Malays from their faith in Islam. The influence of Islam on Malay society has not only persisted, but has in fact been reinforced with Islamic revivalism, especially since the 1970s.

It should be noted that Malay literature also evolved in tune with the cultural developments outlined above. In other words, the exposure to different cultures has had the impact of instigating change in the function and orientation of Malay literature. However, the advent of Islam is seen as having wrought the most significant changes on Malay literature- from its concentration on myth and folklore (during the period of animism and Hinduism-Buddhism), to its jettisoning of these elements, and its resulting focus on matters spiritual and divine.

This change is closely linked to the Islamic belief in the Oneness of God (*Tawhid*) and the potential of the human intellect (*Al-Haiwan Al-Natiq*), thus leaving no room for superstitious beliefs. Parallel to the above context, Syed Muhammad Naquib Al-Attas (hereafter Al-Attas) maintains that Islam played a pivotal role in the history and culture of the Malays, as it was Islam that nurtured the birth of intellectualism, evident in the literary productions of the 16th and 17th centuries. In this context, the acceptance of Islam is seen as having contributed to the emergence of a 'tradition' in Malay literary activity, which according to V. I. Braginsky (hereafter Braginsky) was characterized by a 'literary self-awareness' (*kesedaran diri sastera*).

'Literary self awareness' here refers to the birth of a concrete, comprehensive and systematic awareness of the meaning, function and features of literature. According to Braginsky, such as awareness did not exist in Malay literature during the pre-Islamic period (animism & Hinduism-Buddhism). Islam was thus considered the bedrock of the establishment termed the 'tradition of Malay letters' (*tradisi persuratan Melayu*), in which literary activities centred on the utilization of the text as a medium for the discussion of spirituality and theology. Al-Attas and Braginsky state that this can be seen clearly in the works of Malay authors in the 16th and 17th centuries, such as Hamzah Fansuri, Shamsuddin Al-Sumaterani, Nurruddin Ar-Raniri, and 'Abdul-Rauf Singkel etc.

With the consolidation of colonization, however, Malay literature was introduced to 'modern' concepts of literature by the West, through the implementation of a secular education system. The introduction of 'modernist' genres and concepts created an impact on the Malay literary scene, when new genres such as novels, short stories and dramas began to sprout. At this point, it can safely be said that despite the widespread acceptance of Western literary concepts and genres, there still exists a literary inclination towards Islam, such as in the emergence of the 'discourse of Islamic literature' (*Wacana Sastera Islam*), an important development of contemporary Malay literature that has paralleled Islamic revivalism.

This begs the question: Is the tradition of Malay letters, that was founded on Islam, still the mainstay of Malay literature, and has the introduction of Western literary concepts failed to create a significant effect on contemporary Malay literature (apart from merely birthing Western literary genres)? This chapter attempts to answer the above question, by examining the conflict between the tradition of Malay letters (grounded in Islam), and the concept of 'modern' literature (as introduced by the West). In line with the above question, my discussion will delve into an essential aspect of literary production- the narrative construction- in contemporary Malay literature.

The need to highlight this aspect is necessitated by the fact there is a distinct difference between narrative construction in the tradition of Malay letters, and that of Western literature. This distinction will then be used as a guideline to understand the two traditions (Islam and the Western), and subsequently the conflict between Islam and the West in Malay literature. To further explore the above dichotomy, this chapter will examine Shahnon Ahmad's (hereafter Shahnon) novel titled *TIVI* (1995) as a case study. The choice of this work is based on certain authorial and textual considerations relevant to the issue at hand.

Apart from his prominence as a leading writer in contemporary Malay literature, Shahnon's Islamic commitments and his educational background make the choice of *TIVI* even more relevant: Shahnon (an Emeritus Professor) has been directly involved in the development of the discourse on Islamic literature, whilst his academic training has been of the Western mould. With such a background, it can safely be assumed that his literary activities would be 'sensitive' to both traditions examined here, that of Islam and the West.

Furthermore, *TIVI* was published subsequent to his involvement in Islamic literature discourse, making the choice of the novel even more apt. Shahnon has also touted *TIVI* as a '*karya mithali sastera Islam*' (an exemplary work of Islamic literature). This label is relevant to the question raised earlier: How far can traditional Malay letters (grounded in Islam) defend itself after the onslaught of Western literary concepts? On the one hand, the label reflects Shahnon's claim that *TIVI* was indeed created within the framework of traditional Malay letters, which would explain his estimation of the work as a *karya mithali*.

On the other hand, the label denotes to an extent that *TIVI* is free from Western literary influence. Commenting on his work, Shahnon says: '*TIVI* should not be viewed as an obscene novelette; to me it serves as a reminder. It is in the divine retribution brought down by Allah that the work integrates elements of education, *jihad* and Sufism.' Interestingly, some literary critics have also acknowledged *TIVI* as 'an exemplary work of Islamic literature'. Rahimah A. Hamid (2004), for example, states that 'whatever the public may feel about *TIVI*, I concur with Shahnon's stand that the novel reflects the spirit of Islam.

In fact, this slim novel espouses Islamic mysticism and Sufism'. Sohaimi Abdul Aziz (hereafter Sohaimi) has also come out in defence of *TIVI*, reiterating Shahnon's contention that the novel is indeed a *karya mithali*, as will be discussed later. This makes *TIVI* an apt choice to embody the conflict central to this discussion, that between Islam and the West. The ideas of Mohd Affandi Hassan (hereafter Mohd. Affandi) in his notion of 'Persuratan Baru' (or Genuine Literature) (hereafter PB) been chosen because it also (partly) evolves around the question of conflict between Islam and the West in Malay literature: it offers a substantive understanding of both the philosophy that forms the basis of traditional Malay letters (grounded in Islam), as well as the concept of 'modern' literature (as introduced by the West).

This enables PB to identify and compare the features of literary works produced in accordance with the two systems and finally to critically evaluate the works of Malay literature. It is therefore evident that the breadth of ideas contained in PB offers a framework for the discussion of the conflict between Islam and the West in Malay literature. For a closer understanding of PB, this chapter will also refer to the works of other scholars including Al-Attas, V. I. Braginsky, Pitirim A. Sorokin, Rene Welleck and Austin Warren since these writers have had a bearing on the generation of PB.

TRADITIONAL MALAY LETTERS VS. WESTERN LITERATURE

It has to be stated from the outset that PB, as a literary concept, aims at nurturing intellectual values in Malay literature. This is deemed necessary, as the current crop of works in the eyes of PB, are judged as being devoid of features which qualify it to be considered works par excellence. The idea of 'excellence' itself- a quality which PB holds as the mark of literary productions of the Islamic period- is called into question. Thus, one of the central tenets of PB is that Islam has made significant contributions to Malay letters, specifically in the infusion of intellectual values.

According to PB, traditional Malay letters are rich in intellectual values partly because of the understanding of the first verse in the Qur'an, i.e.: Surah Al-Alaq Verse 5, which clearly refers to the predominant position of 'knowledge' as a basis for literary creations, encased within the notion of *Qalam* (Divine Pen). Mohd. Affandi states: 'the use of *Qalam* in the Qur'an is related to knowledge, and the objective of acquiring that knowledge is always shown in its execution, that is to enable man to read *ayat-ayat Allah* (Allah's words), and in doing so, place himself in the right perspective'.

The notion of *Qalam* in PB lends credence to the importance of the human intellect (*Al-Haiwan Al-Natiq*), a faculty which enables the processing of complex and intellectual ideas. This understanding was instrumental in changing the meaning and function of 'literature' amongst the Malays. No longer bound by myth and folklore, literary activity was able to immerse itself in matters of 'knowledge', without the abandonment of beauty and artistry. 'Knowledge' here refers to a spiritual knowledge that enlightens Man on the Reality of the Creator, which will then prompt Man to do good deeds and distance himself from evil.

Literature in this context, according to PB, becomes an act of *ibadah* (devotion) that needs to be carried out in accordance with the teachings of Islam. This philosophy formed the basic features of traditional Malay letters; it was didactic, for it would convey the truth as taught in Islam, but was artistic in that conveyance. Mohd. Affandi states: 'such literature that is based on Islam would be didactic, teach that which is truthful, beautiful, and harmonious and complete, which would make Man realise himself and know Allah'. On a practical level, the didactic element in traditional Malay letters is manifested in works of an intellectual nature, including discourses, sermons and critical commentaries in prose form.

These forms are considered intellectual, for they allow matters related to ideas and thoughts to be expounded upon and debated, as Hamzah Fansuri, a leading author of the Islamic period who forwarded the Sufi doctrine of '*Wahdathul Wujud*' (Unity of Existence) in his literary works, had done. Whilst it is true that Hamzah also made use of *syair* (a verse form) to convey his ideas, Al-Attas notes that commentary was also a basic component of *syair* during the Islamic period. As he states: In poetry, perhaps it is only the *syair* that remains as a heritage of the Arab-Islamic poetic form...; but even in this field we see that prosal commentary on the *syair* is generally the most integral component of the *syair* concept-reaffirming the importance of the explanation element in the Malay language of the Islamic period.

The precedence given to intellectual works has had an important bearing on the function and position of the narrative in traditional Malay letters. It is amply clear that since the primacy of knowledge forms the foundation of the philosophy of Malay letters, then the function of a narrative would be to convey 'knowledge' (to reiterate, 'knowledge' refers to spiritual knowledge that enlightens Man on the Reality of the Creator). This means that the utilization of narrative devices, such as characters and characteristics, events, conflicts, plots, and the like, are only relevant in the context of conveying ideas and thoughts, and not for the mere purpose of developing a story, implying a subordination of the narrative to knowledge in traditional Malay letters.

Mohd. Affandi, in explaining the subordinate role of the narrative, states: The position of poetry as the most popular genre of Arabic literature in the pre-Islamic period declined with the introduction of Islam. With the coming of Islam, new prose forms like the *al-rasa'il* and *al-munazarat* gained prominence.

A 'literary work' *karya persuratan* does not merely narrate, it needs to propound an idea or thought.... I am not interested in merely telling a story, since my study shows that the Qur'an does not merely tell a story for its own sake. Stories are employed to convey an idea or thought, to remind or warn. We now turn our attention to the concept of 'modern' literature as introduced by the West. As stated earlier, the introduction of the Western concept of literature was the direct result of colonization, and the channel for this was the colonial British education system and the resultant exposure to Western literary works.

At this juncture it is necessary to take a cursory look at the development of Western culture to understand some of the main concepts of 'modern' literature. With full awareness of the complexity of the topic, my discussion will only draw from the relevant points needed for the analysis. The birth of 'modern' literary concepts was the manifestation of the rise of modernism in the West, and this in turn is linked to historical developments in the West approaching the 15th century. At the time, the West was freeing itself from the Dark Ages which was marked by the paucity of intellectualism. It was the Renaissance movement, which strove to revive the glory of the Greek intellectual tradition that ignited intellectual growth.

The West then identified some of the sources of its backwardness, one of which was traditional values. Subsequently, some of the institutions which were the custodians of these values were challenged. One of the institutions that came under scrutiny was the Catholic Church. This opposition to the Catholic Church- the Christian Reformation- was significant as it signalled the decline of religious values in Western society. It was at this juncture that modernism surfaced to free Western society of traditional values, and this included the belief in matters of a metaphysical and transcendental nature.

The new emphasis was on the function of the human intellect. The recognition of this function, the need for rationality, and the abandonment of the metaphysical and transcendental, gave birth to a modern Western culture that was worldlier, in that there was now a separation between worldly and religious matters. Pitirim A. Sorokin (hereafter Sorokin) who describes Renaissance and Reformation culture as 'sensate', states: Beginning roughly with the sixteenth century, the new principle modernism became dominant; and with it the new form of culture, modern culture that was based upon it. In this way the modern form of our Western culture emerged- the sensory, empirical, secular, and this 'worldly' culture.

It may be called sensate culture. Modernism, as described above, subsequently gave birth to the concept of 'modern' literature with its own unique features. It is in this context that PB argues that concepts such as naturalism, romanticism and realism came to the fore, and that all these centre on the concept of mimesis, known to us since the ancient Greek age. According to PB, under this umbrella of mimesis, 'modern' literary works have become a tool to record the 'reality' of human existence; and 'reality', after the abandonment of the metaphysical and transcendental, mostly focused on events seen as empirical that could be experienced by the five human senses.

We can examine one Greek concept of literature that is prominent in 'modern' literature- the concept of 'entertaining whilst teaching' (referred to this concept demands that a literary work should emphasize two elements, namely 'pleasure' and 'utility'. According to PB, 'pleasurable is defined as something that is not boring, not burdensome, and is its own reward. Useful is defined as something that is not a waste of time, not a form of passing the time, but one that deserves serious attention'. And these two elements, according to Rene Welleck and Austin Warren, had not only to coexist, but more importantly, to coalesce.

This means that any form of teaching (*utile*) had to be sprinkled with elements of entertainment (*dulce*) so that the reader is not bored, or does not feel as if he is being lectured to. Thus, works that are intellectual in nature, such as discourses, sermons and critical commentaries (which are basic to a tradition Malay letters) are now deemed irrelevant, since they appear overtly didactic with moralistic tones, and this would run counter to the objective of 'entertaining whilst teaching' (*dulce et utile*).

In PB, it is based on these considerations that 'modern' fiction places emphasis on the narrative for it is this component that is able to entertain the reader. To realize this objective, narrative devices are manipulated so as to make the story as realistic as possible, and this manipulation then has the effect of making the element of 'teaching' more subtle. The 'modern' emphasis of the narrative, and the aversion of preachy and moralistic tones, is summed up in Richard M. Eastman's definition of the novelist's role in accordance with 'modern' literary conventions: A novelist, however, is not a preacher, nor a systematic philosopher.

He cannot develop his life's wisdom primarily through direct exhortation or reasoned essays. His first business is to show the lives of imaginary people, through which his wisdom must appear dramatically, in the vital terms by which his characters discover or lose their own worth. Another of the assertions of PB is that a story, as a tool for entertainment, has to accentuate 'differences' or the unusual to avoid boredom. Most stories, therefore, tend to portray characters not normally encountered in our daily lives. The characters tend to be sub-social types, often evil and immoral. By portraying these characters, one is able to bring in elements of sensationalism, eroticism and concupiscence, all of which are able to excite the reader.

The employment of these narrative devices is strengthened by the use of other techniques, such as caricature, satire and comedy. The ultimate aim of the full manipulation of narrative devices is thus to create a story that is more interesting and pleasurable to read. The following quote from Sorokin explains this sensate element in 'modern' literature: Sensate art lives and moves entirely in the empirical world of the senses. At its overripe stage, prostitutes, criminals, street urchins, the insane, hypocrites, rogues and other sub-social types are its favourite 'heroes'.

Its aim is to afford a redefined sensual enjoyment: relaxation, excitation of tired nerves, amusement, pleasure, entertainment. For this reason it must be sensational, passionate, pathetic, sensual, and incessantly new. It is marked by voluptuous nudity and concupiscence. Since it must amuse and entertain, it makes wide use of caricature, comedy, farce, and debunking, ridiculing and similar means. The above discussion clearly demonstrates the dissimilarity between the two literary traditions: the tradition of Malay letters, and Western literature.

Although both traditions recognize the role of literature in 'teaching', their priorities certainly differ. The tradition of Malay letters places a high premium on didacticism, thus subordinating the element of having to amuse the reader. On the other hand, Western literature gives priority to the narrative aspect so that the 'teaching' element is projected in a more subtle form. Premised on the above discussion, this chapter analyses *TIVI* to identify its main function: to teach or narrate; and to evaluate its claim to be considered as a *karya mithali*.

THE POSITION OF SHAHNON AHMAD'S *TIVI*

Since Shahnon has positioned his novel as a *karya mithali*, it is necessary to review his ideas on Islamic literature, and more so, his criteria of *karya mithali*. To this end, this chapter will examine his *Azab Allah: Juzuk yang Digeruni dalam Sastera Islam* (1997), which was written with the objective of clarifying his position on the novel. In the work, Shahnon raises the idea of *juzuk azab* (scene of divine retribution), which he considers an essential criterion of a *karya mithali*.

Shahnon states that a story must explicitly depict punishment from Allah for evil deeds committed, so as to instil fear, and in doing so, to serve as a lesson to readers. *Juzuk azab*, explains Shahnon, must represent two elements: portrayal of extreme suffering and the arrival of this suffering without any forewarning. Shahnon further elaborates that this idea originates from his reading of the Qur'an, in which Allah punishes wrongdoers for their misdeeds. He states: 'the stories in the Qur'an which depict frightening pain, unbearable torture, as well as calamities from the land, sea, and sky, are numerous and we are expected to ponder upon and learn from it.'

The fact that Shahnon admits that his ideas on *juzuk azab* are of Quranic origin demonstrates his approval of traditional Malay letters; as he states: 'This depiction of divine retribution in Islam *juzuk azab* should become an important source for the production of Malay literary works' Shahnon's ideas on *juzuk azab* need to be understood in relation to the narrative devices used in *TIVI*. As a novel claiming to be a *karya mithali*, readers can expect *juzuk azab* to be an important component in the novel.

A cursory reading indicates that the novel does indeed include a chapter depicting *juzuk azab*. The presence of *juzuk azab* is significant, for it does reflect Shahnon's cognisance of the need to convey moral teaching through his novel. Next, we need to examine how Shahnon imparts his teaching: whether it adheres to the traditions of Malay letters that gives precedence to didacticism, thus subordinating the narrative, or whether he imparts his teaching in an 'amusing' fashion as prescribed by 'modern' literary concepts. *TIVI* is about the evil committed by a Muslim family, which then results in the frightful occurrence of *juzuk azab* (divine retribution). It is important to note that in the context of constructing the narrative of *TIVI*, there is a coalescence of evil and divine retribution (*juzuk azab*).

In other words, the novel has to include the scene of human evil, for which the scene of *juzuk azab* is meted out. In accordance to this principle, Shahnon introduces incest into the fictive world of the novel, which irrefutably necessitates *juzuk azab*, since it is a most heinous deed, and is against both the teachings of Islam as well as human nature. Incest and *juzuk azab* have a predominant role in the narrative construction of *TIVI*, and to display these elements, the author exploits a number of narrative devices, such as the introduction of the character and characteristics. Thus, the character of Chah is introduced in the fictive world of the novel, and assumes the character role of an innocent village girl who moves to the town to be employed in a factory. Chah is rendered as a very impressionable girl who is easily influenced, and allows for her transformation from innocent village lass into immoral urban worker plausible.

To evoke incest and *juzuk azab*, the new Chah is represented as bold and capable of not only influencing other family members, but also exhibiting offensive behaviour. Obviously, Chah has been introduced into the fictive world of *TIVI* as an 'agent of change' who transforms the god-fearing family into one that betrays the teachings of Islam. Chah executes this role effectively, as can be seen in her act of sending a nude calendar to her home, persuading her sister to appear in revealing outfits, as well as openly hugging her male companion in the presence of other family members.

These drastic changes in Chah and other members of the family are vital to the further development of the plot, which culminates in incest and *juzuk azab*. It is also significant to note that Chah, who works in the city, only makes periodic visits to her village home, and in her absence there is a vacuum in her role as 'an agent of change'. Logically, her absence should prevent the plot from developing into a tragedy that ends in incest, and subsequently retribution. But this does not happen, for her role in bringing evil influences from the city is taken over by television, which exposes the rural family to hitherto unseen sexual conduct. The novel thus skilfully brings in the television to ensure that the progression towards incest is not disrupted.

The paper will now examine another narrative device in play, namely episodes and events. As mentioned earlier, Shahnon introduces *juzuk azab* to impart moral teaching, but that only occurs at the end of the novel: Chah, her father, mother, younger sister and brother are all struck by lightning, and the television is swallowed by the earth. This retribution is an embodiment of the cause-and-effect element, a commonly used narrative device in plot development, and its appearance at the end is sound, since evil deeds have to be portrayed prior to the punishment. Thus, the narrative structure of *TIVI* begins with Chah moving to the city, which provides the backdrop for her to evolve into an immoral person.

And this change is necessary to expose Chah's evil, as well as her influence on other members of the family, which ultimately results in incest. Her father, Mat Isa, commits incest with two of his daughters, Chah and Hasanah. This series of developments makes it imperative that the novel be filled with heinous acts to necessitate retribution. The excessive representation of evil turns the novel into a text soaked in sex and eroticism. This can, for example, be seen in the vivid descriptions of Chah's and Hasanah's physique, Chah's sexual display with her male companion, and the even more blatant depiction of sex in a pornographic video. Added to that is the element of suspense that originates from the father's sexual fantasies, which leads readers to await the probable conclusion of the father committing incest with his daughters.

In this way, the author is able to create suspense and deliberately delay the actual occurrence of incest. Furthermore, the text is generously littered with suggestive and salacious language, all with the single purpose of creating an atmosphere of heightened sexual anticipation. Yet another device is the use of caricature and lewd humour, as in the scene when Chah's parents first get the television. Hence it is evident that Shahnon has manipulated the narrative devices purely with the intention of spicing the story with eroticism.

What further contribute to thickening the sexual atmosphere of the text are the two scenes of incest: one between the father and Chah, and the other between him and Hasanah, despite one act being sufficient to qualify for divine retribution. It is clear that the excessive portrayal of sex serves only to intensify the erotic element, as Shahnon himself admits: '*TIVI* does contain episodes that are obscene and erotic, that sometimes even slips into the pornographic'.

This admission by the author certainly raises questions about the function of the sex episodes, especially if one is to evaluate it as a *karya mithali*. In this context, it is necessary to examine Shahnon's rationale. Firstly, he states that the episodes are necessary as they reflect the 'reality' in society. Those obscene elements had to be presented for that is the reality. Don't be enraged if you find the novel obscene, erotic, or pornographic, for I am only acting in accordance with the demands of the reality of society. I cannot lie and turn readers away from the realities of society.

Obscenity, eroticism and pornography are real. Shahnon also claims that these portrayals serve to convey his moral message of divine retribution for sin. He argues: It is true that the author Shahnon has explicit representations of sex before the occurrence of *juzuk azab*, but then the objective is not to excite the readers... contemporary life, which is certainly is full of obscenity, is 'bait' for the retribution and torture that Allah would inflict upon sinners. The two quotations are closely related to Shahnon's philosophy and concept of literature as applied in the construction of *TIVI.*

His defence of sex on the grounds that it reflects social 'reality' indicates his sensitivity to the function of literature as a vehicle for recording human behaviour that is empirical, and that which is experienced only by the five human senses, as affirmed by the concept of 'modern' literature (often referred to as 'grounded in reality' by Western scholars). Shahnon's second explanation that sex is 'bait' reflects his inclination towards the concept of 'amusing while teaching' (*dulce et utile*). And in the context of *TIVI*, the explicit portrayal of sex serves to amuse or excite the reader, which then neutralizes the moral message that the novel wishes to impart. Thus it is clear that Shahnon is more attuned to the Western concept of literature, and not to the tradition of Malay letters which places a premium on didacticism, not amusement.

Shahnon himself has admitted that he has avoided 'preaching' in *TIVI*, as he says: 'Perhaps my way of presenting Islamic values is rather different, and society, that is accustomed to being educated through sermons, will not accept my ways.... In *TIVI*, for example, I Shahnon have presented too much sex; perhaps I have overindulged' The fact that Shahnon deliberately waters down the instructional element by avoiding 'sermons', which are a basic element of traditional Malay letters based on Islam, renders his claim that *TIVI* is *karya mithali* untenable.

But again, Shahnon's reluctance to resort to preaching is not entirely surprising, for he has described being overly didactic as a 'sickness' to be avoided. In another instance, Shahnon states that 'some writers are too eager to instruct their readers; the works are so didactic that art is sacrificed. Such a sickness should be strictly avoided'. The presence of eroticism and obscenity in a work that professes to be a *'karya mithali sastera Islam'* or an exemplary work of Islamic literature ignited considerable controversy both among critics and readers. Sohaimi, a literary critic, attempted to explain the presence of sex in such an 'exemplary' work by invoking Sigmund Freud's theory on sexuality, which he says places sexual instinct as most important element in the development of human psychology.

Based on Freud, Sohaimi claims that the presence of excessive sex in *TIVI* is 'normal', as he writes: 'Based on Freudian theory, when Shahnon portrays sexual elements in his works, his actions are normal for he channels sexual instincts through the creative process' The question to be raised here is the suitability of Freudian theory as implemented by Sohaimi, for Shahnon has asserted, in his own words, that *TIVI* was written 'in accordance with what is demanded in Islam' (*ukurtara seperti yang dituntut oleh Islam*). Such being the case, the yardstick of measurement has to be an Islamic framework. In this context, Mohd. Affandi's evaluation should be looked upon as more valid, as his is based on an Islamic framework (*Tawhid*).

In an article titled 'Persuratan Baru dan Cabaran Intelektual: Menilai Kembali Kegiatan Kreatif dan Kritikan', he challenges *TIVI's* claim to be 'an exemplary work of Islamic literature'. Unlike Sohaimi's 'process of sublimation', which permits the presence of eroticism as a manifestation of the writer's psychology, Mohd. Affandi, whose views are based on *Tawhid*, claims that the sexual depiction is merely aimed at providing pleasure, and not aimed at instructing man to the right path of Islam. Mohd. Affandi also states that what is presented as *juzuk azab* by Shahnon contradicts the spirit of the Qur'an, for Islam primarily focuses on education (*tarbiyah*), and not retribution and punishment, which he says stresses only the anger of God (*ammarah*).

In Mohd. Affandi's judgement, the writer's bold depiction of man's most despicable conduct- incest- makes *TIVI* a worthless novel, and not a *karya mithali*, as proposed by

Shahnon. Writes Mohd. Affandi: 'It is most inappropriate for the writer to stake the claim that his work *TIVI* is an exemplary work in Islam, for the Islamic elements are non-existent, and its content centres on human desire at its lowest level, and the storytelling too is crude'.

This chapter shown that in contemporary Malay literature, there is an ongoing conflict between the tradition of Malay letters and Western concepts of literature while not in denial of the fact that there is still a tendency to appreciate Islam, the fact remains that literary productions do not fully subscribe to the genuine Islamic values. While colonisation did little to shake the faith of Malays towards Islam, Malay literature, however, is not completely free from the influence of Western concepts and philosophy. And even novels that label themselves as 'Islamic', such as in the case of *TIVI* are genuinely closer to Western concepts of literature.

RADICAL NOVEL CHALLENGES

Salam Maria is a radical novel as it provides a critique of the nation-state for turning its back on the less-privileged and marginalized communities, mainly women who are old, poor, single, disabled, victims of incest and rape, says prominent literary critic Dr Wong Soak Koon. She expressed this view during the recent launch of Dr Fatimah Busu's *Salam Maria* by Malaysia's Poet Laureate, Prof Muhammad Hj. Salleh. The launch was organised by KANITA, Universiti Sains Malaysia's foremost Women's Development Research Centre.

SPIRITUAL LEADER AND ENTREPRENEUR

The female protagonist in the novel, Maria Zaitun, is a character taken from W.S. Rendra's famous poem *Nyanyian Angsa* (Song of the Geese). Wong added that it was Maria Zaitun, fashioned after women Islamic saints such as Rabeah al-Adawiyah and Sayyidah Nafisah, who provides spiritual leadership, enlightenment and salvation to this group of dispossessed women in Hutan Beringin, a place deep in the interiors. Maria Zaitun is not just a spiritual leader, she is also an entrepreneur: she is the one who encourages these women to start a small cottage industry, sewing and selling specially-embroidered *telekung* or praying attire for Muslim women in the urban centres. This helps provide them with some form of financial independence and security.

A devout Muslim, Maria Zaitun is reduced to a social outcast because she has been misunderstood. Wong highlighted Fatimah's courage in criticizing religious institutions through the character of the village imam, who lacks compassion and humanity for social outcasts such as Maria Zaitun. Instead of helping her, the imam chases Maria Zaitun out of the mosque, where she had thought she could find refuge and spiritual salvation. It is a group of women, old, poor and disabled, who offer her sanctuary in their humble abode in Hutan Beringin. Wong noted that Maria Zaitun's resourcefulness is clearly demonstrated when she takes over the running of the household and provides help to other marginalized women who had sought refuge in Hutan Beringin.

Fatimah didn't spare the media in her novel, noted Wong. One of the characters is Siti Senang, a journalist with *Primadonna* magazine. To please her bosses, gain popularity and reap profits, Siti Senang sensationalises news about Maria Zaitun, her spiritual powers and saintly touch. The novel has several strengths and some limitations, said Wong. Although the writer was brave enough to raise important social issues affecting Malaysian society, in particular Malay-Muslim society, it would have helped if she had attempted to explore the "subjective layer of personal life". It would have been interesting to unravel the underlying tensions, contradictions and anxieties within Maria Zaitun as she juggles several roles and assumes a number of identities.

"The spiritual leader is bound to conflict with the entreprenuerial self," said Wong. Likewise, tensions and conflicts within other characters such as Tasnim and Siti Senang could have been explored. As an educated Malay-Muslim woman living in a modern, capitalist society, Siti Senang too was bound to have faced tensions and anxieties within her. Wong felt it would have been interesting to see how Siti Senang handled them. A pertinent point indeed: by revealing her doubts and insecurities, the character assumes a human identity and "begins to live."

EASILY MALIGNED

Maznah, a social scientist and KANITA director, agreed as she underscored Fatimah's valiant attempts at exposing the "brutal realities of contemporary society" through her airing of issues such as incest, child sexual abuse, religious hypocrisy, superficial religiosity, greed and slander. Maznah argued that Malay women are often "easily maligned" and vulnerable to slander, as in the case of Maria Zaitun, as they are expected to conform to certain State-constructed and -promoted ideals. The writer, Maznah added, deserves to be commended for her efforts in dismantling a "gendered Islamic history".

Reinscribing an alternative history into her narrative, Fatimah has highlighted the contributions and sacrifices of Muslim women saints. Women in this novel, Maznah noted, are portrayed as highly reverent, charitable and non-judgemental in their dealings with incest victims and unwed mothers. These marginalized women are kind, humble, understanding; they have a genuine desire to help fellow women in distress. It's an interesting point Maznah raised as such women are often subjected to shame and scorn at the hands of bureaucratic officers and holier-than-thou religious authorities.

BLURRING THE BOUNDARIES

Salam Maria has provided women with alternative identities that are contrary to the traditional model of womanhood, a model that other writers so often subscribe to, observed another panel speaker, Ruzy, a Universiti Kebangsan Malaysia lecturer. Fatimah provides a critique of such women - whose identities are defined by the men they are married to - through Maria Zaitun. This female protagonist is not portrayed as a subservient wife but as a devout Muslim and a wise and knowledgeable spiritual leader. Like other women in this novel, Maria Zaitun has been given both voice and agency, said Ruzy.

This is clearly shown through the character's interrogations of society's improper understanding and implementation of religious practices. It is also seen in her resourcefulness in setting up home in Hutan Beringin. Ruzy also touched on the technique of magical realism that Fatimah employed to blur the boundaries between fantasy and realism. Using such a technique, she was able to weave in elements of mystery, mysticism, suspense, disbelief through dream sequences when foregrounding real issues of poverty and abuse.

Hanafi Ibrahim, a Language Planning Officer with Dewan Bahasa and Pustaka, viewed *Salam Maria* as an "idealistic novel" as it is reflective of Maria Zaitun's idealism. Her migration to the interiors, he added, was the result of moral and spiritual decay and loss of humanity amongst city dwellers. He felt that the writer had foregrounded several basic issues revolving around religion - issues which have not yet been resolved. Difficulties arise when boundaries that separate cultural and religious practices are blurred in this novel. This, he added, is worrying as uninformed readers will not be in a position to distinguish them.

BOLD TOUCH

In her speech, Fatimah touched on the creative and publishing processes of her novel. She expressed her disappointment with the editor for making unnecessary changes to the manuscript and acknowledged that Maria Zaitun was based on a character in W.S. Rendra's poem. Rendra had depicted Maria Zaitun as a syphilis-stricken prostitute; however, the Maria Zaitun in *Salam Maria* is a devout Muslim woman much hated and maligned by a sick Malay-Muslim society. The writer added that Maria Zaitun is an ordinary person, but she is one who is quite conscious of her temporary existence in this world.

Fatimah Busu's latest novel is certainly radical: it questions and challenges established religious norms and practices by exposing their gaps and inconsistencies. She is highly critical of Malay-Muslim society, its religious hypocrisy and its penchant for superficial religiosity. The novel also highlights the nation-state's failure in providing much-needed support to marginalized women. What is demonstrated is this society's skewed understanding of important religious principles and their improper implementation.

In addition, issues of incest, rape, child sexual abuse and abandoned orphans are real issues that confront this society on a daily basis; hence the writer deserves praise for being bold enough to highlight them, when her contemporaries would have played safe by staying well clear of them. The Malay language which belongs to the Austranesian or Malayo-Polynesian language group includes dialects such as Achenese, Javanese and Sundanese found in the various islands that make up the Indonesian archipelago, the Malay speech of Malaysia and Yawi, a dialect of Malay spoken in Southern Thailand. Also closely related to Malay is Tagalog spoken in the Phillipines.

The local Malay language known as Melayu Bahasa somewhat differs from the standard Malay language of Indonesia (Bahasa Indonesia) and Malaysia (Bahasa Malaysia). Hussainmiya (1987) believes the local Malay language to be descended from a colloquial dialect known variously as Batavian Malay (Omong Jakarta), Low Malay, Bazar Malay etc, a Malay pidgin that originated in the coastal areas of Java. In support he points out that the original Malay settlers, since the beginning of Dutch rule in Sri Lanka were drawn from many East Indian nationalities domiciled in and around the Dutch port city of Batavia (present-day Jakarta).

He notes that the diverse national groups of soldiers such as Amboinese, Bandanese, Javanese and others who arrived in the island to perform military service, were in the main former residents of Batavia and did not always come from the different geographic regions of the archipelago as their names suggest. He contends that ever since the founding of Batavia in 1619, a number of such nationalities settled in the outskirts of Batavia and cites Dr.F.De Han who shows in his Oude Batavia (1922) that there were separate kampungs for each of these nationalities headed by their own chieftains.

He nevertheless notes that assimilation between these various ethnic nationalities from the archipelago which had settled in Batavia had already taken place before their arrival in Sri Lanka and contends that one of the main factors which assisted the residents of Batavia gain a distinct group identity was a simplified Malay language alias 'Batavian Malay' which they adopted as their main medium of communication. In this connection, he cites Viekke who in his Nusantara. A History of the East Indian Archipelago (1945) has this to say: "Gradually this heterogeneous population developed into a new Indonesian national group, distinct from the Sundanese of the west and the Javanese of the East Java and with a simplified Malay language, the lingua franca of the archipelago as their native tongue".

In later times, this Malay pidgin that found its way to Sri Lanka with the early Malay soldiers was considerably influenced by the local languages, especially the Tamil spoken by the Moors, contends Hussainmiya.

Data from the Department of Statistics Malaysia (2005) indicated that out of the estimated population of over 26 million, males outnumbered females by about 104 males to every 100 females. However, enrolments in schools and universities indicated higher percentages of females (74%) compared to males (67%). The female life expectancy is also higher than for males especially for those within the 60-64 age groups. The statistical data also indicated that the proportion of single women aged between 20 and 34 increased from 43.2% in 1991 to 49.1% in 2000 and a higher proportion of young adults tended to marry at a later age.

The statistics therefore indicate that the female population forms nearly half of Malaysia's population, a higher percentage of them are enrolled in secondary and higher educational institutions, and a higher percentage of those of 20 to 34 are unmarried and tend to marry late. This picture makes women's studies essential in order to ensure that women contribute productively to Malaysia's economic growth as they form a large proportion of the nation's potentially available labour force. The business of libraries in this situation is in making sure that serious literature on women in Malaysia is controlled bibliographically and systematically acquired.

The health of research activities in a discipline is often reflected by the amount of literature it generates. For collection development librarians, identifying what has been published can be quite a tricky business especially when the types of literature generated are those not easily obtained from the usual commercial channels of publishers and bookshops. As a result, acquisitions librarians often resort to using compiled bibliographies and listings of resources when ascertaining what is available, so that an educated decision can be made about what to purchase or acquire. Compiling bibliographies or creating listings of documents to support research activities or to enable acquisition and collection development is a traditional role of libraries. Bibliography itself is an ancient genre and is considered a scholarly practice.

Hendry and Carlyle (2006) further explained that this scholarly practice encompasses, scoping and collating the items to a specific domain related to faculty research activities, using clear rules about what to include or exclude, organizing the items into logical categories, using a standard unit of what should be included in describing the items and packaging it in the form of a published monograph, weblogs or web bibliographies. This chapter indicates how the growth and pattern of women's studies in Malaysia can be gauged from resources listed in two published bibliographies on women in development in Malaysia, the first covered literature before 1970 to 1990 and the second covered studies between 1990 and 2004.

The study scoped itself to these two bibliographies for two reasons. Firstly, no dedicated web bibliography on women can be found originating from Malaysia except for one compiled by the Berkeley library, which listed only 98 titles. Secondly, the two bibliographies provide historical bibliographic data by virtue of the period covered, pre 1970s to 2004, and as such, trends and research productivity could be observed. The observed trends of generated literature would be useful for librarians in developing collections to sustain research activities in this area of study. The earliest bibliography compiled on women in Malaysia was published in 1981 by the National Library of Malaysia.

This first bibliography was 31 pages and was updated in 2002. In the same year Fan (1981) compiled a "Bibliography on women in Malaysia" and this was published as a chapter in a book by Hing, Nik and Rokiah (1984). Fan (1982) later extended her bibliography to include women studies in Southeast Asia. This was followed by a 77-page bibliography published in 1984 by the National Development and Family Planning Board, Malaysia, a government agency and this might be the bibliographical manuscript which Jamilah (1991, v) had mentioned locating at the National Family Planning and Development Board library.

The Malaysian government's interest in collating information on the role of Malaysian women in development was manifested through the setting up of a National Clearinghouse on Women in Development under the Prime Ministers Department and aimed at enhancing awareness on the role and needs of women. The Clearinghouse prepared a 167 page bibliography in 1987 (*Women's bibliography*, 1987) to provide a resource base in support of national programmes. Fan's 1981 bibliography was reproduced in Jamilah's 1991 publication and Jamilah herself extended the coverage of literature produced on women up to 1989.

There have been attempts to produce special listings such as on "Women and the media", 1991 and "Theses on women in Malaysia". An annotated bibliography was also published by the Sabah State Library and Khoo (1991a; 1991b) wrote an informative bibliographic essay in which she traced the efforts undertaken to bibliographically control literature on women in Malaysia. A sequel to Jamilah's bibliography was published in 2006 covering literature on women's studies in Malaysia produced between the period 1990 and 2004.

This chapter used the resources listed in both Jamilah's (1991) and Zainab's (2006) bibliographies to ascertain the publication activities on women in Malaysia. Entries from the other bibliographies were counter checked to ascertain complete coverage. However, the earlier bibliographies compiled by the National Library Malaysia and the Population and Family Development Board Malaysia have included high proportion of "popular" resources. The bibliographies by Jamilah and Zainab cover research-based literature from the pre 1970 years to 2004 and have excluded popular articles published in magazines and the newspapers.

Research-based literature refers to works generated from undergraduate, graduate and doctoral research activities, papers presented at conferences, journal articles, and chapters in books, research reports, monographic series and books. Jamilah's bibliography had listed titles under two separate chapters, where chapter 2 was the reproduction of Fan's 1981 bibliography entitled, "Women studies in Malaysia: a bibliography covering the period prior to 1980" and chapter 3 was her own contribution entitled, "Women studies in Malaysia – a bibliography covering the period 1980 – 1989". Zainab's bibliography was compiled as a sequel to Jamilah's work.

The resources listed in both bibliographies will be used to ascertain the trends and growth of the body of literature produced on women in the pre1989 years and up to 2004, as well as to make comparisons between the two broad periods in terms of the total number of publications generated, the active authors, the authorship pattern and subject coverage. This study will use bibliometrical methods to analyse bibliographic data. Bibliometrics is a type of research method used in library and information science, where quantitative analysis is applied to describe patterns of publication within a given field or body of literature and their authors.

Both Jamilah and Zainab have listed resources under fairly similar headings. The resources compiled by Zainab's (2006) bibliography were classified under 13 categories while Jamilah (1991) and Fan (1981) had categorized their listings under 12 broad subject areas. Zainab excluded the category "miscellaneous" as most citations collected could be placed within the 13 categories used and had instead included a new category "Technology and science" as there was a growing number of works produced under this category in the recent years. Due to the similarity in the classification used, it was possible to compare literature produce up to 1989 and those up to 2004.

The categories framed literatures under a broad spectrum of knowledge, basically following the subject classification used by the Library of Congress Classification Scheme: generalia, economics, education, literature and the mass media, law, medicine and health, politics, religion, sociology and technology. The different time frame covered by these bibliographies, with Fan covering studies for the period up to 1980, Jamilah covering the period 1989 to 1989 and Zainab for the period 1990 to 2004, has made it possible to compare and gauge the growth as well as trends of literature generated under the respective categories. This should also help libraries in collection development.

PUBLICATIONS ON WOMEN STUDIES IN MALAYSIA

There was a substantial increase in the publication output of works on women in Malaysia within the 15-year period between 1990 and 2004 compared to those produced before this year span. The quantity of publication refers to the number of publications produced by a researcher or individual in a given field and is used to assess publication productivity. There is a definite growth in published literature on women studies in Malaysia from 691 publications in the years up to 1989 to 3346 between 1990 and 2004, with the latter period contributing 80% of total publications produced.

For most years in the active period between 1990 and 2004, the number of literature produced totals over 200, except for the year 1991 and 2004. The most productive year was 1999 with 296 publications. The low count for 2004 is expected as Zainab's compilation was completed in 2004 and it would take at least two years before the body of literature produced in a particular year is published and recorded in secondary reference resources such as periodical indexes, databases and online or printed bibliographies. Libraries would also take time to receive and process all research publications deposited by academic staff, undergraduates, postgraduates and those purchased from commercial vendors. The average publication was thus computed to be about 258 per year between 1990 and 2004.

PUBLICATIONS BY BROAD SUBJECT CATEGORIES

In all broad subject categories the growth of literature published between 1990 and 2004 increased manifolds when compared to the earlier years. Under Category 1 "General works and history", a substantial number of biographical works on women were written (38 titles). Bibliographical listings began to be compiled between the 1990 and 2004 years (32 titles) as well as writings on the historical aspect of women's social, economics, health and welfare during the British colonial period and Second World War.

The subject concerning women in relation to Category 2: "Crimes and delinquency" was hardly reported before 1989 but this changed between 1990 and 2004 when investigations reported issues such as sexual harassment, domestic violence, abusive and violence acts upon women, wives and girls, rape victims and drug abuse among women. There was a larger body of literature generated under Category 3: "Economic conditions" between the years 1990 and 2004 (667 titles) especially on women in business (136 titles). This was followed by studies about women and careers and employment (96 titles) and the economic contribution of the working women to the industrial and manufacturing sectors (especially the factory workers - 87 titles).

There were also new areas not researched before 1989 such as: women and trade unions and worker's associations, and migrant female labour the latter of which mainly came from Indonesia, the Philippines, Cambodia and Burma. In the education category (Category 4) prior to 1990, research activities covered the general area of women's involvement in education. This which became more focused between 1990 and 2004 to issues concerning female students in higher education (73 titles), women teacher's attitudes, burnout and stress issues among women teachers and the academic performance among female students in schools as well as in higher educational institutions. The category "Feminism and women's rights" for both the pre and post 1990 years covered issues such as women's emancipation, feminism and rights of women in general and in particular the rights of divorcees and wives.

In Category 6: Health and welfare, more literature appeared on family planning, birth control, maternal health care, breastfeeding, child care, women's diseases, especially breast and cervical cancer among Malaysian women. A large body of literature in this category was published in journals. The next category, Category 7: "Legal status, women and family law" for the years 1990 to 2004 continued to cover issues on women's legal protection or lack of, family laws and legal rights. In Category 8: "Literary aspects, women in literature" in the post 1990s years indicated greater interest on analyzing women's portrayal in novels and short stories, women in the mass media and about women authors.

In Category 9: "Marriage and divorce, fertility and demography" there were over 200 titles covering marriage and divorce issues, reproductive rights, child birth, birth control and family planning rights and attitudes. Over 400 titles were concerned with socio-cultural issues such as traditional practices during child birth and pregnancies, the issues on late marriages and unmarried women, the obstacles faced by single mothers and the support systems available for them. Psychological aspects of the urban women were also the focus of studies, such as stress and women's ability to cope with their work and their home responsibilities.

A section for the 1990 to 2004 period warranted the addition of a new category – 13: Technology and Science, to cover studies on women's role in the science and technological world especially in academia and the school system. In general, the total count of publications between the pre 1989 years and post 1989 years according to the broad subject categories, totaled to about 4037 publications. Economic and socially-related issues were the most actively researched areas, making up to approximately 35% of total titles generated. Health and welfare issues literary aspects were equally popular.

TYPES OF PUBLICATIONS GENERATED

It is important for libraries to identify what are collectable items and which items could be solicited on exchange basis. The resources listed revealed the type of publications produced by authors on women studies in Malaysia.

The highest type of publications produced were academic research reports generated by staff and students of universities, especially in the form of final year research project reports mainly produced by the Arts and Social Sciences faculties of Malaysian public universities, Masters' dissertations and Doctoral theses. This pattern is similar for both years before and after 1989.

Academic research reports amount to about 30% of total types of materials produced. The data indicate the distribution of academic research reports produced by selected public universities in Malaysia. In all instances, Universiti Malaya and Universiti Kebangsan Malaysia were the main contributors, indicating active research on women's studies in these universities.

The number of academic reports, dissertations and theses from Universiti Malaya, Universiti Kebangsan Malaysia and Universiti Utara Malaysia was high because these items were catalogued and access was available from the respective online library catalogue. The other types of publications produced by rank order were conference proceedings, journal articles, books and book chapters.

THE ACTIVE AUTHORS: PRE 1970 - 2004

Knowing the active authors in any field of study helps the acquisitions librarian to acquire the core literature in a discipline. The resources listed in the two bibliographies provided the necessary data to identify the authors who have actively contributed to women's studies in Malaysia. Between 1990 and 2004 a total of 2797 authors contributed works on women in Malaysia, either as single authors, joint authors, editors or compilers. Multiple counting of publications was unavoidable as a large number of the single author also authored joint works. An overwhelming majority of authors were one time contributors (2417 or 86%).

This is a common trend among researchers in the social sciences and humanities. Those producing 4 or more articles constituted merely 4% (108) of total authors involved. A total of 18 authors contributed between 10 to as high as 54 publications. Wazir Jahan Karim who was with the Universiti Sains Malaysia contributed the highest number with 54 publications, followed by Jamilah Arifin and Cecilia Ng from Universiti Malaya with 34 and 32 publications respectively. In Universiti Sains Malaysia, the Kanita Project was started in 1978 and had successfully spearheaded research activities, seminars and workshops, which subsequently resulted in a number of journal articles as well as conference presentations on matters concerning women issues in Malaysia.

At the University of Malaya, the Population Studies Unit, at the Faculty of Economics had initiated research activities and generated a substantial body of literature in the form of conference papers, books and journal articles. The strength of research on women studies at the University of Malaya have further progressed with the establishment of the Gender Studies Programme at the Faculty of Arts and Social Science. This indicates that the existence of research centres did help to promote and trigger women studies. In comparison, the titles listed in Jamilah's bibliography (1991) for the period pre 1970s to 1989 revealed that a total of 449 authors contributed to published works.

Authors who were productive during the early years remained productive after 1990s. This is exemplified by authors such as Jamilah Ariffin who contributed the highest number of publications (18), followed by Nik Safiah Karim (17), and Ahmad Ibrahim (9). In the period 1990-2004, most authors (370 out of 449, 82%) were published once. Only 9 authors published 5 times or more. This comprises 2% of total authors. More foreign researchers were involved in women's research in the pre 1989 years than in the later years.

COLLABORATION PATTERNS

Collaboration is an important factor in research especially if the domain is multidisciplinary in nature and the trend of collaborative research is increasing. Often multi-authorship is taken as an indicator of collaboration. The data reveal that about 87% of total publications produced were singly authored. As most of these studies encompassed the fields of Humanities and Social Sciences, this authorship pattern is not surprising, as researchers in these disciplines often prefer to work alone. Most of the publications that were authored by 5 or more authors were in the field of "health and welfare of women in Malaysia".

This predominance of single authored works also the case for works listed in Jamilah's bibliography (1991), where only 32 (4%) titles were jointly authored by 2 or more authors. The majority of works were singly authored, indicating that researchers on women studies mainly work alone and collaboration is not the norm.

The data provided by the bibliographical works indicate the following:

- There was a substantial increase in the number of literature produced on women in Malaysia between the 1990s and early 2000s. From totals of over 300 publications every 10 years in the pre 1989 years, the amount of publications generated has increased about 8 times to 3346. This indicates a healthy and active research environment.

- There continued to be high interest in studying women in the work place and the focus was on the economic status of those working in factories on the assembly lines, the entrepreneurial ventures and the available support systems for working women.

Two other areas that continued to be of high interests were the social-cultural aspects in terms of rites and ceremonies where women were the key players especially in marriage ceremonies amongst the diverse ethnic groups in Malaysia. The problems faced by single mothers and the community support systems available were also highlighted in graduate research studies. Women in the mass media were actively addressed by researchers in Universiti Kebangsan Malaysia and Universiti Malaya. One area highly studied was the problems faced by women who were subjected to abuse and harassment in the home and the work place. This indicates area that warrants further study to ascertain why this is happening and how women's organisations and governance can provide adequate support to address these issues.

- Collaborative works are uncommon in the field of women studies in Malaysia. This may be because a large number of women studies are socio-economic based and studies in this field have indicated that researchers often worked alone or in very small groups. The authorship characteristics differ in the Science and technological fields where single authored works are on the decline.
- Those who were active in the years before 1970 to 1989 continue to be active between 1990 and 2004. The latter years saw an increase in Malaysian researchers and less contribution from foreign researchers.
- One contributing factor to the growth of studies on women is the setting up of centres for research and learning on women studies such as the KANITA project centre in Universiti Sains Malaysia and the Gender Studies Programme at the Universiti Malaya. These two moves have made it possible for women's studies to be managed and promoted to initiate greater research activities in order to sustain the current and future needs and interests.

The Kanita Centre for example is offering Masters and doctoral degree programmes.

- Although there have been various bibliographies compiled by individuals especially between the years 1999 and 2004, there is no cohesive collaborative institutional effort. This has resulted in bibliographies which are static and not dynamic.

To support research, a dynamic listing would be most helpful. This is feasible and viable in the Internet environment and extremely important in sustaining research activities in any of the subject fields.

The Internet can provide a complimentary avenue in the purposeful effort of collating, building and linking "like" and "related" resources both old and new. In reality collaborative bibliographical initiative could be initiated and maintained by a single compiler or a group who would rigorously select items bound by a topic. The framework for such a collaborative bibliographic system was proposed by Hendry and Carlyle (2006) who highlighted the main characteristics of such a system.

Firstly, the system would (a) allow for groups of people to participate in the selection decisions, to decide what to include or exclude; (b) enable incremental contributions and growth; (c) support a structured collections of impressive overall size; (d) organize contributors into a structured division of labour; (e) select items based on clear selection policy; and (f) design the system to support an "open bibliography" (allowing anyone to submit and rate items) or a "moderated bibliography" where a single reviewer or a group of reviewers blind-review submissions. Bibliographies are usually compiled by professional librarians or scholars and therefore could be easily differentiated from the listings compiled by amateurs or lone enthusiasts.

Kerriemuir (1999) and Bawden and Robinson (2002) evaluated subject gateways and lamented on the large number of people and organizations creating lists or links to resources without any quality control criteria, standard of descriptions and often do not meet the normal standard of bibliographic creations.

- Academic public institutional collaboration is becoming feasible in the case of women' studies in Malaysia, since for the period 1990 to 2004, 38% (1271) of the 3346 titles come from research activities at the universities in the form of Ph.D. theses, Masters dissertations and final year academic reports.

The remainders were literature generated from academic research activities in the form of journal articles and conference papers (40%) and books and book chapters (20%). Mutual exchange programmes on a title per title basis or non-restrictive inter-library loans could be advantages to institutions serving active researchers in this field. Collaboration and professional intermediation also becomes necessary to support purposeful bibliographic compilations to provide effectively for those seeking information, help sustain researchers' needs and promote possible networking.

2

Novels in English by Singaporean Women

The form of feminist agency we encounter in popular Anglophone women's literature from post-colonial Singapore (Mingfong Ho's novel, Sing to the Dawn, 1975; Lee Tzu Pheng's poem "My Country and My People, 1980; the novel, Serpent's Tooth 1982, and some short stories 1990's by Catherine Lim). All the stories address what is a stock theme of Singaporean women's literature-how Western-educated women deal with changing times and their different allegiances to modern and traditional (neo-Confucian), urban and rural Asian values. To an extent, the pieces conform to dominant nationalist narratives about the benefits of modernity and role of tradition in contemporary Singaporean women's lives. The seeming conformity to cultural narratives in these popular expressions should not be read as conventional women's submissiveness to patriarchal nationalist norms.

For intertwined in these acquiescent voices are strategies women adopt to re-form the masculinist values and practices of the culture to which they stake their loyalty. The difficulty of discerning these strategies, it seems to me, has to do with the absence of an adequate framework for reading the feminist claims that underlie nationalist women's voices. Post-colonial theories of female identity and agency by and large fail to account for the range and complexity of these feminist stances that arise under anti-colonial nationalisms. Here, I sketch one framework for discerning agency in these writers' imaginations, and discuss which assumptions underlying Post-colonial studies have to be rethought to provide this account.

Influential historiographies of anti-colonial nationalism suggest that women's cultural identities-laid out in codes by which they belong to their kin group and share in its collective future-are determined by the male elite's contentious relationship with imperialist modernity. Elaborating on Subaltern historian Partha Chatterjee's argument, for example, R. Radhakrishnan suggests that the nation's modern-educated new woman becomes the symbolic resolution to men's "schizophrenic" consciousness, their split reaction to a "temporality of modernity that authorizes" the progress-oriented white male as the best form of human.

The woman serves to repress this schizophrenia and enable her nation's new people (men and women) to step out into historical time to vie with Western man for material progress by symbolically taking on the preservation of a timeless inner self. Construed to be spiritually superior to the materialistic Westerner, this traditional self posits an alternate racial-cultural hierarchy against the dominant one. These Orientalist sexual politics of nationalism give men some flexibility in experimenting with modern concepts and tools; but they confine the new woman's identity in a spatiotemporal dichotomy. She has to keep tradition in the home and community and superficially adapt to the nation's social and economic teleologies in the private and public spheres.

Kumari Jayawardena suggests that although feminist ideas-women's education, voting rights, sexual rights-enter anti-colonial contexts in the course of nationalist reform movements, they do not necessarily enable women to correct the dichotomous construction of femininity. Geraldine Heng goes further to assert that women's issues are manipulated as "ideological and political resources" in national liberation struggles, and that this historical trend "commonly develops, in contemporary contexts, into the manipulation of women themselves as socioeconomic resource in Third World nation-states".

The consensus is that in the phases both of national liberation and nation- state development, the modern-educated woman plays a central role in the male-dictated patriotic 'causes' of competing with yet rising above dominant Western temporality. Women who are embroiled in these identity politics of male nationalism fail to command what is perceived to be the Western woman's "politically enabling" marginal position in the nation-the margin from which a feminist habitually critiques "centered capitalist ideology".

The implication of such studies is that the new woman's investment in her people's goals of gaining freedom from racial-masculinist domination and building independent nations inhibits her ability to self-actualize and intervene in patriarchal national history. This raises the central question of this chapter: To what extent cans a woman claim agency in her personal thought and practice and over her historical role without discarding commitments to her cultural community and its ongoing liberation struggle, during and after colonization? The challenge to attaining this political stance within, not outside, the communal realm is that the woman must stake her affiliation according to the terms defined by a community-reconfigured-as-nation: she must define herself and her role in terms of a past she shares with her people, and a future she collectively imagines.

However, the dominant version of the past and future, distorted by contentions between masculinities in an anti-colonial present, is precisely what imposes contradictions on women's everyday spaces. If the modern woman is to envision a feminist future in common with her people, she must speak both to these distortions and contradictions and their ideological premise, the schizophrenic split in male nationalist consciousness, but also for her nation's principal ideals and goals. She must speak with mainstream articulations of communal progress and cultural liberation yet retain the reflexivity to critique the manipulative aspects of the discourse and re-form its underlying ideology. To elaborate how and to what extent the Singaporean women writers find this reflexive voice, and why key assumptions of prevalent theories have to be reworked before we are able to think feminist historical agency in these terms.

One strand of Post-colonial theory entirely depends on the Foucauldian assumption that rational consciousness is a self-referential product of linguistic and social power structures in modernity. On this basis, some scholars suggest that women's acquiescence to imposed symbolic and material roles indicates an outright loss of historical agency. Through his reading of Indian women's texts Subaltern scholar Partha Chatterjee, for example, attempts to expose the "subjection of women" to a double patriarchal regime in anti-colonial contexts. He argues that Western-educated women's control over language "is doubly vitiated by their subordination at one and the same time to colonialism as well as to a nationalist patriarchy".

As a result, women are even less capable than their male nationalist counterparts of claiming an "autonomous subjectivity" that struggles against domination and constitutes power as a relation. Chatterjee's framework effectively recenters regimes of patriarchy, race, and class in emerging nations by way of obliterating signs of women's dissenting rationalities. As against this, many feminist Post-colonial scholars explore ways to theorize women's agency in nationalist contexts. They also avoid Western postmodernists' liberalist faith in individual agency, and the allied binary model in which feminist subjectivity is "synthesized from fusions of outsider identities" positioned on the utopian margins of masculinist-racist regimes. Instead, Post-colonialfeminists explore how knowledge/ power works pervasively and invisibly in capitalist modernities, constituting and "enabling" every subject position-dominant, subordinate, oppositional.

Many concur with the argument that "to speak from the margin is to be already complicit with the discourse of the nation-state... that creates and censors the margins". Within this feminist poststructuralist paradigm, agency is claimed through "muddying the pure positions". It has to do with demystifying all knowledge claims and exposing how these are constructed through hegemonic discourse and its various processes of centering the subject. It also is a matter of "performing" (Bhabha, "Introduction"; Butler) in the Derridean interval of historical time the contradictions and aporias in masculinist-capitalist discursive forms.

This means, however, that Post-colonial feminists tend toward yet another binary paradigm. According to this, agency consists only of subversively responding to a centered and all-encompassing episteme, and not at all of reconceptualizing mainstream concepts and tools in more empowering ways. Their rigidly anti-essentialist approach to the self and rationality does not allow critics to attend to those uneven and partial ways in which consciousness reforms ideology, impelled by other ways of knowing the present and connecting with the past that may exist around the dominant.

This approach denies that the development of agency has a cognitive component-that any political struggle to re-vision oppressive conditions has to be accompanied by a moral epistemological one. It fails, that is, to acknowledge that the possibility of "accurately interpreting our world and grasping what is going wrong in it, "fundamentally depends on our coming to know what it would take to change it". The extent of a subject's political agency depends on her coming to rationally think about which social arrangements and cultural practices manipulate her reality together with her community's, and how else these may be rearranged in "more productive ways".

It depends, in a nutshell, on an at least partial re-orientation of both thought and practice. The poststructuralist denial of this moral cognitive component of political agency quite commonly leads to a reaffirmation of binarism. Failing to account for the complex and uneven processes through which a subject struggles toward epistemic agency, critics tend to settle for differentiating already politicized agents from interpellated subjects. Some scholars do emphasize that "ideological boundaries" surround feminists of color, and that it is important in the interest of progressive politics to reconstruct differently "the raced and gendered 'I's' and 'We's'". But in general, Post-colonial studies of feminist agency fail to elaborate on the extents and limits of self-reconstruction and epistemic re-orientation.

Critics do not address how subjects break out of dominant nationalist ideologies, what the material and emotional constraints are to the reconstruction of female identities and roles, and how oppositional knowledge conducing positive change in the lives and worlds of women arises from within these constraints. These Post-colonial models do not allow me to explain the way that popular Singaporean writers address women's traditional and modern selves. For the writers look upon women's dominant identities and roles not so much as confusing fabrications that must be disrupted, or exposed for their constructedness.

They treat them as repositories of practical knowledge about how women struggle under dominant values and commitments but also strategically select from the old and the new to empower themselves together with their communities. In these literary representations, the women writers, together with reading publics who consume and enjoy the narratives, engage in minimally systematic reinterpretations of the existing life conditions of modern Singaporean women. The stories constitute a site for rethinking women's worlds-on the basis both of traditions (organic and reinvented) and of modern innovative ideas-in more productive and empowering ways. It seems to me that we can provide an account of how these narratives develop feminist agency if we begin by considering, as Geraldine Heng suggests, how women's "adaptations" of modern feminism are "mediated" by their social roles and cultural identities in anti-colonial nationalist contexts.

An emphasis on cultural mediation requires that we attend to both visible and submerged ways of knowing the self in relation to the present and past of a community.

Therefore, this emphasis requires that we extend Heng's framework in a way that allows us to explore two different things: firstly, how Singaporean women's adaptations are constrained by the nationalist paradigm of reformed/ traditional woman because of the security of belonging this affirms; secondly, how they may be inflected by different communal legacies of responding to and appropriating new knowledges as well as altering the familiar. I show below that one way to explore how these self-mediations occur in literary representations of everyday lives is to unravel the various levels at which the stories re-represent and "process" information about Singapore women's embodiment of dominant values and commitments.

In these popular literary pieces norms of feminine self become aesthetic products that constitute a locus of women's desire to gain advantage by conforming to social standards, and are marketed as such. But as symbolic re-creations of everyday selves, these also permit women-the writers themselves and their reading publics-to reflect on and rework imposed identities.

As Charles Taylor points out, a society's symbolic expressions lie between the levels of "explicit doctrine" and "embodied understanding" or the habitus; they bring together "images as yet unformulated in doctrine". In other words, symbolic understanding is somewhat fluid.

It represents and experiments with embodied forms of being and knowing, exceeding the doctrines/ formalized meanings that exert control on a particular cultural domain. In Singapore, whose daily life is strongly regulated by doctrines of Asian nationhood and capitalist progress, popular literature is one site in which women cultivate a "bifurcated consciousness". They begin to think in oppositional ways about the identities they embody and the roles they play in national history. These women's narratives are made up of conflicting strands that capture the multiple acquiescent and reflective voices in which the writers respond to modern and traditional femininities.

They show how women situated in positions similar to their own desire and adhere to them, and become embroiled in contradictory and distorted forms of reality. Through the partially reflexive practice of storytelling, writers also unevenly cultivate an understanding of why these distortions occur and how they may be rectified by drawing on non-conflictual practices of cultural exchange. In short, these narratives present inquire into how women struggle to claim cognitive agency over their embodied values and commitments. They interpret in a minimally systematic way what it takes to change the oppressive aspects of dominant selves.

These critical reflections on embodied femininities cumulatively produce a divergent history of Singapore life. This centers women who attempt not to synchronize their lives with prevailing nationalist agendas, but to transform existing social and symbolic conditions in a way that enables women's participation in communal interpretations of ideals and goals. Speaking to the common interest of decolonization, the writers persuade compatriots in overt or covert ways to seek in the interaction of modernity and communal memory not a hierarchical relationship producing totalized notions of adversarial humans, but intersectionalities between different cultural times, spaces, and epistemes of the human (ways of knowing the self in relation to the family, society, the cosmos, the good).

They draw on female cultural legacies of survival to sketch a Singaporean subject who is conceptually mobile, who selectively adapts new ideas and tools to change yet conserve traditions. This subject finds in no social arrangement unconditional freedom from sexualized hierarchies. But she seeks in all of them concepts and tools for a new society liberated from gendered forms of oppression. Before turning to the works, I consider them in their historical context.

DISJUNCTIONS AND INTERSECTIONS

The creative writings investigate how modern-educated women of Singapore are able to find their voices in a national history that surrounds them with contradictory constructions of the self. Since the establishment of independent Singapore in 1965, patriarchal nationalist discourse produced by the Chinese-dominated ruling elite has dexterously controlled the temporal and spatial conditions under which middle-class, predominantly ethnic Chinese, female citizens belong to the nation and practice citizenship. It has dictated that women will perform instrumental functions in the time and space of production; but they will truly belong only to the reproductive sphere.

Moreover, the latter's temporalities periodically have been manipulated to revive a stable (gendered and ethnicized) Singapore subjecthood. In the first phase of national development under the PAP government-People Action Party led by Cambridge-educated Lee Kuan Yew-there were obvious commonalties between the values and commitments ascribed to women's productive and reproductive identities, with undercurrents of contradiction. In the later, neo-Orientalist phase of ideological formation, the disjunctions became acute. After Singapore's expulsion from Malaysia and the common market in 1965, the government discursively constructed a nation caught in a "crisis of survival"; this demanded that every member be "transformed into a tightly organised and highly disciplined citizenry all pulling in the same direction of socioeconomic development".

In this first phase of social engineering, economically privileged women were made into both efficient workers and modern citizens whose progress vindicated the nation's rejection of its 'barbaric Oriental' past. They received English and technological education equally with men, and were encouraged to selectively modernize family arrangements and sensibilities. Government propaganda discredited such traditional values as preference for large and extended families, sons over daughters, and dependence on children for old age care.

Intending to enhance women's productivity in the workplace, Lee encouraged companionate conjugal relationships by urging men to partake in housework. Singaporean people were already living in nuclear forms of family due to their migrant status.

Now, they were indoctrinated in the bourgeois capitalist idea of the nuclear family comprising upwardly mobile male and female individuals. As early as 1961, this ideology of modern Singaporean womanhood had been institutionalized by the Women's Charter that showed unmistakable influence of Western feminist concepts about women's progress. It granted women unprecedented rights of societal participation and self-definition: enfranchisement, property-ownership, increased education and employment opportunities, divorce rights, and autonomy over their sexuality (through the prohibition of polygamous liaisons and marital rape).

Throughout this period of modernization and urbanization-extending from 1965 to the early 80's-the nation's elite Chinese new women also were reminded that their primary duty lay in socializing children in what were nativist hybridizations of modern Western concepts and values. They were to teach children a form of "individualism" that combined economic competitiveness with a citizenship "conceived less in terms of rights - as enshrined in the liberal-individualist tradition of Western societies-than in terms of community-defined duties".

These duties in turn were understood in Confucian-patriarchal terms, as these were being redefined by Singapore's Chinese elite. Women's task of nurturing dutiful individualists did not clash, in the arguments put forward by the leadership, with their other responsibility, that of preserving communitarian values against the "cultural and moral pollution" of the West. The next ideological phase of nation-building began around 1980.

In this period, there was systematic reaction against the "excesses" of individualism and consumerism perceived to have been bred by economic success. In the view of the ruling elite, these trends foreboded a decline in the state's control over its hypersubjective citizens. The contradictions between

Singapore's modernity and its re-invented traditions were now spotlighted as moral polarities.

Alarmed by the decline in marriage and fertility rates of university graduate women (largely Chinese) in comparison with less-educated women (largely Malay Muslim, also Indian Hindu) the government vilified 'hyper-individualist' graduates for failing to fulfill the familial and patriotic duties of marriage and child-bearing. As he defended the government's infamous social eugenics program-which gave tax-incentives to university-educated women to marry and have babies-Yew grew nostalgic about the past when families retained control over their daughters' biological destinies by arranging marriages. He also spoke admiringly of the "virile Chinese patriarchs" who had retinues of wives, mistresses, and illegitimate children, and even speculated on the possibility of reviving this virility in Chinese men through reintroducing polygamy.

The process of producing and legitimating nationalist female identities that had begun with the legal definition of the modern Singapore woman by the Women's Charter now was harnessed to the neo-Orientalist patriarchy of the evolving capitalist-racist state. These ascriptions of conflicting times and spaces to female identity have been integral to the elaboration of a national hegemony that upholds gendered and racial stratifications of social labor in the capitalist state. Yet a "lived" hegemony, even when based on outright propaganda and intellectual coercion as in Singapore, is always a "process": "it has continually to be renewed, recreated, defended, and modified... and is also continually resisted, limited, altered, challenged by pressures not all its own".

The spread of modern education and diverse progressive influences has produced many dissenting voices throughout the periods of Singapore's birth and development. The PAP government has been rather successful in coopting or marginalizing such dissenters, notably feminist and Marxist radicals. Through legislation, penalties, and restrictive libel laws, it has tried to curtail freedom of foreign and local presses, of parliamentary discourse, and of political opposition in general. Moreover, these censorship codes enforced by the one-party state have deeply influenced the everyday attitudes of Singaporean citizens. Viewing alternative political voices as illegitimate, the majority engage in acts of "self-censorship and/or the censorship of others".

Nonetheless, this stringent structure of governance has had to deal with an increasingly independent-thinking electorate. It has partially yielded to persuasions from below and periodically attempted to rebuild consensus. As is often the case, symbolic expressions, because of their reflective and processual nature, capture the "hegemonic in its active and formative but also its transformational processes". There are "counter-traditions" of literature that run against the grain of the "aesthetical ideology" that pervades the canon of Anglophone writing in Singapore.

The canon itself is produced by English-educated professionals who hold prestigious jobs in the state and want to avoid intellectual coercion. But many texts by Chinese-Singaporean women who hold such jobs carry the counter-traditions as well. In some instances, as in Catherine Lim's, these literary projects are intertwined with political reflections (discussed below). As a whole, women's counter-traditional literature presents an arena of hegemonic struggle between doctrinal meanings of Singaporean femininity and women's practical consciousness-i.e., lived relations of domination and subordination, and opposition to oppressive ideas and practices.

As the writers depict and reflect on everyday lives, they speak in conflicted voices about the status of new Chinese women in a world of shifting times, spaces, and ontologies. Their protagonists attempt to embody both traditional and modern roles and sensibilities, and find their lives fragmented by spatial and temporal contradictions: segmentations of families and communities into advanced-backward and authentic-inauthentic cultural sectors and the fractures of female bonds; temporalized hierarchies of upwardly mobile and backward classes and ethnicities, and of urban and rural peoples which also break down intra-community and intra-family bonds.

Through these symbolic portrayals of Singaporean lives, however, the writers also struggle to achieve cognitive agency over women's fragmented selves. They refuse to treat modern and traditional values and underlying social arrangements as the moral polarities defined by patriarchal nationalism. Instead, they draw on women-centered practices and communal legacies of non-confrontational exchange between different cultural rationalities. The pieces look through gendered lenses on the various intersecting and conflicting epistemic positions their protagonists learn or expect to embody.

They examine the individualist self participating in a "common action in profane time"; the rational subject claiming rights and reparations in the body politic; the mobile subject of a market economy; the monogamous nuclear family woman seeking companionate relationships. They also look into the implications for women of a collective self and its principle of communal-over-individual-good; a self attaining fulfillment in sacred time, a ritual, not purposive, rational subject; a non-individualist resistant self; and women's practices of self-empowerment in patriarchal and polygamous communities.

What these works attempt is to discriminate between ways of knowing the self and its community on the basis of the beneficial or oppressive impacts these produce on contemporary women's lives. Thus, these writers enter into the "temporal action or progressive, future drive" which Homi Bhabha considers to be a "value" of modernity. But they also resist the homogeneous times of dominant modernities. They contribute to the vision of a new nation whose progressive past contributes to a gendered decolonized future. They demonstrate that, from the standpoints of modern Singapore women's fragmented lives, insights may be garnered about a trans-temporal agent of national progress. This subject turns critical eyes on conceptual and material innovations, foreign and native. She seeks ideas and tools that enhance-rather than compete with or obliterate-communal histories of survival, self-actualization, and liberation.

WOMEN REINTERPRET PROGRESS

The poem, "My Country and My People" (1980), is written by Lee Tzu Pheng, a Ph.D. in English Literature and a faculty member at the National University of Singapore. Well-known for its advocacy of nationalism, the poem captures a socially privileged Chinese woman's perspective on nation-building at the height of Singapore's first spate of modernization, before the backlash against the West gained momentum.

Overtly, it concurs with the dominant nationalist agenda of controlled progressivism for Singapore's elite women. It suggests that modernization and urbanization have emancipated women like the narrator from oppressions of rural Chinese patriarchy and have granted them participatory citizenship in the new, egalitarian nation. Further, the narrator agrees that she must practice citizenship not only by "driving" into the city with the current of economic progress, but by nurturing the essentially human sentiment of neighborliness at the heart of a diverse nation:

> Yet careful tending of the human heart
>
> may make a hundred flowers bloom;
>
> and perhaps, fence-sitting neighbour,
>
> I claim citizenship in your recognition of our kind.

Put differently, the educated woman's productive role in the urban economy must be complemented by her role as reproducer of the spirit of national culture: she must nurture the transcendent human sentiment of togetherness in the hearts of racially disparate (also unequally privileged) citizens. Generically, this poem belongs with other celebratory development narratives produced by elite Singapore women in the first decades following independence. Noteworthy among these is the first novel by a Singapore woman, expatriate author and activist Mingfong Ho's Sing to the Dawn (1975; first published in New York and later in Singapore).

Although set in Thailand, the novel is a Singaporean period-piece in its choice of theme. It deals with how urban migration and modern education improve women's lives. The work is a commentary on the agenda of urbanization that was central in the first phase of Singapore's development. In this phase, the PAP government was erasing traditional habitats of ethnic groups-Malay kampungs, Chinese villages-and exposing selected segments of the population to modern education. The dominant voice in Mingfong Ho's children's tale is a didactic one, telling about a potential reformer of rural Asian social oppressions and evils. This reformer is a village girl who strives to reach the city and higher modern education in order that she may return to the village and uplift the backward conditions of her community.

Like Lee's poem, the novel imagines the development of the modern woman in teleological terms. It suggests that women become legitimate members of the community and trailblazers of progress only by moving to metropolitan centers of advancement. However, closer inspection reveals that both authors are only partially indoctrinated in the ideology of urban progressivism. Different strands of the narratives capture the other voices in which the writers persuade audiences. The narratives suggest that patriarchal modernist notions of progressive self and citizen fill women's lives with contradiction, and fracture communities. But they also show that these notions alter when women embody them and try to garner the benefits they promise: dignity and care for one's self and participatory membership in a non-hierarchical community.

Sing to the Dawn opens with the young protagonist, Dawan, receiving from her village school teacher the unexpected news that she and not her brother, the top male student of the class, has won the scholarship to pursue higher education in the City School. Because of the social and economic opportunities that come to her with this award,

Dawan is singled out for spearheading the changes her Marxist school teacher has envisioned for the villagers. She is expected to bring back to the villagers not only modern knowledge and technological tools ("how to raise new crops and use better fertilizers,") but new ways of analyzing and demystifying the socioeconomic institutions that perpetuate inequities in the village.

Notable among the institutions she must challenge are the land ownership and revenue systems which routinely cause lands and labors of the poor to be seized by feudal landlords who have now accumulated capital. In the words of the schoolteacher, if the scholarship-winner wants to be useful to her own people, she must acquire from progressive intellectuals of the City school a new critical perspective, the ability "to think, to perceive what is wrong with the society, to analyze and understand the rules which create these injustices... "

Although she is educated in the intellectual tradition of dialectical analysis by her school teacher, Dawan is depicted as being unable to move forward in the path of revolutionary social change until her grandmother steps into the enterprise of sending her to the city. The school teacher is one of a new breed of urban Asian men influenced by radical strands of modern European thought. He has traveled to the village to organize at the grassroots against rural inequities. His class-centered analysis is, however, limited by an elite male perspective that fails to take into account the specificities of how gender biases intersect with class, and what village women must combat in order to become agents of liberation.

The novel both complements and contrasts the teacher's bird's eye view of villagers' oppressions with the knowledges of village women. It depicts the oppositional wisdom of a multiply-marginalized villager, an illiterate and aged woman. Through her portrayal of Dawan's aged grandmother, the modern author symbolically revivifies progressive legacies of women's conceptual mobility and adaptation. She attempts to draw these legacies out of a collective/ personal memory overrun by the notion that progress constitutes a teleological movement away from the rural past toward a modern metropolitan future. Since the character of Grandma forms a symbolic bridge between the progressive pasts and the future of women, it also counteracts the dichotomy of static rural tradition and dynamic urban modernity presented by the novel's didactic narrative.

Grandma "has a way of sensing things". She is the first one at home to pry out of Dawan the facts that the girl has won a scholarship but that her brother and bosom companion, Kwai, sorely begrudges his defeat by her. Grandma then inspires women to mobilize against the patriarchal figures-the brother, the father, the monk in the local Buddhist temple-who obstruct Dawan's progress. She urges Dawan's mother to break her habit of ventriloquizing her husband's sexist biases and take independent charge of preparing for her daughter's journey to the city. She also breathes into the girl herself the empowering insight that women's courage to stand up to patriarchal bullies like Dawan's father wells up from deep within the wombs that produce these "big fierce men". In these and other actions, Grandma clearly represents the modern-educated expatriate author's effort to recall grassroots traditions of women's activism, self-definition, and participatory group formation.

The basis of Grandma's activism on behalf of her granddaughter is a non-individualist and relational notion of feminine self. She indirectly advises Dawan that to win over her father she must temper her courage with the recognition that his ferocity stems in part from the "burdens and worries" the impoverished peasant has borne. Grandma's principle of compassionate opposition counteracts the Orientalist stereotype, also present in the novel that unenlightened Asian men tend to be despotic and ought to be rejected by women seeking progress. Instead, the principle is shown to enable rural women's bonding with men who also suffer diverse forms of oppression, such as poverty and classist exploitation. Following Grandma's lead, Dawan wins over to her cause not only her brother and companion, Kwai, but the overbearing father.

Later in the novel, Dawan's father is shown to be strongly supporting his daughter's emancipatory vision "to do great things for them all... the village, and the country, even the world". Practicing this non-individualist philosophy of collectivizing the community against various kinds and levels of oppression, Dawan finally brings about a re-grouping of villagers across gender lines. On the eve of her departure, men and women alike gather on her doorstep; they symbolically converge on the goals of acknowledging the dignity of the female individual and looking forward to her visionary leadership of society.

Still, the novel does not present a utopian vision of a community homogenized on women's causes, nor an unqualified affirmation of the collectivist ethos of compassionate opposition. It shows that women who try to self-actualize and claim equal membership in making communal history must continually strategize in old and newly-acquired ways against dominant communitarian agendas that attempt to erase or co-opt their individualities. For example, there is no indication that Dawan succeeds in quelling the ferocity of all patriarchs who, like her father, react against economic and social oppressions by clinging to the last bastion of their privilege, possessive authority over family and community women. Posing an odd contrast to the communal assembly at the novel's close is an earlier scene. This depicts Dawan's schoolmate, Vichai, brutally attacking his own rebellious sister, Bao, for her support of Dawan's aspiration for a life independent of patriarchal control.

To celebrate the rare opportunity Dawan has earned of "flying to a bigger world" free of impositions by brothers and husbands, Bao permits Dawan to free one of the few caged birds she herself is vending. When Vichai learns of this, he attacks Bao on the charge that her whim will cause financial hardship for their family of impoverished pavement vendors as Dawan is unable to pay for the bird. But his plea of disciplining Bao in the cause of the collective good of the family turns out to be a cover for reactionary masculinism. As Bao is quick to note, Vichai grows angry because women like herself and Dawan assert their individual self-worth. This threatens his control over the one thing he owns, the birds he 'caught' and the women these symbolize.

This episode implies not only that the approach of compassionate opposition will not work in all cases, but that its underlying principle of placing the collective over an individual's good needs to be rethought in regard to women's well-being. The criteria for the collective good may well be determined by dominant men like Vichai who want to stifle germinal efforts of self-definition by women like Bao. If malevolent patriarchs like Vichai, whose viciousness is exacerbated by social inequalities in the present, stand outside the influence of Dawan's vision, so does their temporal opposite in the novel's map of patriarchy, the Buddhist monk who keeps the gate of the community's spiritual past.

Through her feminist depictions of malevolent and benevolent men, Mingfong Ho scrupulously avoids romanticizing the supposedly resistive knowledges of underprivileged or unmodernized people. Earlier in the narrative we see this monk's customary "gentleness" turn to authoritarian recalcitrance when Dawan tries to marshal to her cause his paternal authority over villagers. He reminds Dawan that her spiritual self will attain fulfillment and Nirvana only if she strives to rise "beyond" profane time, when suffering is inevitable, into sacred; it is pointless learning how to achieve material improvements in lives and times that must pass when all that is really valuable to know is not out there but in his "tiny temple".

To an extent, the monk stands for the nativist who wants to impose on the woman a static spiritual identity that signifies the timeless inner core of the community. But the scene resists a monolithic reading. Mingfong Ho presents not simply a pedagogic situation that the subordinated disrupts, but a polemical one. She pits a static against a dynamic vision of time, and ends the scene in a breakdown of communication that unsettles both parties. Dawan is embittered that she fails to communicate with her spiritual father, and the monk slightly saddened that such a "good-hearted" follower should rebel against his concerned guidance. This mutual sense of failed communication is conveyed through a poignant metaphorical image: "for a brief moment a glint of sunlight on his smoothly shaven skull seemed to catch and reflect the shiny tears from the young girl's face".

The scene underscores the intellectual struggles women face as they cultivate a purposeful way of understanding their roles in historical time-seeing themselves as transformers of oppressive social and cultural formations-and realize that their moral rationality has become incommensurable with the ritual reasoning that is presented to them as the core of their heritage of faith. It also sets the stage for a response. This response once again comes from Grandma. She implicitly argues that when women embody faith they rework the dichotomous male understanding of religious morality that separates the sacred/ ascetic realm from the profane/ worldly one. The implication is that the woman adapts spiritual sensibilities and rituals of faith to the dynamic ethical purposes of empowering herself against manipulation and reconstructing her community.

In characterizing the growth of progressive spiritual awareness in women, Grandma invokes a central Buddhist symbol of spiritual permanence, the lotus. But she presents the lotus in temporal and spatial movement. She suggests that women must be lotuses that "endlessly... unfold" across the inside and outside, the village and city and, by implication, cultural memories and modernities. This means that women self-actualize and grow resistant to gendered oppressions only when they cease to be afraid of newnesses, of what lie "outside" the circles of familiar time and space (cultural and religious customs, homes and temples) in which they are placed. Women ought to remain conceptually mobile because no singular cultural space or time affords freedom from patriarchal institutions.

In important ways, Grandma is a didactic portrayal that depicts the combination of knowledges progressive village women carry in them but must also acquire. Her words imply that custom-bound women such as her should draw upon the "future drive" that inheres in many women's histories of survival and empowerment. This is the drive to select from and adapt newly-acquired ideas and tools to empowering legacies from the past. The larger implication is that only when women refrain from a supremacist affirmation of one communal tradition and its culture of struggle are they able to avoid the risk of compromising their emancipatory visions. When they do not, they very well may be complying with family and community traditions manipulated by malevolent and benevolent powers.

In the novel's feminist schemata, visionary Grandmas from the past see the full potential of their legacy realized through the unprecedented opportunities modern offspring get for thinking cross-culturally about revolutionary change. The first of these is the scholarship that comes to the village girl and indicates the democratization of economic resources in a modern nation. It also shows, however, that capitalist distribution systems limit the democratic process by maintaining urban centers and rural peripheries of economic privilege. As Koh Tai Ann points out, only one scholarship reaches the village, and causes rifts in the family and the community.

What the single scholarship does afford Dawan is access to innovative intellectual resources for challenging the capitalist hierarchy that intersects with and rigidifies existing feudal patriarchal inequalities. The essential complement to Dawan's lessons from the past is her educational travel to an urban locus through which global cultures flow, and carry both hierarchy-forming and liberation epistemologies cultivated in other sites of struggle. These include Marxism and, implicitly, Western feminism which clearly informs this novel. Equally important, however, is the symbolic return of the new woman, Dawan, to rural Asia to rethink and re-contextualize her hybrid modern and traditional knowledges.

Sing to the Dawn presents a symbolic assessment of the temporal and spatial conflicts rural-tradition-bound women negotiate as they attempt to embody the ideology of urban progress in rapidly modernizing Asian contexts such as Singapore. It endorses the unprecedented intellectual and economic opportunities for resisting old and new social hierarchies that urban growth and ancillary global flows bring to women. But it transforms the very notion of 'progress' from a teleological to a cumulative temporal-spatial process-an ongoing cross-fertilizing and cross-critique of familiar and new theories and practices of gendered liberation. By contrast, "My Country and My People," the poem I briefly discussed above, overtly repeats nationalist ideology.

The elite Chinese author's ability to critique her dominant identity seems severely restricted, not only by the race and class privileges this identity gives her in Singapore but also because of her location within a repressive regime that censors dissent. In this respect, her location is in contrast to the expatriate Mingfong Ho's geographical and political positioning. Lee Tzu Pheng appears to concede to hegemonization also by writing about nationalism in the poetic form. Poetry, unlike the novel, constitutes the canon of Singapore literature. Nonetheless Lee speaks, as Ann Brewster rightly notes, in an "ambivalent" voice. She covertly re-tells Singapore's past and present to selectively concur with and differ from her poem's dominant narrative. What she aims is to find her voice and place her body in the history of national-urban progress.

The work reveals that its author is deeply invested in her people's struggle for decolonization. She indicates that her own life-story is inextricable from her people. Neither her people nor she has had the "comfort of their preferences" because conflictual processes of domination, subordination, and reaction-colonization, nationalism, modernization, reactionary traditionalism- have impinged upon the lives and times of all Singapore people. While she stakes her loyalty to her people, however, she also asserts right at the outset that her kind of patriotism is at odds with "fanciful" constructions of pasts and futures.

My country and my people
are neither here nor there, nor
in the comfort of my preferences,
If I could even choose.

At any rate, to fancy is to cheat;
and, worse than being alien or
subversive without cause,
is being a patriot of the will.

It is soon evident that she is re-telling history through re-defining the terms of her affiliation with her countrypeople. Being the "daughter of a better age," a Singaporean woman learning the lessons of modernity and progress, she was trained in English books. But this also was the day of militant anti-colonial nationalism, when "those foreign devils/ whose books she was being taught to read" were being cut down everywhere. Thus, although she entered the new Lion City (Singapore) with the "privilege" of a modern education, she was "sent... back fast to her shy forbearing family." She succumbed to the contradiction patriarchal nationalism bred and returned to village traditions in her 'authentic' Chinese home. There, she faced a rigidified patriarchy:

The city remained a distant way,
but I had no land to till;
only a duck that would not lay,
and a runt of a papaya tree,
which also turned out to be male.

If she does reaffirm the ideology of a new nation that arises from decolonization, then, the narrator also reflects on this ideology and why it must be reworked. She begins to understand that her person and body are contradictorily used as symbolic labor in the patriarchal discursive economy. On the basis of this partial knowledge of manipulation, she sets about reinterpreting her role in the nation. The poet reclaims the privileges of her education and class status and "drives," in real and metaphorical terms, on urban highways of opportunity.

But she seems to suggest that the city too does not offer her a supportive community, one that is free of sexual oppression: "They built milli-mini flats/ for a multi-mini society, / the chiselled profile in the sky/ took on a lofty attitude..." The implication is that the lofty phallic profiles of modern urban institutions give not much more room than the reinvented traditional home to her progressive, gendered individuality. It seems that the symbolic phallus is ubiquitous in all the cultural times and locations that surround her. In the course of the personal/ communal historical narrative she presents, however, the narrator still searches across her past and her present, her urban and rural experiences to find ideas and tools that will enable her participatory agency in determining her nation's future.

The last stanza, which claims citizenship by asking from neighbors "recognition of her kind"(quoted above), is multi-level in meaning. In the obvious sense, it reproduces the dominant ideology of multiracialism by making visible and overt the different "kinds" of racial cultural groups dwelling in Singapore. Propounded by the People Action Party, this ideology tailors the principle of racial pluralism that had thrived in British Singapore, under entrepot trading, to the interests of the nation-state. If we set Lee's claim of citizenship against the historical narrative that precedes it, we also note that the reproduction of multiracial nationalism veils a feminist voice that criticizes the exclusions this communitarian nationalist framework enforces.

The poem presents an argument about how the kind of citizen the narrator is can achieve recognition and participation in the nation. What she demands is that the nation be reconfigured in a way so that she is known not only as a Chinese citizen with her own customs, but as a gendered Chinese citizen. She must be un-circumscribed and un-threatened by masculinist "runts" of frozen traditions, and other such phallocratic "lofty" forms of sexual and psychic domination. Although this vision is gendered, it refrains from a binaristic feminist stance that interprets women's progress into citizenship as also the rejection of (Orientalized) traditions of despotic patriarchal communities. The vision includes all those like-minded countrywomen and men who want to join. The narrator reaffirms in the last lines

> My people, and my country,
>
> are you, and you my home.

In the stanza previous to the last, the narrator invoked the feelings of racial and cultural tolerance that had once existed in Singapore. As she put it: "I grew up in China's mighty shadow,/ with my gentle brown-skinned neighbours..." But she also implied that Singaporeans had progressed beyond the discrete composition of the pluralistic colonial society in which different ethnic groups had peacefully co-existed "because crossing over racial lines was near impossible"; post-colonial Singaporeans strive for a feeling of community among racial groups. In the last stanza, the narrator calls for revivifying the pre-existing organic spirit of tolerance in this new multiracial community-as-nation.

But also implicit here is her doubt about the ambivalent attitudes of her "fence-sitting neighbours." She attempts to speak to the feelings of racial and cultural alienation that underlie this ambivalence, and thereby to dispel the tensions riddling Singapore's reinvented multiracialism. Moreover, for the feminist nationalist narrator, speaking to the common interests of communal progress and racial harmony is not enough. She substantially reinterprets the legacy of tolerance and its significance in modern Singapore by introducing in it her idea of feminist-democracy-as-country-and-home.

Although this elite Chinese woman's depiction of a feminist citizen is more restricted in its vision of social justice than Mingfong Ho's class-sensitive reflections on revolutionary feminist change, the two writers come together in taking an important first step in the cause of feminist nationalism. Both

Lee Tzu Pheng and Mingfong Ho depict how women reconstruct themselves as active agents of history by becoming at least partially aware of and resistant toward their oppressive dominant identities, and how they try to build communities that support their trans-temporal vision of the future. In the overarching ethical objective of caring for oppressed female selves through resisting binaristic identitarian commitments, they are joined by a different category of female author, the commercial fiction-writer, Catherine Lim.

TRADITION IN FEMININE IMAGINATION

Like Lee Tzu Pheng, Catherine Lim holds a Ph.D. degree in Linguistics. She has taught in schools and served as a high official in Singapore's Curriculum Development Institute. She is best known, however, for her mass-produced novels and short stories. These address another strand of nationalist doctrine about Chinese Singaporean women. They consider what is involved in women's attempts to reproduce a frozen set of traditions while they also participate in the production of progressivist capital. Lim is a highly successful writer who thrives, like other commercial producers of culture, on instrumentalizing and packaging for entertainment popular desires and anxieties.

The fiction she produced through the '80's overtly responds to the growth of sexist neo-Orientalism in Singapore. The works assuage prevailing cultural anxieties about the social and sexual autonomy college-educated Chinese women were commanding, and the decline this was causing in the fecundity of their elite ethnic bodies.

They pit the decadent materialism and threatened desexualization of educated and upwardly mobile Chinese women against the social and sexual 'reliability' of rural females and women of bygone days, who kept the homes and bred the progeny of virile patriarchs. But nested within Lim's skillful "management" and repression of male nationalist schizophrenia are elements of another narrative about modern-educated women's critical engagement with the temporality of native traditions.

In recent years, Lim has spoken out against the lack of "freedom of expression in political debate, in the arts and the media" in Singapore, and how this is symptomatic of the "emotional estrangement between the ruler and the ruled" (Latif). Her literary works are related to the growth of these political views. In effect, they explore how modern-educated women can work across the "emotional" divide and speak freely for and to the Asian traditions the rulers attempt to revive and uphold. Her fiction suggests that for women preserving heritages and practicing the traditional self does not comprise memorized routines of 'timeless' values and commitments. Tradition-bound women constantly revivify as well as redefine habitual ways of relating the female self and body to its family and community.

The objective still is a mainstream Singaporean one, of preserving-not revolutionizing-family and community structures in a context where both men and women cope with rapid material and conceptual changes. Her first novel, Serpent's Tooth (1982) is illuminating in this respect because its protagonist, Angela, cultivates a dynamic understanding of traditional identity beneath her fragmented modern-traditional self. I discuss this work and connect it with some short stories Lim also wrote around this period. On the dominant level, the novel constructs a neat temporal-spatial binary of moral and decadent Chinese femininities.

Angela, a consumerist new woman who is the wife of a businessman-aspiring-to-be-bureaucrat and an entrepreneur in her own right, is openly blamed for destroying the timeless moral harmony reigning over rural Chinese female spaces, emblematized by her aged mother-in-law. Living in an exclusive private residence and driving around in an imported Toyota Corolla, Angela performs memorized routines of filial piety and kin-keeping, but utterly fails to connect with her rural and Chinese-custom-bound relatives. The narrative clearly blames her for causing fragmentation in the family.

She is shown to be identifying Old Mother with a valueless, past way of life filled with numerous irrationalities and superstitions. She denies the old woman the right to participate in raising the children and determining the family's future, her argument being that any association her children have with their grandmother's erroneous thoughts will retard the children's education and upward mobility. For betraying her venerable heritage, Angela also is fittingly reprimanded in course of the dominant narrative. Ancestral spirits haunt her dreams-of her dead father-in-law who will not recognize her dutiful rituals of respect, and of the rural patriarchal home that turns into a graveyard.

In this respect, the novel merely repeats a stock theme that appears in best-selling short stories by Lim. One of her early successes, "The Mother-in-Law's Curse" (later reprinted under the title, "Or Else the Lightening of God") depicts how the Westernized Margaret is cursed for her arrogance by her mother-in-law. Later, she is haunted, in her dreams and in waking hours, by both filial remorse and fears about the supernatural consequences of the curse. Driven to the brink of losing both her sanity and the child she bears, Margaret finally succumbs to the authority of her mother-in-law and her magical beliefs.

Another short story, "The Journey," narrates how a wealthy, professional Chinese man who learns that he is terminally ill chooses to leave the elegant abode of his materialistic and individualist wife to return, in search of physical and emotional solace, to elderly female relatives in the village. It is clear from these narratives that Lim markets her books by capitalizing on a particular nativist-patriarchal desire that pervades the rapidly changing context of modern Singapore, the desire to reappropriate woman as a cultural sign into the transcendent roles of keeper of a reified traditional Chinese home and breeder of a (male) progeny. Moreover, this centripetal pull of traditions, as defined by patriarchal nationalism, is even stronger in the prevailing ideology of female sexuality.

Modernized women are shown to be decadent and symbolically desexualized. In the bitingly ironic short story,

"The Awakening," Lim narrates how Peony pitifully fails in all her anxious efforts (which include investing in French negligees) to rekindle her aging Chinese husband's sexual desires because she is being soundly defeated at this game by the voluptuous Filipino maid. The story provides an ironic outlet for the ruling elite's anxiety that female fecundity resides only on the ethnic-sexual peripheries of Singapore, in the racially tainted bodies of lowly Malays and Filipinos. But it also implicitly exhorts elite Chinese women to reclaim their sexual energies and so regain their rightful positions in the racialized hierarchy of female sexualities in Singapore.

Serpent's Tooth, like "The Awakening," reproduces the center-periphery model of female sexualities. But other strands of the narrative introduce a significant alteration in the reproduction, capturing the author's bifurcated perspective on Chinese female sexuality. Angela's husband is lured away by their rural Malay maid, Mooi Lan; but Angela herself and her consumerist individualism are not blamed for this loss. The novel suggests that her husband's promiscuity is inherited from age-old customs of polygamous liaisons and concubinage that pervade Chinese patriarchy, and were rampant in Singapore until the institution of the Women's Charter.

This important point is made through the depiction of one of Angela's nightmares in which ghosts from the past come to haunt her, as if preying on the modern woman's independent existence. In this central episode of the novel, Angela is visited by the vision of the ancestral bed of her parents-in-law. On this bed, her father-in-law's body is twice replaced, first by a profligate grand-uncle's who is raping a Malay Muslim maid, and then, by her own husband's who is "locked in pleasure" with her maid, Mooi Lan. In this instance, Angela is by no means a conventional nationalist who gazes with Orientalist eyes on the sexual barbarities-the wild masculinities and exploited femininities-pervading her Chinese past. She suffers the same form of sexual domination, and moreover, must cope with it on her own, without the female support groups that existed in rural Chinese spaces.

This lack of a support group stems, on the one hand, from the nuclear framework Angela has sought to impose on her family life by casting 'backward' and uneducated relatives onto its periphery. On the other hand, it arises from Angela's partial disagreement with Chinese women's traditional tactics of resisting male promiscuity. These tactics are invoked by Old Mother. The only instance in which Old Mother openly bonds with Angela is when she offers supportive counsel about dealing with her own son's, Angela's husband's, profligacy. Old Mother recognizes, before the monogamy-oriented Angela admits so to herself, that Mooi Lan is a "snake" who must be disposed of (140-141).

Through Angela's dream, the narrative symbolically suggests that Angela herself values this ancestral legacy of resistant wisdom symbolized in Old Mother's counsel; for she sees Old Mother as a supportive figure in that central nightmare about old and new profligate patriarchs. Still, Angela cannot fully endorse the form of resistance Old Mother represents. In her dream, Angela is discomfited to see that the old woman silently comes in to clear away the stained sheets after Grand-Uncle's rape of the servant girl. Old Mother's dream behavior suggests that what underlies her covert attempts to bond with Angela in organizing resistance against the man's irresponsibility is acquiescence to the patriarchal structure that institutionalizes male promiscuity and blind faith in this structure's stability.

This faith stems from women's habitual lack of the opportunity to exert choice. The new generation professional woman, however, does have the right opportunities for economic and, at least partial, social independence. Concomitantly, she has cultivated an independent sense of sexual dignity. Therefore, Angela is uncomfortable with Old Mother's acquiescence to a social structure that institutionalizes the sexual degradation of women. Because Old Mother's form of resistance fails to engage this structure it is, in Angela's view, limited at best. Angela symbolically takes a step beyond Old Mother's partially progressive female legacy of collective survival and suffering.

She claims control over her own experience of sexual exploitation by selling the ancestral bed immediately after she gets this nightmare. Catherine Lim's depiction of Angela's partial disagreement with the resistive traditions Old Mother carries poses a contrast to Mingfong Ho's celebratory revivification of progressive female Chinese legacy. Lim exposes the strategic ways that women learn to be trans-temporally mobile to improve their own and the community's conditions. She shows that they evaluate and selectively discard oppressive traditions, they draw on and also add to enabling legacies of women's resistance whenever they get the opportunity to exert that choice.

The symbolism of the ancestral bed in Catherine Lim's fiction is critical to understanding Angela's response to Old Mother's legacy of resistance. The bed is a recurrent and ambivalent sign in many stories by Lim. Quite often; it is identified with a dying breed of Chinese matriarchs, specifically, with their fecund bodies that demand social authority because of the male progeny these have produced. The new generation of modern-educated Chinese women violates this authority by commodifying the beds as exotic relics of the past, and thus underscores their own materialistic decadence as well as the possibility of decline in their procreative energies.

However, on close inspection, stories about the bed ("A Bed: A life," "Monster") also suggest that the ancestral bed is a dynamic, not frozen, symbol of how Chinese female sexuality survives and is collectively nurtured by generations of women. In "A Bed: A Life," Chan Ah Keow's four-poster "absorbs the blood of her birth, her reaching womanhood, her being broken into". On it, she is suckled; she joins her sisters in making body pads out of rice paper when they start to menstruate, and storing these beneath the four-poster for "communal use"; she is raped by a profligate Chinese man; and, on her wedding night, she is camouflaged as a virgin by a resourceful grandmother (who supplies her with pig's blood for this purpose).

Defying the aversion her modern offspring show for the bed that carries these "terrible stories of sweat and pain and dark superstitions from the past," Chan Ah Keow clings to the memories of collective nurturance it evokes. She strives to revivify the dignity these memories give to her body. She dies in contentment only after she is brought back from the immaculate modern hospital to this bed which reeks with "sweat, urine, saliva, vomit". Angela's dream of the ancestral bed in Serpent's Tooth does give symbolic value to the tradition of communal nurturance of female sexuality by including Old Mother as a supportive figure.

But the novel also suggests that women like Angela who cultivate a sense of individual sexual and social worth restore themselves to dignity by attempting to change histories of degradation and domination, not by merely learning to survive within the seemingly stable social structures these histories reproduce. Tactics of survival within oppressive structures do not exhaust these women's claims to resistance and agency. Modern-educated Singapore women who seek to maintain traditional family and communal ties are portrayed to be adapting the epistemic positions acquired from new intellectual influences to inherited notions of social stability and the collective good.

Angela's assertion of individual self-worth takes a non-sovereign form. She acts according to Old Mother's guidelines, without explicitly acknowledging this, in trying to resolve the problems in her family life. She gets rid of the Malay maid and refuses to blame her husband for his promiscuity. Moreover, she stands by her husband when he is frustrated in his professional ambitions, and even takes some of the blame for this on her. However, she is depicted, on a meta-narratival level, as being critically aware of and politicized against patriarchal sexual and social oppressions. The narrative of her life is en-framed by a commentary in Angela's own voice, which perhaps captures the author's own bifurcated response to the story of an upwardly-mobile Chinese new woman she markets.

In this voice Angela declares that her family is in a "mess" which she alone can "clean". She also says that she cannot afford to "remember," live in fear of, the paternal ghosts who accusingly haunt her dreams. The implication is that she must forge ahead to re-stabilize herself and her family on her own terms. The large question posed by the novel seems to me to be exactly this, how the stability of Chinese family life can be preserved by women whose ways of knowing themselves in the present and thinking of the collective future have altered. The answer appears to be that women must critically redefine the criteria of the stable family. They must simultaneously evaluate and select from inherited and new ideas about women's survival and self-empowerment in patriarchal family contexts.

FEMINIST AGENCY AND CROSS-BORDER DIALOGUE

Above, I consider the productions of three writers who are unequally reflexive toward power structures in their feminist visions of social change. If Mingfong Ho's and Lee Tzu Pheng's come together in the quest for different forms and degrees of change in cultural, social, and economic structures, Catherine Lim's vision resists fundamental structural change. All want to preserve the overarching form of the heterosexual, ethnically and economically dominant Chinese family of Singapore. But they also underscore how modern women recast this form from within. My objectives in juxtaposing these works are two.

The Singapore women's emancipatory visions not only are constrained by the social and economic privileges that impose psychological blindness on subjects. In some instances they are restrained by choice. The subjects attempt to conserve communal heritages, and to partially align themselves with 'country people' who also struggle for this conservation against the manipula-tions of communal memory that accompany cultural colonization (during and after political colonies). Secondly, I have tried to underscore where the writers share common ground. They garner from the everyday lives of modern Singapore women a trans-temporal future drive. This constitutes the specific form of feminist challenge modern Chinese-Singaporean women thinkers pose to the gendered temporality of anti-colonial ethnic nationalism.

As a whole, these literary works underscore the point made at the outset, that when modern Singapore women speak for communal liberation and progress, they substantially redefine the constitutive terms of the ideals. In this light, it is useful to re-consider the question with which began the discussion and think through its adequacy for this and similar explorations of feminist histories. It seems to me that these women's works have demonstrated what is misleading about the question itself, and how it ought to be rethought by asking about the extent to which a woman can claim agency without discarding her commitments to her national cultural community.

To frame the question in this way really is to look at the problematic of feminist agency and national culture from an either/or perspective. Driving the binaristic perspective is skepticism about a woman's ability to think and act for self-empowerment so long as she abides by the roles and ideals dictated by male-dominant national culture. If we are to arrive at a notion of agency that accounts for the practical and conceptual struggles women undergo to recast such ideals and rethink their communal roles, we must revise the investigative query. We must ask: To what extent is a nationalist woman able to claim the agency to rethink what her commitment to the community means, and accordingly redefine the terms of her participation in communal history?

This revised question enables a fruitful investigation of the various community-centered feminist claims that arise in contexts of decolonization. It permits us to consider in what ways women intervene in the dominant national episteme and which factors constrain or otherwise limit these re-visions. In closing, I stress what the significance is for cross-border feminist debates of recognizing how different forms of feminist agency arise out of dominant nationalist subject positions. This recognition can produce more fruitful exchanges, across historical divides, on the common struggle for social justice if we take note of both its implications.

On the one hand, it reinforces the point many Post-colonial feminist thinkers make, that it is highly problematic to search for "a transparent or transcendent feminism... a space outside... patriarchal formations". Feminist consciousness arises at different intersections of sexual, racial, imperial, and class formations, and always struggles against interpellation by dominant discourses. Progressive selves are circumscribed by different privileges or their lack-which incites desire-and different loyalties. It is critical to the enhancement of cross-cultural feminist solidarity that we do not overlook the factors that circumscribe agency, or seek an essential legacy of women's liberation.

For if we do so, we impose centers and peripheries on women's histories, tending to separate those who are always on the path of emancipation from others supposedly victimized by despotic patriarchal regimes. Recognition of some forms feminist agency takes in anti-colonial cultures, on the other hand, also reinforces why the Post-colonial model of interpellation-and-response itself is only partially adequate for understanding different feminist struggles and achievements.

To discern these differences, and share concepts and tools between women's histories, we must be attentive to what motivates women in their advocacy for emancipation and how these motivations change with the context of domination-and-struggle. We must first acknowledge that an at least partial moral self-consciousness motivates political struggles, enabling subjects to selectively "break and reform ties to ideology" as they set objectives for their advocacy. We also must distinguish between the different assumptions, ideals, and aspirations that drive moral consciousness in diverse contexts of struggle.

This means that we must be alert to where and when a woman's aspirations for personal emancipation and improvement are mediated by her responsibility toward her community's on racial and cultural freedom, and to the ways that this sense of responsibility inflects her own liberation thought. This is not to assume that a loyal woman's objectives will be tailored to patriarchal visions of liberation, and constitute a predominantly "contributive history". It is to explore, as sought in the study of Singaporean women's voices, the uneven ways in which women re-determine the objectives of their contribution to their community's ideas about liberation and progress. My hope is that this study of struggles for epistemic determination in Singaporean women's literature paves the way to further cross-border dialogues on feminist emancipatory visions.

The way we, as feminist thinkers and researchers, can guard against imposing theoretical models of feminist agency, or its lack, on women's voices is by collaboratively examining how progressive subjects re-orient specific constellations of oppressive thought and practice, and where and why they meet their limits. What are called for, then, are conceptualizations of feminist agency that both focus on specific contexts and also initiate broader comparisons between contextual histories. These comparativist dialogues will reveal the specificities of feminist agency in different contexts. Moreover, they should enable mutual critiques of the factors that constrain feminist emancipatory thought in different contexts, or drive women to restrain their efforts to reform dominant ideology. It seems to me that a shared critique such as this of diverse women's struggles for epistemic agency will substantially advance the cross-border pursuit of feminist justice.

AN ANALYSIS OF TWO STORIES BY SINGAPOREAN WOMEN

If literature is the mirror to life, questions inscribed within literary texts have an important bearing on life situations. Thus, in the context of Singapore and indeed in many other countries where sensitivities regarding political governance can close off or closely guard many possible channels of articulation, the impact of silence emerges as particularly relevant. Very often this enforced silence is associated with an authoritarian system of government. Such a conception of power as essentially centralized is critiqued by Foucault.

He disagrees with the notion of power that locates it as an overarching structure. This model of power suggests the ability to compel obedience resides in a centralized authority. In contrast, Foucault argues that power is tolerable and is tolerated only when it masks a substantial part of itself. Power can be effective only when it is exercised at multiple sites and by no one particular agent. Thus the power to silence 'an other' may emerge as a strategic rather than a juridical model, where power is seen not as emanating from a central point, but rather as being produced by unstable familial and other communal relationships.

We get an opportunity to glimpse these strategic power points and how they successfully silence 'the other' in the two short stories by Lim and Tessensohn. Power acts to exclude and marginalize. From this act of exclusion, however, crucial significations can emerge. In order to comprehend these subtleties we need to understand the political and social setting of these stories, namely Singapore. Singapore-the modern island nation state situated at the southern tip of the Malay Peninsula is a nation of immigrants (mostly from China and India), with also a sizeable proportion of Malays, native to the peninsula.

Singapore has over the last three decades emerged as a remarkably successful capitalist economy following its separation from Malaysia. So successful has its economic experimentation been that many countries around the world have taken it as their role model for economic progress. This remarkable progress (which has been realized in the form of vast reserves in the world bank, very low unemployment figures and one of the highest per capita incomes in Asia) has been accomplished through a system of 'communitarian democracy,' as it has come to be termed, and a climate of multiculturalism.

The major races that inhabit the island according to the last census figures released in 2000 are the Chinese who form the majority with around 76.8%, the Malay, who form the second largest segment with about 13.9%, and the Indians, the third largest section forming a minority of about 7.9%. The rest-1.4%-is made up of what official terminology specifies as 'Others'-mainly constituted of Eurasians, Caucasians and the expatriate community. Economic growth has enabled remarkable social changes to be fostered, particularly in the areas of education and health.

This in turn has brought about notable changes in the lifestyle of both men and women in Singapore. Women have excellent access to jobs, education and have progressed steadily over the last thirty years. There is no doubt, however, that the speed of change has made it impossible for all sections of society to benefit equally, and inevitably some social groups have been left behind. This is particularly the case for orthodox and working class sections of the three Asian communities. The two female protagonists in "Bandong" and "Kumari," from Chinese and Indian communities respectively, inhabit the narratives, imprinting their presence strongly within them.

They are, however, portrayed as completely silent from the beginning to the end of the narrative, throughout the entirety of events set into play by their initial actions. This chapter sets about analyzing how and why silence as a strategy holds sways in the lives of these two women and seems to become their only mode of expression. Predictably enough, silence has never been considered alien to women in any patriarchal society. Feminist theorists such as Felman point out how Derrida and other deconstructionists, who critique the logocentrism of Western metaphysics, perceive it as based on the principle of the repressive predominance of 'logos'-primarily speech over writing.

This perception gives a privileged status to voice and valorizes 'presence.' This presence-to-itself of a centre (given the name of Origin, God, Truth, Being, or Reason) centralizes the world through the authority of self-presence.

Consequently, it subordinates to itself, in a hierarchical manner, all the other cognizable elements of the same epistemological (or ontological) system. Thus thought (presence/absence, being/nothingness, truth/error, self/other, identity/difference, etc.) is identified in fact as a subtle mechanism of hierarchization, which assures the unique valorization of the positive pole and the subordination or repression of the negative.

Feminists claim that this binary division therefore privileges masculinity over femininity, speech over silence and so on. The implication follows that within Western discourse is inscribed a latent design which works to exclude women from the logical production of speech. However, though speech generally means empowerment and silence is more often than not arraigned on the side of powerlessness, the equation is not always straightforward. This is because, traditionally, in Western societies, a strange ambivalence exists with regard to silence as a concept. In society at large and in educational institutions in the West, there is, without doubt, a great premium placed on verbal assertiveness.

By contrast, silence is often perceived negatively as absence or, as Tannen and Saville-Troike (xi) point out, 'an out-of-awareness phenomenon.' In other words, silence is merely the background against which talk takes place. Even in the Bible, several of the allusions regarding speech and silence are mostly negative. Paradoxically, however, within the Bible itself, and in Western philosophical tradition at large, there is also a strain of sentiment that valorises silence. In the Ecclesiastes we are abjured that there is "a time to keep silence and a time to speak".

Furthermore, in the philosophical tradition many, starting with St Augustine, and continuing with others, including Heidegger and Wittgenstein have valorized forms of silence. Also, from proverbs that exist in English and several European languages ("Speech is silver, silence is golden;" "Empty vessels make the most sound;" "Still waters run deep"), it is clear that Western folk culture attaches a positive value to silence.

WOMEN AND SILENCE

This ambivalent stand with regard to silence is also apparent in feminist discourse. On the one hand, when opposed to speech, silence seems to imply powerlessness and yet, on the other, when opposed to chatter it seems to indicate power. Ironically, feminist theorists point out how within texts in patriarchy, women have always been ranged on the side of powerlessness. Thus, we can point to the enduring social and literary stereotypes of the chattering bird-witted woman who is opposed to the strong, silent purposeful male or, in contrast, to the forceful, articulate male who is thrown into relief by a silent (often passive) woman, whose silence then comes to signal sullenness, stupidity or cunning. These stereotypes are played out extensively in Hollywood films of the fifties and sixties as well.

This idea of silence as a largely negative entity that conveys variously inscrutability, docility, passivity and submissiveness has also led to minority groups living in the West being labelled in certain distinctive ways. In Articulate Silences, a study of silences in fictions by Asian-American women, King-Kok Cheung makes the link between women and minority groups when she points out that "the quiet Asians are seen either as devious, timid, shrewd, and above all 'inscrutable'-in much the same way that women are thought to be mysterious and unknowable-or as docile, submissive, and obedient, worthy of the label 'model minority', just as silent women have traditionally been extolled".

In many Eastern cultures, however, silence contains complex significations. Cheung for instance, analyzes different kinds of silences that prevail in distinct Asian Cultures such as Japan and China. Silence therefore need not necessarily be the result of prohibition either by patriarchal structures or a dominant culture. On the contrary, silences can carry meanings that vary with individuals and cultures.

The two women protagonists are Ah Fah-wife of Ah Lai, the acknowledged 'village idiot' in "Bandong," and Kumari, the central figure in the story by that name, both located geographically in the Malay/Singapore peninsula. While "Bandong" is set in an earlier pre-colonial Chinese settlement, the "Kumari" is very much the product of the modern, present-day nation-state. Despite this contrast in the stories, which should inevitably reflect the different social circumstances within which the women exist, the writers still foreground silence as an innate yet indefinable element of the 'self' in the two women protagonists. "Bandong" relates the tale of a woman being punished for adultery. The omniscient narrator of "Bandong" presents the adulteress first from the perspective of Wong Tuck Heng, an immigrant and a newcomer from the Chinese mainland to a tin mining settlement in the Malay Peninsula.

On his arrival Wong witnesses the torture and pillory of a young woman, Ah Fah, by the Cantonese community of men and women who punish her for adultery with a man from a rival Hakka clan. The woman is finally drowned in a basket used to carry pigs to the market. We thus enter the episode from Wong's male perspective. He is the spectator; the woman is the spectacle, the object of the androcentric gaze. As Wong's companion and guide, an older miner from the settlement gleefully informs him: "The gods, ah! You're in luck, young dog! They are going to drown the bitch tonight. Come, come! You can watch it with me".

Ah Fah is both figuratively and literally at the receiving end of the community's wrath. When Wong first comes upon her, she is at the centre of an angry mob that is circling her ominously, "splattered with mud and dung, and bleeding from several lacerations on her face and arms", we are told that "it was obvious that she had been whipped and the lashes had cut deep into her flesh". Verbally too, she is abused ("slut, slattern"), and thereby reduced to her sexual parts. At the end when she is being carried to the sea in the pig basket, the sex-starved men also sexually abuse her. Throughout all these experiences, however, she never utters a word.

In Tessensohn's short story "Kumari" we encounter another mute woman. The narrative relates the story of how the young Indian girl Kumari, who serves at the till in a local

National Trade Union Congress NTUC supermarket is persuaded by a Malay social do-gooder Arif Mydin to steal from the store in order to replenish the rapidly diminishing stock of a neighbourhood home for the elderly that is very short of funds. Kumari's theft is discovered and a move is made to bring her to trial. But the situation is speedily resolved by the timely intervention of the inmates of the home who represent the case to their Member of Parliament who, in turn, intercedes successfully on Kumari's behalf.

Kumari is freed through no active representation on her part. A progressive young man comes forward to marry her, who she passively accepts, and she is set for a happy future. The two short texts complement each other in significant ways. In both, the central protagonists never utter a word throughout the narratives. Their plights are conveyed to us through the narrative voice. This strategy, however, offers no insight into their minds. Kumari is shown as rather slow and incapable of absorbing the actual significance of her act.

She is shown as eminently persuadable and as blindly following the instructions of her friend Arif Mydin. Therefore, her inner thoughts when presented show themselves to be infantile, confused and illogical.

Lim's protagonist in "Bandong" is even more of a problem for the reader because her inner thoughts or opinions are never probed or displayed. She goes to her death with her thoughts a complete mystery. Readers, however, do not perceive this young adulteress as either dim-witted or submissive as a person.

In intriguing but contrasting ways in both narratives, silence becomes an aspect of the feminine expression or 'voice.' It becomes interesting to analyze the process through which a subjective self is constituted in the complete absence of speech in the two stories. The women writers seem to signal sympathy for completely silent characters in their texts. The strategies used and significations that emerges out of these become important to our considerations. One possible point of entry for our analysis could be Bakhtin's 'dialogics.'

VOICE IN SOCIETY

In The Dialogic Imagination Bakhtin points out that "the novel always includes in itself the activity of coming to know another's word, a coming to knowledge whose process is represented in the novel". According to Bakhtin, language offers many social voices. These voices construct both selves and characters-as-selves. Because all language is inherited and because it is all socially and ideologically charged, the conflict of voices in a novel can reveal power structures and potential resistances to those structures.

Each character's voice within a dialogized novel, Bakhtin claims, represents ways of seeing the world; that voice competes for ascendancy to power or, at least, seeks an intense relationship on the threshold where boundaries between the languages of self and other break down. Though Bakhtin was, in effect, talking about the novel, it could be usefully applied to the fictive world of the short story as well.

Where the story-teller is loyal, eternally and unswervingly loyal to the story, there in the end silence will speak. Where the story has been betrayed, silence is but emptiness. But we, the faithful, when we have spoken our last word, will hear the voice of silence. (Isak Dinesen, The Last Tales 100)

The above lines are spoken by an old, wrinkled, gypsy storyteller in Isak Dinesen's short story, "The Blank Page." The story addresses one of the paradoxes central to literary studies-the significance of silence in making meaning. Literature is ever primed to explore the nuances of language. It deals with, among other things, the precision and subtlety in various kinds of articulation. In "The Blank Page," however, it is precisely the limit of articulation that is explored: how at times silence can become a more important signifier than speech.

In this chapter I explore how the silenced can make this removal of voice an important way of communicating their resistance. These two short narratives deal with the poor, hence parochial, community and the working classes of two Asian races, Chinese and Indians. "Bandong" and "Kumari" are of interest because they are written by two Singaporean women hailing from two of the four identified racial groups in Singapore. Christine Suchen Lim is a Chinese who can claim antecedents from two different Chinese dialect groups-her Cantonese mother and her Hokkien father. Denyse Tessensohn is of Eurasian descent. "Bandong" is an extract, from a longer novel by Lim that is forthcoming while "Kumari" is a short story.

POWER AND SILENCE

If literature is the mirror to life, questions inscribed within literary texts have an important bearing on life situations. Thus, in the context of Singapore and indeed in many other countries where sensitivities regarding political governance can close off or closely guard many possible channels of articulation, the impact of silence emerges as particularly relevant. Very often this enforced silence is associated with an authoritarian system of government. Such a conception of power as essentially centralized is critiqued by Foucault.

He disagrees with the notion of power that locates it as an overarching structure. This model of power suggests the ability to compel obedience resides in a centralized authority. In contrast, Foucault argues that power is tolerable and is tolerated only when it masks a substantial part of itself. Power can be effective only when it is exercised at multiple sites and by no one particular agent. Thus the power to silence 'an other' may emerge as a strategic rather than a juridical model, where power is seen not as emanating from a central point, but rather as being produced by unstable familial and other communal relationships.

We get an opportunity to glimpse these strategic power points and how they successfully silence 'the other' in the two short stories by Lim and Tessensohn. Power acts to exclude and marginalize. From this act of exclusion, however, crucial significations can emerge. In order to comprehend these subtleties we need to understand the political and social setting of these stories, namely Singapore. Singapore-the modern island nation state situated at the southern tip of the Malay

Peninsula is a nation of immigrants (mostly from China and India), with also a sizeable proportion of Malays, native to the peninsula.

Singapore has over the last three decades emerged as a remarkably successful capitalist economy following its separation from Malaysia. So successful has its economic experimentation been that many countries around the world have taken it as their role model for economic progress. This remarkable progress (which has been realized in the form of vast reserves in the world bank, very low unemployment figures and one of the highest per capita incomes in Asia) has been accomplished through a system of 'communitarian democracy,' as it has come to be termed and a climate of multiculturalism.

The major races that inhabit the island according to the last census figures released in 2000 are the Chinese who form the majority with around 76.8%, the Malay, who form the second largest segment with about 13.9%, and the Indians, the third largest section forming a minority of about 7.9%. The rest 1.4% is made up of what official terminology specifies as 'Others'-mainly constituted of Eurasians, Caucasians and the expatriate community.

Economic growth has enabled remarkable social changes to be fostered, particularly in the areas of education and health. This in turn has brought about notable changes in the lifestyle of both men and women in Singapore. Women have excellent access to jobs, education and have progressed steadily over the last thirty years. There is no doubt, however, that the speed of change has made it impossible for all sections of society to benefit equally, and inevitably some social groups have been left behind. This is particularly the case for orthodox and working class sections of the three Asian communities.

The two female protagonists in "Bandong" and "Kumari," from Chinese and Indian communities respectively, inhabit the narratives, imprinting their presence strongly within them. They are, however, portrayed as completely silent from the beginning to the end of the narrative, throughout the entirety of events set into play by their initial actions. This chapter sets about analyzing how and why silence as a strategy holds sways in the lives of these two women and seems to become their only mode of expression.

Predictably enough, silence has never been considered alien to women in any patriarchal society. Feminist theorists such as Felman point out how Derrida and other deconstructionists, who critique the logocentrism of Western metaphysics, perceive it as based on the principle of the repressive predominance of 'logos'-primarily speech over writing. This perception gives a privileged status to voice and valorizes 'presence.'

This presence-to-itself of a centre (given the name of Origin, God, Truth, Being, or Reason) centralizes the world through the authority of self-presence. Consequently, it subordinates to itself, in a hierarchical manner, all the other cognizable elements of the same epistemological (or ontological) system. Thus thought (presence/absence, being/nothingness, truth/error, self/other, identity/difference, etc.) is identified in fact as a subtle mechanism of hierarchization, which assures the unique valorization of the positive pole and the subordination or repression of the negative. Feminists claim that this binary division therefore privileges masculinity over femininity, speech over silence and so on. The implication follows that within Western discourse is inscribed a latent design which works to exclude women from the logical production of speech.

However, though speech generally means empowerment and silence is more often than not arraigned on the side of powerlessness, the equation is not always straightforward. This is because, traditionally, in Western societies, a strange ambivalence exists with regard to silence as a concept. In society at large and in educational institutions in the West, there is, without doubt, a great premium placed on verbal assertiveness. By contrast, silence is often perceived negatively as absence or, as Tannen and Saville-Troike point out, 'an out-of-awareness phenomenon.' In other words, silence is merely the background against which talk takes place.

Even in the Bible, several of the allusions regarding speech and silence are mostly negative. Paradoxically, however, within the Bible itself, and in Western philosophical tradition at large, there is also a strain of sentiment that valorises silence. In the Ecclesiastes we are abjured that there is "a time to keep silence and a time to speak". Furthermore, in the philosophical tradition many, starting with St Augustine, and continuing with others, including Heidegger and Wittgenstein have valorized forms of silence. Also, from proverbs that exist in English and several European languages ("Speech is silver, silence is golden;" "Empty vessels make the most sound;" "Still waters run deep"), it is clear that Western folk culture attaches a positive value to silence.

Ah Fah's predicament is presented to us through a complex set of competing discourses. On the one hand, her sexuality is shown to be excessive and therefore threatening to the community. She has been bought from a brothel keeper and she has committed adultery with a man from a rival clan knowing full well the dire consequences if she were discovered. This seems to point to an excessive passion/lust threatening the stability of her community. The community is enraged: "Let the whore die!' 'Without coffin or mourners!'... 'Not so fast!'... 'Strip and whip her first! Death is too sweet for traitors like her!".

The miners and their families pelt the accused woman with lumps of pigs' dung and shout abuse at her. However, we are told that The woman who was bound hand and foot showed no sign that she had heard. Her eyes were glazed and fixed at a point above the heads of the mob. Her impassive face was oblivious of her tormentors. A miner went forward and gave her a violent kick. She fell on to her side but no sound escaped her lips. No cry. None. She lay where she had fallen.

Despite the fact that the crowd is angered and frenzied by her silence, she refuses to satisfy them by uttering any sound except that of pain when she is goaded and physically hurt beyond endurance. Moreover, we are also shown the feeling of compassion she arouses in Wong, the newcomer:

"Tuck Heng trotted beside Chan Ah Fook, his heart torn between pity and excitement".

Later on her death opens up the voices of the other women in the community, who speak up in sympathy: When you locked him in the bedroom with Ah Fah, he kicked Ah Fah and bit her. She showed me the teeth marks all over her body. Bit her like a dog. We heard her cries. Our whole village heard her cries. How to bear you a grandson? You blamed her and you caned her. Every night you caned her... But, aye, a mother-in-law is the sky and we daughters-in-law are the earth.

Here, her initial positioning as the adulteress seems to be contested. She is positioned more as a woman to be pitied. But her identity as a victim, we realize, is precariously constructed. As readers who are outside the narrow codes that rule the community we are inclined to sympathise with her sad predicament. This would perhaps predispose us by and large, to be 'on her side'. However, we also understand the codes that rule the commune and the strong sense of threat that her action poses to the community.

In all of this, what is carefully glossed over is her sexuality, the very issue at the centre of the narrative. Her silence conceals the excess of her sexuality investing her nature with mystery and pathos. The precise nature and reason for her adulterous acts is left unexplained. The silence of the adulteress is in the interest of the narrative. For, if we had access to Ah Fah's inner thoughts we would have known the reason for her adultery. Then the danger would arise that her motivations for adultery would be out in the open perhaps emphasizing her excessive sexuality.

In this case, the precarious balance of power achieved between the community at large and Ah Fah would be ruptured, one way or the other. If she is shown as having committed the adulterous act only to fulfil her mother-in-law's desire for her child, she would emerge as undeniably more powerful than the indicting community. On the other hand, if it is revealed that Ah Fah formed the adulterous liaison for her own pleasure then the power would unequivocally shift to the community condemning her for her excessive sexuality.

However, as it stands in the narrative, with no clue to Ah Fah's motivations there is a tight opposition set up between the surveillant gaze of the repressive, parochial community and the disruptive silence of the female protagonist. This tension constitutes the structure of the text. Her death or 'sacrifice' is a metaphor to be conscripted into the dialogue of the interpretive community. Her death forces her internal dialogue into the open raising questions rather than closing them, about the norms in place in the community.

It is only after her death that Wong returns to the temple where the women are seated awaiting their men's return from the river and witnesses their heated debate about Ah Fah's distressing life. Her silence therefore paradoxically becomes Bakhtin's 'resisting voice' challenging dominant codes. The contradiction between her will and the authoritative will of the community inform the events of the novel. In the ultimate analysis, it is crucial to grasp the fact that she evades being caged or imprisoned by language. It is through silence that she sets up an effective dialogue with the rest of the interpretive community.

This contradiction places her in the ambivalent position of belonging to neither class of Freud's daughters. Ah Fah is not quite the 'obedient daughter,' the hysteric almost always identified as a woman ('hysteria', significantly, is derived from the Greek word for uterus) who uses only her body language to communicate and who depends on her patriarchal father to be released into speech. This obedient daughter speaks only with her body and does not aspire to challenge the hierarchies in place in patriarchy.

We know, from the discussion above, that Ah Fah in "Bandong" does not fade into muteness like the obedient daughter, but precisely through her silence challenges the status quo. Nor does she exactly emerge as the 'rebellious daughter,' who dares to match the patriarch word for word, for she firmly remains in the realm of silence never emerging into the zone of speech shared by the rest of the interpretive community.

French feminist literary theory associated with theorists such as Cixous and Irigaray, introduce the interesting figure of the madwoman who they interpret as redemptive. She is taken to be not what an oppressive culture has made of women, but rather what women have managed to remain in a society that marginalizes the disruptive revolutionary force of the female. Christiane Makward, one of the important translators of and commentators on French feminism, describes the female language as open, non-linear fluid, involving silence.

From another perspective, Domna C. Stanton points out that the recurring identification of madness, anti-reason and mystery only goes to revalorize traditional female stereotypes. She points out that It is an essentialist definition making women incapable of speaking as a woman; therefore, the most female course of action is to observe an hour of silence, or to scream... Women are resigning themselves to silence and to nonspeech. The speech of the other will then swallow them up, will speak for them. In the above definition, the normal premise prevalent within Western metaphysics that ascribes nothing but powerlessness and disempowerment to silence is prominent. What marks the unique position of Kumari and Ah Fah is that through their efforts they dare to radicalize this premise.

In the final analysis, the determination that both women display to remain silent against all odds emerges not as passivity but as subversion, subversion not ascribed to the function of the character, but to the function of the narrative. Through their silence, the normal hierarchy of Western metaphysical thought gets overturned. Speech and meaning becomes replaced with silence and meaning and the usual correlation between presence and signification gets altered here into absence and signification. This disruption in effect points to a new, radical functioning of narrative.

3

Filipino Women Novelists and their Novels

The history of Filipino women writers is an account of how Philippine women became literary "mistresses of the ink" and "lady pen-pushers" who created works of fiction or factual and historical storybooks, poetry, novels, short stories, essays, biographies, autobiographies and other known writing genres. Writing in English, Spanish, Filipino and other local languages and native dialects, female writers from the Philippine archipelago utilized literature, in contrast with the oral tradition of the past, as the living voices of their personal experiences, thoughts, consciousness, concepts of themselves, society, politics, Philippine and world history.

They employed the "power of the pen" and the printed word in order to shatter the so-called "Great Grand Silence of the Centuries" of Filipino female members, participants, and contributors to the progress and development of the Philippine Republic, and consequently the rest of the world. Filipino women authors have "put pen to paper" to present, express, and describe their own image and culture to the world, as they see themselves.

Among the principal influences to the Filipina image of herself and to her writings include four women in Philippine history, namely: Gabriela Silang, Leonor Rivera, Imelda Marcos and Corazon Aquino. Often mentioned in Philippine literature, these four represents the struggle, perception and character of how it is to be a woman in Philippine society. Gabriela Silang was a *katipunera* or a revolutionary a representation of female bravery who fought against the Spanish colonialism in the 1700s. Silang was a contrast to the chaste and religiously devout image of the Filipino lady as portrayed by Jose Rizal through his Spanish-language novels, *Noli Me Tangere* and *El Filibusterismo*.

Within the pages of these novels of the 1800s, Rizal depicted Leonor Rivera - a girlfriend of his - through the fictional character of *Maria Clara* as the epitome of virtue, the ideal Filipina. Then there was the arrival of Imelda Marcos – the "beauty queen… dictator's wife… the power-seeking kind of a woman…" – and then there was the advent and the rise of Corazon C. Aquino, the first woman president in Asia and the Philippines – the elected 1986 replacement of a male despot, Ferdinand Marcos. Gloria Macapagal-Arroyo, after two male presidents (Fidel V. Ramos and Joseph Estrada, respectively), followed the footsteps of Corazon Aquino into becoming a leader and political figure of an Asian nation.

In later years of modern-day Philippine literature, from the 1960s to the 1980s, feminism became the focus of Philippine women writers – first in poetry and then prose – in order to break away from what is termed as the "Great Grand Silence of the Centuries". The creation of an image unique to themselves – through their own individual efforts – became the norm. There were criticisms against the *Maria Clara* image portrayed by the Philippine paladin, José Rizal, as well as critiques and female disapproval of how Filipino men writers wrote about women.

Contemporary feminist female writers were also inclined towards breaking away from the traditional, idealized and typecast image of Filipina women of the past, being matriarchal mystics, and figures that perform sacrifices, undergo suffrage and works of martyrdom which were expected from their pious upbringing. Women writers also passed judgment against the typical portrayal of women as sex symbols.

Among the first lady writers to break away from the old style and genre exemplified in the works of past female writers such as Paz Latorena's traditional "teachings" about the ideal Filipina was the feminist poet, Marjorie Evasco. Other women writers like Kerima Polotan Tuvera, Rosario Cruz Lucero, Ligaya Victorio-Reyes and Jessica Zafra even stepped forward to boldly make it a "fashion" to discuss aspects of womanhood that were previously regarded as taboo in Philippine society, such as subjects about female anatomy, erotica, divorce or separation from former husbands, abortion, premarital affairs, and childless marriages. An example is the 1992 publication of *Forbidden Fruit*, a bilingual volume combining Filipino and English language works of women.

LANGUAGE AND EDUCATION

Contrary to the treatment received by Filipinos during the Spanish colonialists' period, education of the Philippine citizenry was prioritized during the times of American occupation, such as the activities of the Thomasites and U.S. military personnel in the islands beginning the early 1900s. Thus, only the elite classes of society – those known as the Ilustrados – preferred the use of Spanish rather than enhance and develop the native ancient scripts (*baybayin*), languages and dialects. Filipinos of both genders were able to obtain school and learning opportunites resulting to being educated in the English-language and a high literacy rating for a developing country like the Philippines.

However, despite of this advantage, grants and similar forms of funding were not immediately available to Philippine writers, for both men and women. But in turn, in contrast to this lack of pecuniary support for writers, many works in the Filipiniana style proliferated and were written dominantly in Philippine English, but fewer however in the local maternal languages. During the four-year Japanese occupation of the Philippines during the Second World War, the Japanese delivered the concept of "Asia to Asians," an idea that halted the proliferation of English as the language of literature in the Philippines, because it sparked the publication and media broadcasts by means of the exclusive use of the vernacular or the "childhood languages" of Filipinos.

This Japanese contribution to the Filipino's linguistic enlightenment reawakened the already existing move towards uplifting the status of the local languages as forms of literary expression prior to the introduction and propagation of English in the Filipino archipelago. The common "languages of childhood" of the Filipinos, in general, include Tagalog, Visayan, Hiligaynon, Cebuano and Ilocano, among others.

Still, despite of the Filipino's reawakening to their "languages of childhood", the status of the English language returned and elevated. This rejuvenation was due in part to the spread of English-based Philippine magazines, in conjunction with the publication of serial "romantic and melodramatic" novels by women writers who wrote in their "mother tongue" through the pages of comics and magazines such as *Liwayway*, *Bannawag*, *Bulaklak*, *Aliwan* and *Tagumpay*.

The competition between the use of English and Filipino as main modes of communication was unrelenting even after the end of World War II, the proclamation of Philippine Independence in 1946, and the official adoption of Filipino as a second official language other than English in 1987. The persistence of this competitive phenomenon had been accounted for the economic, military and cultural association of the Philippines to the United States, the encouragement of the use of English in combination with the dialects in schools and universities, and also the need to gain a larger audience of readership. As a result, bilingualism and even multilingualism became the linguistic style and norm.

THEMES, CHARACTER, AND GENRE

Literature penned by women authors in the Philippines embark upon the many realities and faces of Filipino society: the gap and the friction between the rich and the peasantry, personal experiences and dilemmas, love stories, their formative years, married life, employment; culture, beliefs, religion, rituals and tradition, womanhood, livelihood, family and motherhood, the duties of a female spouse; periods in history such as the Second World War, the war for Vietnam, the presence of the American military bases, nationalistic ideals and questions of cultural identity, the Marcos despotism, the EDSA revolution of 1986; poverty, prostitution, the effects of globalization and pollution, volunteer work, and the need to migrate for economic survival.

Philippine literature is the literature associated with the Philippines and includes the legends of prehistory, and the colonial legacy of the Philippines, written in both Indigenous, and Hispanic languages. Most of the notable literature of the Philippines was written during the Mexican, and Spanish period. Philippine literature is written in Spanish, Filipino, English, and other native Philippine languages. Compared to other Asian nations, the Philippine Islands has very few artifacts that show evidence of Asian writing.

However, a script called *Baybayin* was used in Luzon when the Spaniards settled the islands in 1521. The Spaniards recorded that Indigenous people in Manila, and among other native groups in the Philippines, wrote on bamboo, and specially prepared Arecaceae palm leaves, using knives, and styli. They were using the primitive Tagalog script which had basic symbols. These were the vowels a/e, i, and o/u. Each basic consonantal symbol had the inherent *a* sound: ka, ga, nga, ta, da, na, pa, ba, ma, ya, la, wa, sa, and ha.

A diacritical mark, called "kudlit", modified the sound of the symbol. The kudlit could be a dot, a line, or even an arrowhead. When placed above the symbol, it changed the inherent sound of the symbol from *a/e* to *i*, placed below, the sound became *o/u*. Thus a *ba/be* with a kudlit placed above became a *bi*, if the kudlit was placed below; the symbol became a *bo/bu*.

CLASSICAL LITERATURE IN SPANISH (19th CENTURY)

In 1863, the Spanish government introduced public education. This had an important role in the rise of an educated class called the "Ilustrado" (meaning, well-informed). Members of this group included the Philippine national hero, José Rizal, who wrote literary novels in Spanish. His novels included "Noli Me Tangere" (Touch Me Not), and "El Filibusterismo" (The Reign of Greed), considered a Philippine classical literature. Other popular Philippine writers include Francisco Balagtas who is recognized for his novel called "Florante at Laura" (Florante, and Laura).

The Philippine historical documents such as the national anthem, the Malolos Constitution or Constitución Política de Malolos, and the revolutionary propaganda are also considered a classical literature.

Philippine literature propagated in the Spanish language, especially in the writings of Marcelo H. Del Pilar, who produced the La Solidaridad (The Solidarity). In Cebu City, the first Spanish newspaper, "El Boletín de Cebú" (The Bulletin of Cebu), was published in 1890.

MODERN LITERATURE (20th AND 21st CENTURY)

The greatest portion of Spanish literature made by Philippine scholars was written during the American period. One of the Philippines' famous writers, Claro M. Recto, continued writing in Spanish. Other well-known Spanish language writers were Isidro Marfori, Cecilio Apostol, Fernando Guerrero, Flavio Zaragoza Cano, Jesús Balmori, Enrique Fernandez Lumba, and Francisco Zaragoza.

Among the newspapers published in Spanish were "El Renacimiento", (The Renaissance), "La Democracia" (The Democracy), "La Vanguardia" (The Outer Works), "El Pueblo de Iloilo" (The People of Iloilo), "El Tiempo" (The Season), and other titles. Magazines such as "The Independent", "Philippine Free Press", and "Philippine Review" were published in Spanish, and English. In 1915, the Philippine newspapers began publishing writings in English. Cebu produced writers in Spanish, most of who flourished during the decades of the 20th century. José del Mar won a Zobel Prize (Premio Zobel) for his work "Perfiles" in 1965.

Precolonial to Spanish Colonization

Prior to the surge of Spanish conquerors and colonizers, Filipino women were already creating and recording poetry using perishable materials such as banana leaves. Indigenous Filipino women were also singing tribal songs, at a time when they were of equal status to their male counterparts. They can own property, become rulers themselves in place of the men, act as ritual leaders or *babaylans*, and had the right to divorce husbands. But this ancient social image of the Filipino female changed upon the arrival of the Spaniards.

Through this transition and foreign intervention, the liberal women of ancient Filipino society were silenced and confined to the home. They were trained, based on the "European model", to become passive and obedient members of society, performers of domestic tasks, preservers of personal attractiveness, and to prepare for married life. The nunnery and the teaching occupation became their only careers outside the home. Therefore, their literature became either centered on religion or "reproductions of stories" derived from Spanish models, with the exception of a few brave women such as Leona Florentino, a female poet who refused to be silenced during the final moments of the 19th century, thus now regarded as the "founder of women's literature" in the Philippines.

Revolution against Spain

During the final stages of the 19th century, Filipino women participated in the nationwide revolt against the governing Spaniards, although less prominently than their male counterparts. Among their role and contributions were "to influence" the state of affairs of an "emerging republic" and to claim equal opportunity in education, which includes learning the Spanish-language.

An inspiring group of women, who debated against and pushed for the eradication of discriminatory laws, particularly the right to be educated in schools, was the so-called "21 women from Malolos, Bulacan".

Another would be Leona Florentino (1849-1884), who eventually became "the mother of Philippine women's literature", and who was also regarded as the conduit from "oral to literary tradition". Born in Vigan, Ilocos Sur, Florentino was a poetess of Ilustrado background who wrote in Ilocano and Spanish. Her poems were recognized in Europe in 1889 following her untimely death.

American Interlude

From the onset of the early years of the "benevolent" American occupation of the Philippine archipelago after Spain lost control of the islands through war and opted to sell its Asian colony to the U.S. the ambience was approving to the publication of vernacular literature which included the abundance of local magazines. Parallel to this, the United States of America established an English-based public education system. Both men and women were able to study in schools, colleges, universities such as the University of the Philippines. Women were gradually beginning to regain equal footing with men, as it was during precolonial times. Both genders were able to publish works in their newly adopted language.

During this European-Hispanic to Anglo-American linguistic transition, among the women who became active in creating Philippine literature in English were Paz Marquez Benitez, Paz M. Latorena, Estrella Alfon, Angela Manalang-Gloria, Genoveva Edroza-Matute, Loreto Paras-Sulit, Lilledeshan Bose, Cristina Pantoja-Hidalgo, and Lina Espina-Moore. Most of these literary pioneers also wrote simultaneously in the vernacular, although there were also those who became defiant and wrote exclusively in their mother tongue. An example of which was Magdalena Jalandoni, a Hiligaynon-language writer who was able to produce volumes of manuscripts. Among Jalandoni's 24 Hiligaynon novels, two were translated into English.

Those who excelled in both English and their local lingua franca were Lina Espina Moore, who became known as a forefront promoter of Cebuano literature. Moore's 1968 novel, *Heart of the Lotus* was the first Cebuano novel in the English language. Filipino women authors also became active pariticipants in the development of Philippine media.

Japanese Intervention

As discussed, during World War II, the Japanese were able to influence and encourage the Philippine literati in developing the vernacular literature, in parallel existence with the English language introduced by the Americans through public education. The impact of this fellow-Asian intervention lingered through and survived after the Philippines achieved the status of a freely governing Republic.

Exemplars are the Philippine-language works written by Lualhati Bautista and Liwayway Arceo. There were also published manuscripts that confer personal familiarity with events that occurred during the four-year long Japanese period such as those achieved by Estrella Alfon, Maria Luna Lopez, and Rosa Henson.

Marcos and Martial Law Years

The 20-year authoritarian rule of Ferdinand Marcos in the 1970s brought forth literary themes of Cultural Revolution, social awakening and political consciousness, reinvigorated nationalism, opinionated movements and protests, disapproval of the patriarchal society, and mass migration. Women writers began writing about the situations of female domestic helpers and slum dwellers employing their skills in both the vernacular and English.

The purpose of writing also in the native language was to stimulate, educate and awaken consciousness of the citizenry. Many writers were either "detained, tortured," or "killed." Among the women who became writers of this societal, political and activist genre were Gilda Cordero-Fernando and Ninotchka Rosca. Anti-Marcos movements, the "fiery texts" of writers, the People Power movement or the 1986 Edsa Revolution dislodged the despot from the seat of power, and was replaced by an elected first woman president, Corazon C. Aquino.

Modern-day Challenges and Status

Filipino women have been receiving recognition and support from non-governmental organizations, libraries, and other publishers, but despite the efforts of these organizations and the writers themselves there are challenges that still confront Filipino women's literary career. These include literary commercialism that prevents women writers from becoming parallel with so-called "esteemed authors", the struggle for additional acknowledgment of their status as writers, and obstacles related to economics.

MIGRATORY TRENDS AND MOVEMENTS

Migrant Literature

One aspect of Filipino women writings includes the production of the so-called "migratory literature," an account of how and why women had to leave their country in order to excel and express themselves through pen and print. In the 1930s, Filipino women authors opted to travel after obtaining the liberty to do so, and for other reasons such as the lack of a grant system within the confines of a developing country and the "resistance of a patriarchal society".

But the exodus of Filipino female writers during the 1970s differed in purpose from that of the 1930s, because they left the country to survive economically and escape government persecution. One of the first voyager-writers was Paz Latorena. The destinations of journeying migrant settlers were North America - primarily the United States and Europe, Australia, Arab nations, Japan, Singapore and other Asian countries. In general, this "Great Migration" of Filipinos created "films, novels, short stories, poetry and comics" in the Philippines that portrayed wayfarers as economic heroes and heroines of the country.

Yet there were still some of those who chose to remain, instead of abandoning the Philippines, as in the case of Lilledeshan Bose; and there were also home-comers who, after traveling and staying abroad, returned to stay permanently, such as Cristina Pantoja-Hidalgo. Other authors of "migrant literature" are Marianne Villanueva, Nadine Sarreal and Edessa Ramos. In addition, the Filipino settlers who founded Filipino communities in the United States of America triggered the generation of Filipino-American literature such as the works of female novelist Jessica Hagedorn. Migrant Filipino writers Linda Ty-Casper and Cecilia Manguerra Brainard stayed in the U.S., publishing for both Philippine and American readers.

Recognition and Support

Present-day associations that support, endorse, publish and collect works of Filipino women writers include the Ateneo Library of Women's Writings (ALIWW) of the Ateneo de Manila University, and the Philippine Center for Investigative Journalism, among other non-governmental organizations (NGOs) in the Philippines. Outside the country, there is the Philippine-Finnish Society in Helsinki, Finland.

Samples of published Filipino women literature are *Comfort Woman: Slave of Destiny* by Rosa Henson published by the Philippine Center for Investigative Journalism, and *Tulikärpänen - filippiiniläisiä novelleja* or *Firefly: Writings by Various Authors* (*Firefly: Filipina Short Stories*) by Riitta Vartti sponsored by the Philippine-Finnish Society. Another non-governmental human rights organization publication is *She Said No!*, an anthology of stories.

The Ateneo Library of Women's Writings - a part of the Rizal Library at the Ateneo de Manila University and the first of its kind in Philippines facilitates the collection, archiving, preservation, and promotion of Filipino women literature about and written by Filipino women. The program includes the acquisition of related photographic material, and literary promotions are held through lectures, exhibitions, publications and book launchings. ALIWW holds the annual *Paz Marquez-Benitez Memorial Lectures*, a series of lectures established to honor Paz Marquez-Benitez who is considered as the "matriarch of Filipino writers in English". This special program also assists in bringing to light Filipino women who excel in vernacular writings.

The role of women in the Philippines is explained based on the context of Filipino culture, standards, and mindsets. The Philippines is described to be a nation of strong women, who directly and indirectly run the family unit, businesses, government agencies and haciendas. Although they generally define themselves in the milieu of a masculine dominated post-colonial Asian Catholic society, Filipino women live in a culture that is focused on the community, with the family as the main unit of society.

It is in this framework of Philippine hierarchical structure, class differences, religious justifications, and living in a globally developing nation wherein Filipino women struggle for respect. Compared to other parts of Southeast Asia, women in Philippine society have always enjoyed a greater share of legal equality. The pre-colonial social structure of the Philippines gave equal importance to maternal and paternal lineage. This bilateral kinship system accorded Philippine women enormous power within a clan. They were entitled to property, engage in a trade and could exercise their right to divorce her husband. They could also become village chiefs in the absence of a male heir. Before the arrival of the Spaniards, Filipino women could also achieve status as medicine women or high-priestesses and astrologers.

Hispanic Philippines

During the colonization of the Philippines, the Spaniards relegated the Filipinas to a secondary position in society, while glorifying and assigning the Virgin Mary as a model for Filipino women. The arrival of the Spaniards and Catholicism also fixed the native Filipino women's role to the church, the convent and the home.

American influence

When Spain lost the Spanish-American War in 1898, the Philippines was ceded to the United States of America.

America introduced the public education system, a catalyst for the change in women's roles in Philippine society. The democratic concepts of elections and political parties were also influential factors to the psyche of Filipino women. Through the American-patterned school system, Filipino women became professionals.

Contemporary Roles

Modern-day Philippine women play a decisive role in Filipino families. They handle the money, act as religious mentors, and could also arrange the marriages of sons and daughters, striving to improve the family's dynastic connections. The emergence of Corazon Aquino, Imelda Marcos and Gloria Macapagal-Arroyo as political figures shows that Filipino society respects women, in spite of its male chauvinism, and in spite of women being often portrayed as surrogates of their husbands.

Urban setting

In the metropolitan work realm, firms and businesses generally hire Filipino women for less pay and lower positions. Typically, a man is hired for the professional position and the women for the secretarial position, despite their having an equal level of education. The Filipina will not only receive smaller wages, but also additional secretarial functions.

This "servile mindset" begins in childhood. In school, boys are often elected to organizational positions such as president and vice-president, while the girls are either members or holding treasurer positions. Young girls try to justify their worth through hard work and by being responsible pupils. Compared to Filipino men, Philippine women carry the obligation of continuing to support their family financially after their school years and marriage. The man, on the other hand, keeps his salary and holds no obligation to the family.

However, current trends in Human Resources Management paved the way in equalizing this perceived notion of inequality as can be seen by a lot of women holding high ranking positions in both big and small organizations. There are a lot of women holding managerial positions in banks, government and even in multinational companies.

Rural and Tribal clan Setting

In rural areas, the Filipino woman belongs in the home. The children approach her for money and help. She is the family's treasurer. She supports the children's educational needs. For non-family members who require support, the wife is the person to be approached. However, the wife is neither the person who makes the final decision nor the person who hands out the money.

In contrast, however, Juan Flavier, a physician, an authority on community development, and a former Philippine senator, described in his book *Doctor to the Barrios,* that "whether some (Filipino) men are willing to admit it or not"... "Rural women in the Philippines wield considerable authority," the housewife in particular. This is especially if the housewife, who is often referred to as the *Reyna ng Tahanan* (Queen of the Home), is convinced of the benefits that will be gained from a certain practice such as the concept of family planning in the barrios. Flavier also mentioned that "In the Philippine barrio, the one responsible for the home" and its management "is the wife... she holds the key to... household... development."

Marriage and Relationships

In rural areas, it is rare for a Filipino female to stay single. Permanent or prolonged single status is not always possible. It is only recently in ethnic communities that men and women have arranged their own marriages. Traditionally, the tribal council of elders and the family of the boy arranged the matches. The woman's family had little say, and the woman herself had no say at all. For example, based on Subanen tribal tradition, men can take on more than one wife, and the women are treated as the property of men. This interpersonal process, however, is already undergoing change.

In marriage, rural women, particularly those belonging to tribal communities, do not present their feelings to their husbands, particularly regarding love and sex. This is because traditionally the husband owns his wife and makes the decisions regarding her body. She can neither ask for nor deny her husband's wishes. Because of this cultural mindset, women in Philippine rural areas experience higher rates of domestic abuse than those from urban areas. Women have no control over the number of children they have. As a result, rural communities are confronted with the growing global reality of overpopulation. Socio-economically, there is not enough land or alternative means of living.

Culturally, divorce is viewed as negative and destructive in the Philippines, because of a tradition that stipulates and emphasizes that the family is the core social unit, especially for the Filipino wife. Divorce is not perceived as a solution to any matrimonial-related problem because it hinders the development or progress of the basic community unit. Therefore, husband and wife are obligated to fix problems within the boundaries of marriage.

It should always be noted, though, that pre-colonial women in the Philippines enjoyed equal status with men. Prior to colonization, both men and women could get a divorce for the following reasons: failure to meet family obligations, childlessness, and infidelity. Children regardless of sex and properties were equally divided. Since a man needed to pay a dowry to the woman's family, she was required to give it back should she be found at fault.

If the man was at fault, he then lost the right to get back his dowry. The pre-colonial society valued offspring regardless of sex. Female children were as valuable as male ones probably because of their economic implications, which was the family getting a dowry from suitors or prospective husbands and their capacity to help in the family's economic, social and political activities.

Change, Influences and Interventions

Although the Roman Catholic Church has changed its position on the role of women in marriage, the Filipina as a wife is still secondary to her husband. She is the "servant" and the "helper". In urban areas, single Filipinas have become liberal due to western influences. Although it is still culturally unacceptable for a single Filipino woman to ask a man on a date or to show interest in a man, Filipinas have learned to use body language to show their interest and openness to a relationship.

In rural communities, Filipinas are still not allowed to be too liberal. They are required to stifle their personality and sexuality, and should show a total lack of interest in intimacy with men to maintain reputation and self-respect.

FILIPINO WOMEN AND WORK

Traditionally, rural and tribal women do all the work. The scope of their functions include cooking, cleaning, teaching the children, washing clothes, repairs, budgeting, and managing the farm. After the husband has finished tilling the farmland, the wife does the planting, the daily maintenance, the carrying of water, and the harvesting. Normally, the husband helps in the harvesting, but the tribal woman has the responsibility to find food for the family. She also acts as the mediator between her children and her husband.

She manages practically everything but she does not have control over finances or in decision-making. In general, Filipino women find pride in their work. They do not find themselves alienated from their chores because they work with, around, and for their families. This family-oriented mindset gives them a sense of dignity and responsibility. The family and the children are the primary priority in a Filipina's life.

Filipino women and Philippine politics

Despite the introduction of an American-based school system and the transformation of Filipino women into educated and professional members of Philippine society, their participation in Philippine politics was slow. This was primarily because engagement in politics is considered "dirty," and due to the traditional concept that holds that women cannot take positions higher than their husbands. But this idea introduced by colonization that Filipino women historically and traditionally belonged in the home, the church, or the convent, is also changing.

A recent study revealed that there is a re-emergence of the empowerment of Filipino women through the political process, just as they were prior to the arrival of the ancient conquerors from Spain. Philippine women are rediscovering their strengths "even if they are not directly engaged in the electoral process." Filipino women had been successful in implementing policies by becoming executive staff members, advisers to politicians, and as advocates within non-governmental organizations.

Modern-day Filipinas are making strides in electoral politics by initiating more female-oriented programs. They are performing well as leaders, although generally, Filipino women still often earn political seats by having fathers and husbands who are politically connected, a "dynasty system" that hinders other Filipino women from joining the electoral process. Other factors that prevent full-engagement of other well-qualified Filipinas from the Philippine political scene are the expense in politics and the importance of the family name.

Participation of Filipino women in Philippine politics was encouraged during the Beijing Declaration in 1995 at the United Nations' Fourth World Conference on Women. In February 2005, however, a United Nations review on the progress of Philippine women and their role in politics revealed that despite "an increase in the quality of female politicians, there was not enough increase in" the number of women participants in government activities. From 1992 to 2001, Filipino women had been elected as local chief executives, functioning as mayors, governors, and captains of villages. One influential factor contributing to the increasing number of female politicians is the elevation of Corazon Aquino and Gloria Macapagal-Arroyo as Philippine women Presidents.

Filipino Women in Art

In his paintings of Filipino women, the Philippine National Artist Fernando Amorsolo rejected Western ideals of beauty in favor of Filipino ideals. He said that the women he painted have "a rounded face, not of the oval type often presented to us in newspapers and magazine illustrations. The eyes should be exceptionally lively, not the dreamy, sleepy type that characterizes the Mongolian. The nose should be of the blunt form but firm and strongly marked. So the ideal Filipina beauty should not necessarily be white complexioned, nor of the dark brown color of the typical Malayan, but of the clear skin or fresh colored type which we often witness when did we meet a blushing girl."

In 1965, the critic Leonidas Benesa complained that when he was asked to prepare a paper on the Filipino novel in English from 1941 to 1962, he had to spend the greater part of the five weeks given him on "a frantic expedition that looked more archaeological than historico-literary". In the end, he had come up with only eleven novels published during those twenty-one years - half a novel per year. Today, if someone were to construct a list of the novels in English published during the last two decades, he would come up with at least sixty titles roughly three novels per year. Contrary to the gloomy predictions of the militant student-led movements of the late sixties, Philippine fiction in English has not merely survived; it appears to have thrived.

Philippine fiction written in English belongs to a long and rich narrative tradition of literary works in several languages. The novel in the Philippines was modeled after Western prototypes, but its roots lie deep in native soil. There is a tradition of local narratives - oral epics, ballads, tales, and other folk materials - to which were later added other narrative types introduced by the Spaniards, including metrical romances (*corridos*), saints' lives, fables, parables, and folk epics (*pasyons*).

The novel in the Philippines developed by combining elements from these different traditions, producing such noted works as *Florante at Laura* by Francisco Baltazar or Balagtas (1788-1862) and ultimately leading to José Rizal (1861-96), whose novels *Noli Me Tangere* (1887) and *El Filibusterismo* (1891) was the first works of realistic fiction produced by a Filipino.

They are the work of a man steeped in both his native traditional literature and the major European literatures.

By the 1920s English was firmly established as a medium of both education and literary expression. Nonetheless, the early novels in English are not appreciably different from their predecessors in Spanish and Tagalog. For instance, the first Philippine novel in English, *A Child of Sorrow* (1921) by Zoilo Galang (1895- 1959), is a simplistic and melodramatic story of thwarted love - in essence, a Tagalog novel written in English. On the other hand, *The Filipino Rebel* (1927) by Maximo Kalaw (1891-1955) is a historical novel about the American conquest of the islands and the establishment of the new colonial regime, very much in the tradition of Rizal, though far less successful.

With N. V.M Gonzalez *Winds of April* (1940) "the Filipino novel takes on a definite qualitative change, manifesting the stylistic and thematic traits that have been taken to be distinctive of the English branch of Philippine fiction". In the 1950s and early 1960s, the intellectual milieu of the urban, university-educated English writer in the Philippines became even more sophisticated and cosmopolitan.

Foremost among the postwar novelists are Bienvenido Santos (1911-96), N.V.M Gonzalez, and Nick Joaquin. These three offer an interesting study in the different directions which the Philippine novel in English has taken: Joaquin's language borrows the cadences and the exuberance of Spanish; Gonzalez's deliberately attempts to capture the syntax and rhythms of the local languages; Santos's comes closest to American English.

Joaquin novel *The Woman Who Had Two Navels* (1961) is an impressive achievement, both for its dazzling use of English and for its mastery of narrative technique in rendering the search for a national identity. Cave and Shadows (1983) is structured like a mystery thriller, yet it explores the same theme, drawing on a rich store of myth and legend but locating the action in the thick of contemporary events and using a middle-class intellectual as protagonist. Joaquin's style has been described as "tropical baroque," a reference as much to his choice of unusual protagonists in rather melodramatic situations as to his prose.

Contemporary literature may have nothing to do with Tandang Sora as a maternal icon in Philippine history, but with creative mythology on its hood, the beloved "Tanda" becomes more than just an old woman tending wounded men in her hut. With Tandang Sora as protagonist for this fable, a new paradigm is opened in light of the Fililpina's disposition as sugar and salt become condiments of bitter twists in Philippine herstory in Sugar and Salt, wrien's rights organization in the country. Ranillo is likewise an artist in her own terms, who has also done cover artworks for *Am Here*: *Contemporary Filipino Writing in English in New York*. Written in an almost prose poetry form, Sugar and Salt, a modern fable of Melchora Aquino, narrates the highlights of the history of Filipino women in rich metaphor, from the pre-colonial times to the genesis of the colonial period.

The narrative starts off with Tandang Sora giving away nine gifts to her relatives in the face of her death. These gifts, which also serve as the sections of the story, are symbols of knowledge about Filipino women of old, with each object, like the mirror and porcelain jars, affecting the course of events that would later shape the Filipino woman's fate. The oppression begins with the arrival of the "strangers from the edge of the world," who preached to the "indios" that the care of their souls and bodies would depend on the structure of a "church in the volcano's shadow" and a "watchtower on a crag overlooking the seashore," thus signifying the spread of Catholicism.

Episodes of abuse follow as these strangers acquire Filipina wives. They give mirrors to these Filipinas, which become objects of new learning. But as time makes them wiser, the women become more conscious of the underlying oppression of the foreigners: "...he raised his cupped hand to her face so that her eyes fell on the mirror. She looked and accepted." The last gift redeems the woman in the form of an insect hopping from Tandang Sora's death chair as her great granddaughter understands that wisdom is "of the soil and must be left behind, and that the soul could only soar in innocence."

There is only so much to comprehend in a mythological history written in a 64-page book, and though context may give the interpretation away, readers will find some of the images difficult to decipher without research. For example, the lines, "The volcano belched and shifted its feet under the earth. The church stones lost their grip on one another and fell to the ground," is a dead giveaway to the eruption of Mount Mayon that resulted in the burial of Cagsawa town. But the non-historically inclined reader may be lost and confused.

The illustrations are literal and devious, adding to the magical aspect of the tale. The language speaks own with rhythmic fluidity, and its voice consistently narrates with an apparent touch of feminism. Creating mythology out of history may be a new touch of Rosca's, whose works usually dwell on the contemporary issues on human rights, specifically women's welfare.

This seemingly new approach might be easily dismissed as a nostalgic attempt to return to a lost ancestral Eden, but her focus reflects a more complex project of negotiation between past and present, between physical and psychic relocation. Rosca reconstructs the Philippines as a means of reaching back through the barriers and dislocations caused by colonial history and migration, and thus aim at a recovery of the Filipina as one who is conscious of her existence and identity.

FILIPINO NOVELS IN ENGLISH

Concerning the genesis of the Filipino novels, we have emphasized at least four significant things. First, that there are four groups of Filipino novels: those that are written in Spanish, those that are written in English, those that are written in Tagalog, and those that are written in the other Philippine languages. Second, that the shortest lived among the four groups is the Spanish novel, which nonetheless holds the distinction of producing the greatest Filipino novels. Third, that the Tagalog novel holds the distinction of being the most dominant in terms of bulk of publication. Fourth, that the English novel, due to the intricate spindles of the power of American colonization, holds the distinction of having the greatest cultural and ideological hegemony over the other groups of Filipino novels.

Concerning the development of the English novel, we have emphasized at least four important things. First, the Filipino novel in English has gone through three basic phases: the period of its birth and development, the period of interruption, and the period of its rebirth and redevelopment. Second, the novels belonging to the third period, otherwise known as the post-war Filipino novels in English, are dominated by socio-politico critical themes.

Third, that such socio-politico critical themes are shaped by some significant historical forces such as the peasant unrest led by the Hukbalahap, the subsequent defeat of this movement, the student and labor unrest, the declaration of the martial law, and the EDSA/People Power Revolution. Fourth, that our selected novels are all post-war novels are historically situated after these significant events. Concerning the socio-economic profiles of the authors of the selected award-winning Filipino novels in English, we have uncovered at least seven important points.

First, that the novelists are predominantly male. Second, that the novelists' average age by now is 70 years, although their average age at the time of the publication of their respective novels is 57 years, giving us a group of fairly matured and professionally honed writers, who have gone through most of the significant historical events that shaped the socio-politico critical themes of the post-war novels.

Third, the most predominant ethno-linguistic group among the selected novelists is Tagalog. Fourth, there are, however, more novelists who have provincial origins than there are novelists with metropolitan origins. Fifth, that the majority of the novelists are trained in hegemonic centers of literary productions, which are at least currently equipped with centers for creative writing. Sixth, all of the novelists are engaged in professions other than pure creative writing, and most of them are professors of literature and creative writing. Seventh, that most of the novelists are based in Metro Manila.

These socio-economic profiles support the general idea that the Filipino novel in English is an elite and central discourse. Concerning the award giving organizations and publication, we have established at least six important points. First, that among the existing literary awards, the Don Carlos Palanca Memorial Awards is considered the most prestigious one. Second, that the national artist award for literature, though more prestigious than the Don Carlos Palanca Memorial Awards, is conferred not on individual works but on persons for their exemplary lives for the service of art.

Third, that the centennial literary prize that was established to commemorate the first centenary of the Philippine independence from Spain, though not a regular or periodic literary award, created a significant impact on the literary community.

Fourth, that most of the publishers responsible for the production of the selected novels are based in Metro Manila. Fifth, that these publishers are dominated by big publishing firms and a successful self-owned firm, suggesting that the Filipino novel in English is after all not a losing proposition. Sixth, presence of the university presses in the production of these same novels is a guarantee of their literary and aesthetic qualities.

Lastly, concerning the readership and circulation of these same novels, we have uncovered at least three important things. First, that the Filipino novel in English has two basic groups of readership: The school-based readers and the non-school based readers. Second, that the closest estimate that we can deduce for the non-school based readers is that they number to less than 1.5 million Filipinos. Third, that, with the available data, it is not possible to deduce any approximation as to the number of the school-based readers.

IDEOLOGICAL THEMES ON THE SELF

Concerning the ideals on the self and personhood, we have uncovered at least seven ideological points. First, an ideal self that was revealed by our study of character types is that one that has been honed and developed through the exposure of the mind to intellectual systems as well as the reflective exposure of the person to both the local and the global realities. Second, another ideal self that was revealed by our study of character types is that one that deviates from the mainstream models and experiments with historical and real alternatives, such as the female that is imbued with power and the leader that is imbued with godliness and pure inner self.

Third, a counter-ideal of the self that is revealed by our study of character counter-types is that one that consumed by greed and pride, one that is insensitive and malicious, one that looks down on the fellow man, and one that is brutal. Fourth, the novels reveal an ideal psychological profile that prioritize conscientiousness first, then culture, then agreeableness, then extroversion, and then emotional stability, in as far as the basic factors are concerned; and responsibility first, then perseverance, then cooperativeness, then intelligence, and then poise, in as far as the twenty sub-factors are concerned; and prioritize least non-jealousy (18th rank), then calmness (17th rank), then being talkative (16th rank), then artistic sensitivity (15th rank), and then adventurism (14th rank).

Fifth, the metaphors and symbols of the self extol that self that is flexible, hardy, and struggles for survival. Sixth, the metaphors and symbols of the self presented as shining ideals that are worth striving that self that has perceived the contradictory circumscribing forces and consequently threads on non-conformist and non-conventional pathways. Seventh, the metaphors and symbols of the self scorns that self that has grown inauthentic and hypocritical, that self that is domineering and manipulative, that self that has lost its moral principles as it trades its very own essence for some financial considerations or other concessions, that self that is collusive and corrupt, and that self that has grown too flexible and comfortable with its lethargy and inaction.

Concerning the gendering of this ideal self, we have uncovered at least seven ideological points. First, the novels over represented the central male characters, under represented the central female characters, and marginalized the gays and lesbians. Second, the novels reveal differentiated psychological profiles for the central male and female characters, which give higher scores in more and crucial basic factors and sub-factors, suggesting a stronger and more powerful masculine ideal psyche. Third, external beauty incongruously appears as a necessary feature for the female protagonist and antagonist, those points to the masculinity of the gaze that centripetally constructed the female and centrifugally constructed the male characters.

Fourth, the same differentiated psychological profiles, however, already hinted that the feminine psyche is more extrovert, more sociable and more headstrong compared to the masculine psyche. Fifth, a more radical attention to the Filipina psyche implicit or explicit in the novels reveals the fact that there are more main female characters that would not fit into the traditional stereotype of submissive, docile and weak Filipinas than there are traditionally stereotypical female characters.

Sixth, the classification of the female characters into the Franco-Warner grid shows that the traditional Catholic patriarchal order has already been shaken through the proliferation of Filipinas within the formerly illegitimate category of non-virgin-and-non-mother, and through the heightened occurrence of pre-marital and extra-marital sexual experiences of the main female characters. Seven and last, the novels contain at least 16 subaltern Filipinas that could not easily be accommodated into the society's predominantly patriarchal order, and who push to the surface the subjugated feminine desire for sensuality, freedom, meaning, power, and leadership in politics, religion and spirituality.

IDEOLOGICAL THEMES ON SOCIETY

Concerning the dynamics of this ideal self with kinship and its group, we have uncovered at least three ideological points. First, the significance of kinship for the ideal ego has been thematically represented in the selected novels. Second, this overt thematic representation, however, is challenged by a more covert process of individualization of the Filipino ego that was revealed by our proximity analysis.

Third and last, the process of individualization of the Filipino ego is validated by the analysis of the cardinal virtues, cardinal sins, ideas of the self and art form following the Bernstein-Douglas grid that shows the loosening of the grip of the group or kinship over the individual. Concerning social classes, social mobility and social justice, we have uncovered five ideological points.

First, the majority of the novels are aware of the social issues and problems of the Philippine society. Second, the Philippine social arena is predominantly seen by the selected novels from the perspective of the middle and lower classes. Third, the social awareness of the majority of the novels is predominately conservative in color, though tinged with a significant radicalism. Fourth, upward mobility is seen as negative in the novels, and the Hollywood pattern of accelerated movement to the higher classes is not ordinarily present, giving the novels enough time to critique and examine the plight of the middle and lower classes. Lastly, the novels' social conflict is predominantly agrarian, but suggesting an idea of social justice consisting of the liberation of the masses from the selfish domination of the elites.

IDEOLOGICAL THEMES ON POLITICS AND THE NATION

Concerning the political profile of the selected novels, we have identified some negative political figures, namely, graft and corruption, the self-centered politicians, Marcos, the Martial Law and the Philippine agrarian situation; as well as some positive political figures, namely, the women's cause, student activism, and the underground movement; we have likewise identified some ambivalent political figures, namely the EDSA-People Power Revolution, and the American conquest and colonization.

In the sub-section *The Political Tenor of the Novels* we have determined that the dominant political ideology of the selected novels is liberal that comes with a significant undercurrent that is radical. In the sub-section *Political Utopia,* however, we have discovered that the novel's dominant liberal political ideology does not have a clearly and positively articulated political ideology. What it has is just a collection of critiques of the status quo. The situation is better with the significant undercurrent of radical political ideology, which likewise does not have a clearly and positively articulated political utopia. It is worth noting that in the last analysis the political utopias of the novel's liberalism and radicalism would turn out to be very similar to each other.

In the sub-section *Images of the Filipino Leader* we tried to profile the Filipino traits of leadership in the figures of the socially involved and committed priests, the peasant and urban labor leaders, the organic intellectuals to the lower classes, and the mystical leader of a religious-political community.

These traits are: first, the ideal Filipino leaders are not part of the established order, for they are precisely reactionaries and critical against the oppressive and unjust order; second, they are energized by some metaphysical principles, such as the ideas of justice, equality, freedom from oppression, nationhood, and mystical divine order; third, they do not act in order to grab power, rather power pours out from them; fourth, they are infused with sincerity, cleanliness of the self, and inner goodness; and fifth, they are all concerned with the lower classes, and are one with the Filipino people.

Concerning the novels' ideology on the nation, in the sub-section *Thoughts on Nationalism* we have profiled Filipino nationalism: first, as something that does not intend to return to a romanticized and nostalgic world in pre-colonial times, where the hypothetical and untainted Filipino may be found; second, as something that is no longer as xenophobic as

Abueva pointed it out to be initially so; third, as something that defines our being Filipino in the face of oppressive foreigners as well as persons and historical events, like Marcos and the Martial Law; and lastly, as something that finds time to be proud of the meager symbols of our being Filipinos.

In the sub-section *The Ethnic and the Filipino* we saw how the novels resolve the tension between the ethnic and the Filipino by downplaying the ethnic and emphasizing the Filipino. Filipino identity has been defined more by the critiques and comments than by the positively identified national traits. In the last sub-section *Views on the Other* we revealed that the Spanish and the Chinese characters are predominantly represented negatively in the novels, while the American and Japanese characters are predominantly represented positively. The novels are very precise with the causes of their resentment against the foreigners, which are their involvement either in the colonization or in the continued exploitation and corruption suffered by the Filipinos.

IDEOLOGICAL THEMES ON THE SPIRIT-WORLD AND MORAL VALUES

Concerning the sacred and religion, in the sub-section *Spiritual and Religious Themes, Images and Symbols,* we have established the strong presence of survivals from the Philippine pre-Christianity in the religious and metaphysical discourses of the novels. We have likewise established that the novels' fictive world is more explicitly Catholic than protestant or Islamic, and that this world has hardly a place for atheism.

In the sub-section *The Idea of the Sacred,* we have uncovered four tacit models of the sacred: namely, the metaphysical God of the philosophers; the colonial God; the sacred as guarantor of justice, goodness and bounty; and the deities of the native pre-Christian religions. We have likewise uncovered that the sacred as guarantor of justice, goodness and bounty, and the deities of the native pre-Christian religions are positively represented, while the metaphysical and colonial gods are negatively represented, due to the underlying reason that the first cluster is compassionate, local and agricultural while the second cluster is uncompassionate, alien and non agricultural.

We have likewise uncovered beneath the discursive contradictions among the four images of the sacred a strong connection between religion and nationalism as well as between religion and social justice. In the sub-section *Religion and the Life-World*, we have determined that unlike in the case of the classic Weberian analysis, the role and impact of Catholic spirituality and religion is felt more powerfully in the arena of socio-politics rather than of economics. We have likewise determined that Catholicism turned out to be a polarized discourse, on one side there is orthodoxy and the other there is the folk expression. We have likewise determined that the power and appeal of folk Christianity strongly proves the religiosity of the Filipino.

We have likewise determined that whereas orthodox Catholicism may be powerful, but underneath its eroding surface is the restlessness of the common people's spiritual and religious yearnings that fuses easily with their social and political aspirations. We have likewise determined that the novels present a pathway towards a resolution of the doctrinal and socio-political tensions between Catholicism and folk Christianity through the figures of the socially committed priests on the one hand and the holy leaders on the other hand.

Concerning moral values, in the sub-sections *Moral Transgressions* and *The Foundations of What is Moral and Immoral* we have found out that the most significant and recurrent base of the selected novels' moral ideology is power relations. Transgressions committed by the powerful against the powerless or less powerful are negatively constructed, while transgressions committed by the less powerful against the more powerful are de-emphasized or even positively constructed. We have likewise found out that the mark of being a covert transgression that is motivated by greed, dishonesty and breach of trust is another significant foundational reason that makes an action immoral.

We have likewise found out that the theme of vengeance and the process of infusing some sort of equilibrium in the grossly imbalanced power relations are tolerated in the novels. We have likewise found out that some strands of situation morality are present in the novels in forms of considering the often good outcome of a moral transgression, as well as the psychological circumstances of the agents. In the sub-section *Assessing the Novels' Moral Reasoning from the Perspective of Lawrence Kohlberg's Theory of Moral Development* we have revealed the novels' very high standard of moral judgment and reasoning.

We have likewise revealed their tendency of challenging the old and traditional Christian morality with the new principles and foundations that emphasize the existential notion of the primacy of the self, and the social and political ideas of justice and equality. This study on the ideology of the award-winning Filipino novels in English has demonstrated that there is not a single strand of ideology that runs through all of the selected novels.

Rather there are a number of competing discourses and divergent points of view, some of which constitute the predominant system others form the strong undercurrent, while still others remain the muted minority. It is worth noting that the ideologies revealed in this study may be reflective of the world-view of a particular class of Filipinos. Scholars in Philippine literature have stressed over and again that the Filipino novel in English is a middle class cultural practice.

In the section *Social Classes, Social Mobility and Social Justice* in the second chapter of this dissertation, we have ascertained through an Auerbachian analysis that though the novels are explicitly fascinated with characters from the upper class, their implicit point of view is that of the lower and middle classes. The social matrix of the novel may be understood further using the more articulated framework developed by the French sociologist and philosopher, Pierre Bourdieu. Bourdieu, oftentimes called a *neo-marxist* for the reason of his enduring interest on social classes, goes beyond the theories of Marx when he extends the meaning of *capital*.

Whereas for Marx, *capital* is purely equated with economic capital, Bourdieu demonstrates that there are other types of capital other than this purely material wealth. All in all, he talks about four types of capitals:

1. *Economic capital*, which pertains to Marx's material wealth, property, stocks, shares, and the like;
2. *Cultural capital*, which pertains to knowledge, skills, and other cultural acquisitions as best instantiated by educational or technical credentials;
3. *Social capital*, which pertains to acquaintances, connections and networks; and
4. *Symbolic capital*, which pertains to accumulated prestige, honor, and cultural mechanisms for legitimation.

For our specific concern, the first two capitals, economic and cultural, matter most. Even for Bourdieu himself, these two capitals are essential when he talks about the French social classes. For instance, what he calls proletariat are the people with very low cultural as well as economic capitals. If we are to plot this in an XY graph, with economic capital assigned to the X axis and the cultural capital assigned to the Y axis, the proletariat would be occupying the lower left corner of the four quadrants.

The dominant classes however, would be occupying the topmost as well as the rightmost area- these are the people with low economic but high cultural capitals, the people with high economic and high cultural capitals, and the people with high economic but low cultural capitals. We can more sharply locate the social class that produces and consumes the Filipino novels in English as a cultural practice.

Instead of merely pointing at the middle class, or lower class, we can more specifically identify the first quadrant that is composed of people with low economic capital but high cultural capital, as the locus of this cultural practice. In Bourdieu's social taxonomy, the social class represented by the first quadrant is still a dominant class. The Filipino novels in English as a discourse coming from a dominant class are remarkably radical and critical of the status quo.

The perspective from the social class represented by the first quadrant offers a good vantage point for critiquing the hypocrisies and corruption of the affluent dominant classes, as well as the cultural crudeness and slumbering consciousness of the masses. Though certainly class-specific, the ideologies underpinning the novels are still significant in the sense that they are aspects of the Filipino ideology, in the sense that they are the ideologies of that social class that is supposed to be same social class that is primarily responsible in spinning cultural ideologies, and in the sense they are the ideologies that exert hegemony over the ideologies of the other social classes.

The selected novels contain a fairly strong critical discourse that is energized by the underpinning ideologies of existentialism, liberalism, and radicalism. The presence of such a critical discourse creates a mild theoretical confusion, for the reason that this contradicts our specification in the first chapter of this dissertation that our intention is merely to map out and profile the neutral ideology of the selected novel and to leave aside the matters pertaining to critical ideology.

A problem threatens to emerge with the realization that the critical discourse contained in the selected novels would appear to be pulling us out of our preferred analytic track. But this confusion is merely a theoretical *trompe l'oeil*. A mapping and profiling of the novels' strands of critical discourse will not make the study a critical ideological analysis, for the reason that critical ideological analysis goes much deeper into the power relations imbedded in the concerned texts.

If our neutral ideological study had unnecessarily ventured into the domains of critical ideological studies, then we would have gone into the extent of plumbing the bourgeois legitimation and mystifications woven into the novels' critical existentialism, liberalism, and radicalism. Though cognitive anthropology might be capable of doing so, the dissertation carefully observed its delimited parameter and never wandered beyond. The critical discourses contained in the selected novels were merely mapped out and profiled.

The study also revealed the prominence of the political, social and nationalistic themes. Even the metaphysical thoughts on religion, morality and the self are saturated with these mundane themes. When these themes blended with the novels' vibrant critical discourse with its attendant ideologies of existentialism, liberalism, and radicalism, a distinctive post-colonial discourse congeals. In its own way this discourse analyzes and critiques the hidden assumptions and spindles of power of colonialism and imperialism that construct the native's inferior and marginalized self and society.

The prominence of the political, social and nationalistic themes suggests that they could be the master-codes of the Filipino novels in English. As we analyzed and interpreted the selected novels, the sharp and incisive tools of cognitive anthropology, encountered another mild theoretical problem. Roy D'Andrade in his synthesizing work *The Development of Cognitive Anthropology* defines it as "the study of the relation between human society and human thought," and looks into "how people in social groups conceive of and think about the objects and events which make up their world- including everything from physical objects like wild plants to abstract events like social justice."

Cognitive anthropology has four basic concerns: semantics, the study of knowledge structures, the study of models and systems, and discourse analysis. It would appear that due to the mediation of the English language in the selected novels, the supposedly powerful semantic and discourse analysis could not be fully utilized. This confusion is premised on the tricky assumptions that the English language is a totally foreign medium, that English language has not structured our consciousness, and that we have not structured the English language to suit our usage. Gemino Abad, in his essay *The Language of Our Blood*, asserted.

Our literary works, our textbooks, our mass media- if nothing else- show that, to all intents and purposes, for good or ill, English was in fact, and still is, a national language with us. If language fixes the forms of the world we inhabit and forges there our sense of our own native reality, then it can be said that through Spanish and English *as we had adopted them to our purposes,* we have in fact shaped our Filipino consciousness, with much the same force as through our own native tongues. Indeed, our own vernaculars had also in their own way indigenized the alien grammars so that, over time, the native Indio freed himself through a kind of spiritual homesteading in the imperial backcountry.

Abad was referring to that English that we have appropriated as a people that we transformed in the process, and that transformed and structured our present collective consciousness. Hence, without discounting the immense possibilities of a similar analysis on texts in Filipino and other native languages, cognitive anthropology can be fully and effectively utilized on Philippine English literature. Dr. Zosimo Lee, dean of the College of Social Sciences and Philosophy of the University of the Philippines at Diliman and one of the readers/critics of this dissertation raised a very interesting point concerning the "Filipinoness" of the findings of this same work.

He is anxious that cognitive anthropology may have introduced unnecessary alien categories into the research that could mute the categories that may be present in the selected novels. It is undeniable that when the symbols, metaphors, knowledge structures, models and systems which are both explicit and implicit in the selected novels were studied and analyzed, categories from both cognitive anthropology and the consciousness of the researcher inevitably dialogued with the categories present in the same novels.

A little excursion into the history of the philosophy of interpretation would illuminate further this theoretical problem. The German philosopher, Edmund Husserl (1859-1938), is probably the first theorist who problematized the need to insulate a text from the preconceptions and biases of the interpreter/researcher.

Husserl states his dictum *Zu den Sachen selbst!* ("to the things themselves"), because he considers texts as complete in themselves, and to interpret them means to methodically isolate them from all extraneous things including the interpreter/researcher's own biases and allow them to communicate their meaning to the interpreter/researcher.

But Husserl's own student, Martin Heidegger (1889-1976), questions the possibility of the interpreter/researcher to actually prevent his biases and presuppositions to color his understanding and interpretation. Instead of hypocritically scrapping the interpreter/rese-archer's biases and presuppositions, Heidegger argues for a better use of these cognitive baggages by using them as premises in conversing with texts and objects. Heidegger's student, Hans-Georg Gadamer (1900-2002), elaborates the former's idea with his concept of *wirkungsgeschichteliches Bewusstsein* (effective-historical consciousness). In the book *Truth and Method*, Gadamer asserts:

If we are trying to understand a historical phenomenon from the historical distance that is characteristic of out hermeneutical situation, we are always subject to the effects of effective-history. It determines in advance both what seems to us worth enquiring about and what will appear as an object of investigation, and we more or less forget of what is really there...

The categories revealed and examined by this dissertation therefore, are categories produced by the dialogue between the selected novels, the interpretive frame of cognitive anthropology, and the mediated and constructed consciousness of the researcher. The theoretical problem of the findings' "Filipinoness" is therefore part of the limitations packaged into our selected interpretive frame. Had the researcher opt to use the more purist frame of Husserlian phenomenology, or the similar Malinowskian ethnography, other categories may become foregrounded and visible.

THE CONTRIBUTIONS OF THIS STUDY

To the humble opinion of the researcher, the study has made some few contributions. First and foremost, in attempting to understand the Filipino ideology within the literary discourse of the novels, this study may be considered as one more step in our nation's struggle for self-understanding and self-definition. Raul Pertierra, in his essay "The Practice of Theory and the Theory of Practice," argues for the need for Filipino scholars to define and understand our own nation, otherwise our self-understanding and self-definition will be hitched to the Western voice's own understanding and definition of our nation. He stresses, "we realize that the Philippines is also a product of the American imagination just as it had earlier been a product of Spanish intentions."

Our failure to systematically imagine the Filipino identity would amount to a tremendous irony, when even our self-knowledge is tied up to some alien imaginations' terms. Second, in the more specific sphere of Filipino philosophy, this study may be considered as a testimony that the struggle for the search of the Filipino *Volksgeist*- which momentarily runs on craggy shores due to lack of rigorous and sustained theorizing on one hand, and of disciplined and methodic research on the other- need not be left unfinished.

Philosophy in general, and Filipino philosophy more particularly, can remain alive and relevant even in the postmodern condition, and can be greatly enriched by heeding the Habermasian call for transformation and openness to the other disciplines. In fact, Filipino philosophy has to work closely with the other disciplines, not for the reason of the former enriching the latter, but for the former to benchmark the latter's dedication to methodologies and theoretical frames.

Third, in the more specific sphere of the Philippine social sciences, this study may be considered to have offered two things. The first of this has something to do with a percolating bias against western theories primarily perpetuated by the exponents of *Sikolohiyang Pilipino*. Such a bias if pursued seriously to its ultimate logical consequences would place Philippine sociology in a situation worse than where the predecessors of Comte had been, a period with very little conceptual tools and theoretical frames at hand. The bias is a little bit paranoid.

Pertierra suggests that: "theoretical production, like other forms of production, is best improved by building on existing models. As Filipinists, we can contribute to a conceptual dialogue by familiarizing ourselves with the reigning paradigms and testing them against our experience of Philippine society." This study found this pathway more reasonable and may even be considered as a testimony that even western theories can be appropriated and developed to serve our nation's interests. Secondly, this study may seen as an application of the Ricoeurian agenda of understanding man and society in a circular manner through analysis of their literary texts.

This strategy had already been used by Reynaldo Ileto in the field of Philippine history. But we can manage to push this a little further by showing that this same strategy can have other applications in other sociological disciplines as well. Fourth, in the more specific sphere of Philippine literature, this study may have offered a few things. First, as this study focused on the award-winning and critically acclaimed Filipino novels in English during its rebirth and redevelopment, it definitely said some things about this significant period and genre in Philippine literature.

Second, this study may be seen as one more proof that literature can be advantageously studied from non-literary and multi-disciplinary points of view. Third, this study had taken full advantage of the realist world of the Philippine novel, or at least the realist aspects of such world, had erased the chasm between the real and the fictive, and had coaxed Philippine literature to offer a window for other disciplines to peer into the Filipino collective consciousness.

Before finally closing this ideological analysis and interpretation of the award-winning Filipino novels in English, there were topics, issues, questions that were encountered along the way and could not be treated in this work due to the limitations in space and time, as well as to the technical limitations set by the problematique's scope, and therefore have to be manifested. First, as revealed in the preceding section, there is a prominent place reserve for the political, social and nationalistic themes in the selected novel.

These themes, then, deserve a more thorough and focused study, as probable master codes of the Filipino novels. Second, after dealing with each of the 33 selected novels, we cannot but notice the fact that the novels and the novelists vary in terms of breadth and depth of their representation of the Filipino world. While some opted to focus on the inner world of a particular, others opted to gaze at the external social world. While some were very penetrating and incisive, others are not so penetrating and incisive. Along this line of thought, my study has revealed the remarkable way of F. Sionil Jose's way of representing the Filipino world, in terms of depth, breadth, style and sheer number of novels.

Thus, Jose deserves a more thorough and focused study. Third, in the preceding section we have mentioned how cognitive anthropology had encountered technical problems due to the mediation of the English language in our selected text. This powerful, sharp and incisive methodological tool deserves to be tested again using texts that are written in the native language so that its semantic and discourse analysis concerns can be fully exploited. Cognitive anthropology can be used against the Tagalog novels or the Filipino films. Lastly, there are still interesting handful themes on ideological criticism that this study failed to cover such as the interpretation of space and time, understanding the novels' motivational system, assessing their level of discursive abstraction, exploring their narrative structures, and mapping their utopias and nightmares, which can be subjects of further researches.

THE LITERARY FORMS

The diversity and richness of Philippine literature evolved side by side with the country's history. This can best be appreciated in the context of the country's pre-colonial cultural traditions and the socio-political histories of its colonial and contemporary traditions. The average Filipino's unfamiliarity with his indigenous literature was largely due to what has been impressed upon him: that his country was "discovered" and, hence, Philippine "history" started only in 1521.

So successful were the efforts of colonialists to blot out the memory of the country's largely oral past that present-day Filipino writers, artists and journalists are trying to correct this inequity by recognizing the country's wealth of ethnic traditions and disseminating them in schools and in the mass media. The rousings of nationalistic pride in the 1960s and 1970s also helped bring about this change of attitude among a new breed of Filipinos concerned about the "Filipino identity."

PRE-COLONIAL TIMES

Owing to the works of our own archaeologists, ethnologists and anthropologists, we are able to know more and better judge information about our pre-colonial times set against a bulk of material about early Filipinos as recorded by Spanish, Chinese, Arabic and other chroniclers of the past. Pre-colonial inhabitants of our islands showcase a rich past through their folk speeches, folk songs, folk narratives and indigenous rituals and mimetic dances that affirm our ties with our Southeast Asian neighbors.

The most seminal of these folk speeches is the riddle which is *tigmo* in Cebuano, *bugtong* in Tagalog, *paktakon* in Ilongo and *patototdon* in Bicol. Central to the riddle is the *talinghaga* or metaphor because it "reveals subtle resemblances between two unlike objects" and one's power of observation and wit are put to the test.

The proverbs or aphorisms express norms or codes of behavior, community beliefs or they instill values by offering nuggets of wisdom in short, rhyming verse. The extended form, *tanaga*, a mono-riming heptasyllabic quatrain expressing insights and lessons on life is "more emotionally charged than the terse proverb and thus has affinities with the folk lyric." Some examples are the *basahanon* or extended didactic sayings from Bukidnon and the *daraida* and *daragilon* from Panay.

The folk song, a form of folk lyric which expresses the hopes and aspirations, the people's lifestyles as well as their loves. These are often repetitive and sonorous, didactic and naive as in the children's songs or *Ida-ida* (Maguindanao), *tulang pambata* (Tagalog) or *cansiones para abbing* (Ibanag).

A few examples are the lullabyes or *Ili-ili* (Ilongo); love songs like the *panawagon* and *balitao* (Ilongo); *harana* or serenade (Cebuano); the *bayok* (Maranao); the seven-syllable per line poem, *ambahan* of the Mangyans that are about human relationships, social entertainment and also serve as a tool for teaching the young; work songs that depict the livelihood of the people often sung to go with the movement of workers such as the *kalusan* (Ivatan), *soliranin* (Tagalog rowing song) or the *mambayu*, a Kalinga rice-pounding song; the verbal jousts/games like the *duplo* popular during wakes.

Other folk songs are the drinking songs sung during carousals like the tagay (Cebuano and Waray); dirges and lamentations extolling the deeds of the dead like the *kanogon* (Cebuano) or the *Annako* (Bontoc). A type of narrative song or *kissa* among the Tausug of Mindanao, the *parang sabil*, uses for its subject matter the exploits of historical and legendary heroes. It tells of a Muslim hero who seeks death at the hands of non-Muslims.

The folk narratives, i.e. epics and folk tales are varied, exotic and magical. They explain how the world was created, how certain animals possess certain characteristics, why some places have waterfalls, volcanoes, mountains, flora or fauna and, in the case of legends, an explanation of the origins of things. Fables are about animals and these teach moral lessons. Our country's epics are considered ethno-epics because unlike, say, Germany's Niebelunginlied, our epics are not national for they are "histories" of varied groups that consider themselves "nations."

The epics come in various names: *Guman* (Subanon); *Darangen* (Maranao); *Hudhud* (Ifugao); and *Ulahingan* (Manobo). These epics revolve around supernatural events or heroic deeds and they embody or validate the beliefs and customs and ideals of a community. These are sung or chanted to the accompaniment of indigenous musical instruments and dancing performed during harvests, weddings or funerals by chanters.

The chanters who were taught by their ancestors are considered "treasures" and/or repositories of wisdom in their communities. Examples of these epics are the *Lam-ang* (Ilocano); *Hinilawod* (Sulod); *Kudaman* (Palawan); *Darangen* (Maranao); *Ulahingan* (Livunganen-Arumanen Manobo); *Mangovayt Buhong na Langit* (The Maiden of the Buhong Sky from Tuwang-Manobo); *Ag Tobig neg Keboklagan* (Subanon); and *Tudbulol* (T'boli).

THE SPANISH COLONIAL TRADITION

While it is true that Spain subjugated the Philippines for more mundane reasons, this former European power contributed much in the shaping and recording of our literature. Religion and institutions that represented European civilization enriched the languages in the lowlands, introduced theater which we would come to know as *komedya*, the *sinakulo*, the *sarswela*, the playlets and the drama. Spain also brought to the country, though at a much later time, liberal ideas and internationalism that influenced our own Filipino intellectuals and writers for them to understand the meanings of "liberty and freedom."

Literature in this period may be classified as religious prose and poetry and secular prose and poetry. Religious lyrics written by ladino poets or those versed in both Spanish and Tagalog were included in early catechism and were used to teach Filipinos the Spanish language. Fernando Bagonbanta's "*Salamat nang walang hanga/gracias de sin sempiternas*" (Unending thanks) is a fine example that is found in the *Memorial de la vida cristiana en lengua tagala* (Guidelines for the Christian life in the Tagalog language) published in 1605.

Another form of religious lyrics is the meditative verses like the *dalit* appended to *novenas* and catechisms. It has no fixed meter or rime scheme although a number are written in octosyllabic quatrains and have a solemn tone and spiritual subject matter. But among the religious poetry of the day, it is the *pasyon* in octosyllabic quintillas that became entrenched in the Filipino's commemoration of Christ's agony and resurrection at Calvary. Gaspar Aquino de Belen's "*Ang Mahal na Passion ni Jesu Christong Panginoon natin na tola*" (Holy Passion of Our Lord Jesus Christ in Verse) put out in 1704 is the country's earliest known *pasyon*.

Other known *pasyons* chanted during the Lenten season are in Ilocano, Pangasinan, Ibanag, Cebuano, Bicol, Ilongo and Waray. Aside from religious poetry, there were various kinds of prose narratives written to prescribe proper decorum. Like the *pasyon*, these prose narratives were also used for proselitization. Some forms are: *dialogo* (dialogue), *Manual de Urbanidad* (conduct book); *ejemplo* (exemplum) and *tratado* (tratado). The most well-known are Modesto de Castro's "*Pagsusulatan ng Dalawang Binibini na si Urbana at si Feliza*" (Correspondence between the Two Maidens Urbana and Feliza) in 1864 and Joaquin Tuason's "*Ang Bagong Robinson*" (The New Robinson) in 1879, an adaptation of Daniel Defoe's novel.

Secular works appeared alongside historical and economic changes, the emergence of an opulent class and the middle class who could avail of a European education. This Filipino elite could now read printed works that used to be the exclusive domain of the missionaries. The most notable of the secular lyrics followed the conventions of a romantic tradition: the languishing but loyal lover, the elusive, often heartless beloved, the rival. The leading poets were Jose Corazon de Jesus (*Huseng Sisiw*) and Francisco Balagtas. Some secular poets who wrote in this same tradition were Leona Florentino, Jacinto Kawili, Isabelo de los Reyes and Rafael Gandioco.

Another popular secular poetry is the metrical romance, the *awit* and korido in Tagalog. The *awit* is set in dodecasyllabic quatrains while the *korido* is in octosyllabic quatrains. These are colorful tales of chivalry from European sources made for singing and chanting such as Gonzalo de Cordoba (Gonzalo of Cordoba) and *Ibong Adarna* (Adarna Bird). There are numerous metrical romances in Tagalog, Bicol, Ilongo, Pampango, and Ilocano and in Pangasinan. The *awit* as a popular poetic genre reached new heights in Balagtas' "Florante at Laura" (ca. 1838-1861), the most famous of the country's metrical romances.

Again, the winds of change began to blow in 19th century Philippines. Filipino intellectuals educated in Europe called *ilustrados* began to write about the downside of colonization. This, coupled with the simmering calls for reforms by the masses gathered a formidable force of writers like Jose Rizal, Marcelo H. del Pilar, Mariano Ponce, Emilio Jacinto and Andres Bonifacio. This led to the formation of the Propaganda Movement where prose works such as the political essays and Rizal's two political novels, *Noli Me Tangere* and the *El filibusterismo* helped usher in the Philippine revolution resulting in the downfall of the Spanish regime, and, at the same time planted the seeds of a national consciousness among Filipinos.

But if Rizal's novels are political, the novel *Ninay* (1885) by Pedro Paterno is largely cultural and is considered the first Filipino novel. Although Paterno's *Ninay* gave impetus to other novelists like Jesus Balmori and Antonio M. Abad to continue writing in Spanish, this did not flourish. Other Filipino writers published the essay and short fiction in Spanish in *La Vanguardia, El Debate, Renacimiento Filipino,* and *Nueva Era*. The more notable essayists and fictionists were Claro M. Recto, Teodoro M. Kalaw, Epifanio de los Reyes, Vicente Sotto, Trinidad Pardo de Tavera, Rafael Palma, Enrique Laygo and Balmori who mastered the *prosa romantica* or romantic prose.

But the introduction of English as medium of instruction in the Philippines hastened the demise of Spanish so that by the 1930s, English writing had overtaken Spanish writing. During the language's death throes, however, writing in the romantic tradition, from the awit and korido, would continue in the novels of Magdalena Jalandoni. But patriotic writing continued under the new colonialists. These appeared in the vernacular poems and modern adaptations of works during the Spanish period and which further maintained the Spanish tradition.

THE AMERICAN COLONIAL PERIOD

A new set of colonizers brought about new changes in Philippine literature. New literary forms such as free verse in poetry, the modern short story and the critical essay were introduced. American influence was deeply entrenched with the firm establishment of English as the medium of instruction in all schools and with literary modernism that highlighted the writer's individuality and cultivated consciousness of craft, sometimes at the expense of social consciousness.

The poet, and later, National Artist for Literature, Jose Garcia Villa used free verse and espoused the dictum, "Art for art's sake" to the chagrin of other writers more concerned with the utilitarian aspect of literature. Another maverick in poetry that used free verse and talked about illicit love in her poetry was Angela Manalang Gloria, a woman poet described as ahead of her time. Despite the threat of censorship by the new dispensation, more writers turned up "seditious works" and popular writing in the native languages bloomed through the weekly outlets like Liwayway and Bisaya.

The Balagtas tradition persisted until the poet Alejandro G. Abadilla advocated modernism in poetry. Abadilla later influenced young poets who wrote modern verses in the 1960s such as Virgilio S. Almario, Pedro I. Ricarte and Rolando S. Tinio. While the early Filipino poets grappled with the verities of the new language, Filipinos seemed to have taken easily to the modern short story as published in the *Philippines Free Press*, the *College Folio* and *Philippines Herald*. Paz Marquez Benitez's "Dead Stars" published in 1925 was the first successful short story in English written by a Filipino. Later on, Arturo B. Rotor and Manuel E. Arguilla showed exceptional skills with the short story.

Alongside this development, writers in the vernaculars continued to write in the provinces. Others like Lope K. Santos, Valeriano Hernandez Peña and Patricio Mariano were writing minimal narratives similar to the early Tagalog short fiction called *dali* or *pasingaw* (sketch). The romantic tradition was fused with American pop culture or European influences in the adaptations of Edgar Rice Burroughs' *Tarzan* by F. P. Boquecosa who also penned *Ang Palad ni Pepe* after Charles Dicken's *David Copperfield* even as the realist tradition was kept alive in the novels by Lope K. Santos and Faustino Aguilar, among others.

It should be noted that if there was a dearth of the Filipino novel in English, the novel in the vernaculars continued to be written and serialized in weekly magazines like *Liwayway, Bisaya, Hiligaynon and Bannawag.* The essay in English became a potent medium from the 1920's to the present. Some leading essayists were journalists like Carlos P. Romulo, Jorge Bocobo, Pura Santillan Castrence, etc. who wrote formal to humorous to informal essays for the delectation by Filipinos.

Among those who wrote criticism developed during the American period were Ignacio Manlapaz, Leopoldo Yabes and I.V. Mallari. But it was Salvador P. Lopez's criticism that grabbed attention when he won the Commonwealth Literay Award for the essay in 1940 with his "Literature and Society." This chapter posited that art must have substance and that Villa's adherence to "Art for Art's Sake" is decadent. The last throes of American colonialism saw the flourishing of Philippine literature in English at the same time, with the introduction of the New Critical aesthetics, made writers pay close attention to craft and "indirectly engendered a disparaging attitude" towards vernacular writings - a tension that would recur in the contemporary period.

THE CONTEMPORARY PERIOD

The flowering of Philippine literature in the various languages continues especially with the appearance of new publications after the Martial Law years and the resurgence of committed literature in the 1960s and the 1970s. Filipino writers continue to write poetry, short stories, novellas, novels and essays whether these are socially committed, gender/ ethnic related or are personal in intention or not.

Of course the Filipino writer has become more conscious of his art with the proliferation of writers workshops here and abroad and the bulk of literature available to him via the mass media including the internet. The various literary awards such as the Don Carlos Palanca Memorial Awards for Literature, the Philippines Free Press, Philippine Graphic, Home Life and Panorama literary awards encourage him to compete with his peers and hope that his creative efforts will be rewarded in the long run.

With the new requirement by the Commission on Higher Education of teaching of Philippine Literature in all tertiary schools in the country emphasizing the teaching of the vernacular literature or literatures of the regions, the audience for Filipino writers is virtually assured. And, perhaps, a national literature finding its niche among the literatures of the world will not be far behind.

4

Novels by Indonesian Women

Within classical social science literature various inherent assumptions have been associated with the household. It has often been seen as consisting of individuals working for the 'common good', in which relations between members are harmonious and in unity; it is often linked with only one type of family form namely the nuclear family; and its function is designed to prepare the way for the smooth entry of its members into society, either as economic, political, or social actors. The urgency of the theme for the Indonesian context was also felt because of the universalizing tendencies of government policies and projects which still consider 'the household' - as a nuclear family (with women as housewives and mothers) take the only existing form.

It was hoped that the participants in the conference would explore and highlight our own biases as academics as well as those of policy makers in dealing with the various forms of householding. Part of the discussion concentrated on the dominant ideologies and policies regarding households and women's roles. Elsbeth Locher Scholten looked at how male colonial authorities perceived Javanese households through a bi-focal lens: peasant households were seen as units of production and *priyayi* households as units of socialization. Mieke Schouten concentrated on the convergence of the ideology of the Protestant missionaries, the Dutch colonial government, and the ideas current in Victorian Europe.

The biases reflected in government policies in the New Order period were scrutinized by Mies Grijns, Lia Sciortino, and Ines Smyth.

Grijns argued that the biases underlying the planning of the coconut nuclear estate system in West Java, in a community where households vary in size and composition, were heady prescriptions for the failure of the programme. Sciortino and Smyth stated that gender bias by the state, basing itself strongly on Javanese values imbued with the concept of harmony in society and family precluded any discussion of domestic violence.

Government policies did not always prove detrimental to women as Anke Niehof states. Niehof concentrated on income-generating policies and argued that women do benefit from income-generation programmes since they can use their income according to their own priorities. In coming to this conclusion she stresses that 'the domestic' and 'public' should not be separated when looking at the meaning of women's income. The views of women (and men) of the elite and the discourse on representations of women was examined in both a historical and a contemporary light.

Susan Blackburn and Barbara Hatley, concentrating on journals and novels in different periods in history, concluded that despite restrictive norms on the household and women's roles, women themselves showed their inventiveness and explored alternative views and ways for giving vent to their expression.

The prevailing view of the nuclear family as the universal form in Indonesia is also suggested by the middle-class intellectuals of the contemporary period and this affects how husband-wife relationships are perceived (Sita van Bemmelen). Focus on elite women and their ability to manipulate social networks for the enhancement of their positions was provided by Madelon Djajadiningrat (Javanese court women); Gigi Weix (women cigarette entrepreneurs); Frieda Dharmaperwira and Marleen Nolten (elite women of two generations, one living in Indonesia one abroad).

DOMESTIC STRUCTURES

Debates about the usefulness of the household as a methodological tool were brought out unequivocally by the presentations concentrating on the domestic structures themselves. Most of the papers argued that households were not useful for an analysis of domestic structures nor for analysing women's position in them. In Ambon, Frans and Keebet Benda Beckmann stressed that different networks were established for different needs, so that co-residential units beyond nuclear families were more significant than household units. This was also the case for Bali where communal courtyards provided the basis for core networks in undertaking daily reproduction (Ayami Nakatani) and where polygynous relations determined the types of cooperation or conflict occurring between domestic units (Megan Jennaway).

This was equally applicable to the Bhuket of West Kalimantan (Shanthi Thambiah). For Minangkabau, West Sumatra (Joke van Reenen, Carol Davis, Bill Watson, and Martini Jufri), the importance of individual networks rather than households was stressed, in the execution of the daily needs of individuals. Conversely, Juliette Koning argued that in her case study, the Javanese community of Central Java, households were becoming more nuclearized and inward-looking as members are exposed more to urban life styles. It was agreed by most of the authors that domestic responsibility, although ideologically placed on women's shoulders, was always subject to negotiation and the actual roles of women cannot be assumed beforehand.

Although it was clear that dichotomies between 'external' and 'internal' relations between and within households were difficult to maintain, some papers could be grouped according to their emphasis on the interplay between 'external' forces and gender relations 'within' households. Patrilineal kinship systems and patriarchal family values were constraining for women but, as in the case of the Toba Batak, Janet Rodenburg argues it was the women's ability to manage households and farms that made it possible for men to migrate. In contrast,

Tina Yusmadiana and Yusmaini stressed that kinship systems more or less shaped the nature of women's autonomy.

In between these two views, Becky Elmhirst admitted that gender ascriptions were open to negotiation but that different ideas (those held by the Lampungese community and the Javenese migrants) on the role of a daughter's contribution to the household shaped their respective employment patterns. Focusing on the linkages between labour demand and labour supply my own paper looked at how households contract and expand following the needs of the cigarette industry in East Java and the ambiguous position of women workers in the different age groups in the face of these changes.

The role of women becomes highly ambiguous when the workplace converges with the home and thus the 'external' and 'internal' become one, as in the case of the homeworkers in East Java and also in Flores. This ambiguity was also examined by Danilyn Rutherford in Biak, Irian Jaya, where she concentrated more on changes in women's roles and rituals in the face of rapid, and often dramatic social changes. In focusing on the rapid changes among the Dayak, Kalimantan Nita Kariani plainly showed the detrimental effects these have on domestic structures and women in particular.

At the end of the conference it was recognized that the process in breaking conceptual boundaries was much more intricate than at first envisioned and many conceptual strands had to be left unexplored, despite the fact that five days had been reserved for the conference including the open day and the closed sessions. Twenty-nine participants from seven countries came to present their papers. Twelve papers have been selected for a future book publication.

The conference, which took place in Leiden, was a joint undertaking of the WIVS (Interdisiplinary Forum on Indonesian Womenþs Studies) and the KITLV. Although modern Indonesian literature originated as a response to the Dutch colonial regime and later often butted heads with the post-colonial state, the use of Bahasa Indonesia has tended to isolate it from mainstream post-colonial cultural studies. This book attempts to redress this deficiency by subjecting an extensive range of Indonesian writing to post-colonial reading strategies.

Originating from a conference on 'Post-coloniality and the question of modern Indonesian literature' held at the University of Sydney in May 1998-coincidentally just at the time of Suharto's forced resignation from the post-1965 New Order regime, which has been compared to the Dutch colonial state at the height of its power-the book directs itself to the scrutiny of identity and language issues concerning the cultural condition of Pos-coloniality.

Seizing a metaphor from Kwame Anthony Appiah in his In my father's house: What does it mean to be an African today, the editors state that the essays are intended to 'clear a space' for a critical approach that could be beneficial in creating new possibilities for Indonesian identity and literary expression as well as enabling future comparative research with literatures of other post-colonial societies.

SITTI DJAOERAH: A NOVEL OF COLONIAL INDONESIA

In her amply and thoughtfully introduced and annotated translation of a largely forgotten novel first published in 1927, Susan Rodgers opens to readers who do not command the Angkola Batak language a fascinating example of what she describes as "the short-lived but incandescent and aesthetically quite breathtaking southern Batak fiction literature that thrived in the last two colonial decades" in certain parts of North Sumatra.

Though in the mid-1970s, when Rodgers began her fieldwork on issues of "oratory, literacy, and literature," "many elderly Angkola readers...vividly remembered Sitti Djaoerah," for most Indonesians today the pre-war Batak-language novels it exemplifies constitute "a lost literature," eclipsed by the much better-known Indonesian-language novels sponsored and published by the colonial government's publishing house Balai Poestaka. Indeed, for me it was a complete surprise to learn that in the 1920s, in the midst of the nationalist fervor to develop an Indonesian-language literature, novels were being written in regional languages such as Angkola.

We must be grateful to Susan Rodgers for her effort in translating this long novel from Bahasa Angkola; for her introduction, which is remarkably helpful in situating the work within its Angkola context; and for asserting the claim of this author, Soetan Hasoendoetan, to a place in the history of Indonesian literature of the colonial era. The novel falls into two parts. The first lays out the background of the novel's main events.

It begins with a description of the geography, economy, and social and cultural character of the city of Padang Sidempuan. Then two important characters, Pandingkar Moedo and his wife Taring, are introduced. Pandingkar Moedo is a man left behind by changing times. Raised in a family that (like most families of that time) did not value formal education, he is unequipped to flourish in the agricultural boom economy of North Sumatra in the 1920s. The first part of the novel ends with his tragic death.

The second part is dominated by Djahoemarkar, Pandingkar Moedo's son with Taring, and by his beloved, the title character, Sitti Djaoerah. Djahoemarkar, a child at the time of his father's death, is raised by his mother. While Pandingkar Moedo belonged to a bygone era, Djahoemarkar and Sitti Djaoerah are young people of the present (i.e. the new colonial world of the 1920s). The first, crucial step toward the new world is taken by Taring: she decides to send her son to school. "After all," she realizes, "cleverness and knowledge are the greatest heirloom treasures on earth and ones you can never exhaust". As young adults, Djahoemarkar and Sitti Djaoerah embrace education and the knowledge and experience needed to confront the twentieth century.

In its themes, the novel resembles other, Indonesian-language novels of the Balai Poestaka era: it features true love threatened by arranged marriage, the conflict between traditional custom and orthodox religion, and the fresh thinking of a new generation. Susan Rodgers observes that the novel's view of these problems is optimistic, and that the story ends happily. It is noteworthy that the author resolves his story's conflicts mainly through the wisdom of the female characters: Taring, Nandjaoerah (Sitti Djaoerah's mother), and Sitti Djaoerah herself.

The novel's antagonist, whose name (unlike those of the positive characters) is given only in translation ("Sutan Hardwood, the Sutan Ashamed to Grow Old"), affords the author opportunities for social criticism, particularly of the corrupt use of religion as a mask for personal ambition, and of the practice of arranged marriage. Again, some of the strongest criticism, expressing what the author's own views are apparently, is given by the female characters. Nandjaoerah, for instance, delivers a defense of traditional custom (adat) against Islamic law (hukum syariah). She also compares the situation of women in strict Muslim countries ("Arabia or Malaya") unfavorably with that of Angkola women. The women bound by Islamic law are not allowed to work outside the home. Nandjaoerah comments:

> If Angkola women worked only inside the house how in the world could be a hope to make a living for the whole household? And that's why there is no way we can follow the customs they use over in those other lands. The way we do things here is pretty good, I'd say. Tasks are divided up nicely, and the work comes out even. So, when you examine the real situation, you'll see that our own rules are right on target".

At the end of the novel, Djahoemarkar and Sitti Djaoerah settle into life on a plantation in Deli where Djahoemarkar is hired (thanks to his education) as a clerk. There he becomes involved in political activity, organizing a union of the plantation workers. Thus the novel, though focused on the local concerns of Angkola society, reflects larger issues of late-colonial Indonesia: the proliferation of political parties and organizations in reaction to Dutch rule, and the potential for conflict between ethnic groups (particularly in a multi-ethnic context like the Deli plantations, with Melayu, Batak, Chinese, Javanese, Sundanese, and other groups all mixed together).

This novel offers a rare view from the daerah ("the regions," i.e., not the center, Batavia) of the changes taking place in many parts of Indonesia in the late-colonial era. Susan Rodgers has enriched our knowledge and broadened our view of what must be included within the term "Indonesian literature."

ISLAM AND WOMEN ISSUES IN INDONESIA

What a prudent, well-grounded measure the country's founding fathers had taken when they came to decide *Pancasila* (the five basic principles) as the complete outlook on life of our Nation, rather than Islam, notwithstanding the fact that Indonesia's population was predominantly Moslem. Such decision has given rise to the unique characteristics of Indonesia, as being neither an Islamic nor secular country. Although it is not an Islamic country, Indonesia is in fact the home of the world's majority Muslim population.

According to the latest population census, the country's total population is some 220 millions, and 85% of which is predicted to be Muslims and if more than half of the total population is woman, it can be as sure as fate that the Muslim women will account for more than 110 million people of the total Indonesia's population, which is a quite huge number and even larger than the population of South East Asian's countries combined.

The majority of Muslim women lead a wretched and miserable life and this is observed from the following indicators. Low education level, poor health quality as evidenced by high mortality rate of mothers in childbirth, low economic level because many of them are only absorbed in manual labor as very badly-paid blue collar workers, discouraging level of human rights protection and legal system which does not side with them.

This very unfortunate condition has given rise to a number of crucial and phenomenal issues, such as migrant labor, trafficking in women and children, acts of violence, especially domestic violence, abortion, prostitution, polygamy, living environment, and HIV/Aids. In addition, the biggest problem faced by Indonesia as the world's fourth most populous country, like the one prevailing in the Third World, is poverty, blindness of ignorance, backwardness.

This situation is made worse and more intricate as the religious understanding of Indonesian people is highly influenced by conservative point of view which tends to show little or even no appreciation of humane, egalitarian and democratic values. Religion is much more understood and practiced as an act to "please God", rather than an effort to uphold and foster sense of humanity.

Due to the constraint and barrier of language and insufficient education, the majority of Muslim people have no sufficient capability to distinguish which religious teachings are God-revealed that are absolute, ultimate, and immutable in nature and which tenets generate from prominent Ulamas' products of reasoning *(ijtihad)* that are relative, inconclusive, and changeable in nature, which are geared to the need and benefit of mankind.

To the greatest extent, the experiences have shed light that it is indeed the second type of teaching (in Islamic terminology referred to as *fiqhiyah*) which are widely practiced, especially in the context of relationships between man and woman. Worse still, the understanding of *fiqhiyah* which ignores women's aspiration and experience have colored many of the Indonesian statutory laws as portrayed in the National Marriage Law (1974), Regulation of Civil Registration (1962), Citizenship Law and Manpower Law (1985).

Some articles stipulated in the aforementioned laws are deemed as contradicting human rights and democratic values. The problem is that, as national laws, the discriminating provisions contained therein bind all citizens regardless of their religions. This means that the *fiqhiyah*-inspired provisions of laws have exasperated and irritated women's sense of justice, not only felt by the Muslim women but also by non-Muslim women.

GENERAL PERSPECTIVES ON ISLAMIC TEACHINGS

The historical fact reveals that the interpretation of Islamic sacred texts since the lapse classical period was predominated by males, and as a consequence,, woman's experiences had been neglected in theologically-based reflection. Marginalizing women's experiences in the theological interpretation was embodied, among other things, by means of banning women from taking an active role in public arena.

The prohibition meant hampering women's involvement and excluding the participation of their aspiration and experience from a wide variety of Islamic traditions-formulating processes. As a result, a number of teachings, especially those which pertain to the relationship and interaction of man and woman are gender-biased and patriachally-biased value laden.

Many centuries later there emerged an awareness of the necessity of feminist-oriented interpretation, one which paid more prominent attention to women's experiences and which in turn strived for freeing women from the confinement of various types of exploitation, discrimination, marginalization which oftentimes passed under the excuse of the legitimating of religious teachings. Muslim Women's awareness of the necessity of emancipation was driven by the shifts that occurred due to the change in the world's political and social arrangement.

The West and the West-inspired ideas has become a fashionable model which has given birth to a new direction of the world's civilization. The East, generally inhabited by Muslim people, has been trying to escape from the narrow confines of backwardness, destitution, and ignorance. To pursue the above objective, Muslim women began to adopt the West's ideological concepts, including the idea of emancipation.

There is no gainsaying the fact that the empirical experiences in the West which have set forth the concept of emancipation have exerted at least two important excesses: First, it poses a menace to the deep-rooted domination of men over women which has so far prevailed in the society; and second, it triggers moral decadence in the society. Alarmed by the possible occurrence of these two bitter effects, the Muslim society, especially the ulamas have staged strong objection to the very idea of the West-initiated emancipation.

Alas! The resistance offered by the ulamas in many countries, much the same as the one made by the Afghanistan-based Thaliban, has been accompanied with systematically-engineered efforts to deliberately reinstate Muslim women in the confines of the engraved tradition which, just exactly on account of that, has all this time effectively brought them to the state of backwardness, ignorance, and poverty.

As far as Indonesian context is concerned, this phenomenon is marked with the promulgation of Local Regulations which put Islamic *shariah* (sacred law) into force such as ones administered in Aceh, Tasikmalaya, and in several other regions. Unfortunately, in effort to formalize the said Islamic shariah, what has come to the fore has been anything but the issue of *jilbab* (head veil) and the displacement of brothels, nothing at all that taps and addresses the very basic need of the Muslim society, such as the promotion of welfare, the improvement of health and education, and the betterment of public services.

To avoid the excess of the application of the said emancipation concept, like the one which has befallen the West, Muslim women do not have to adopt the West-inspired concepts especially as regards emancipation. Islamic teachings, stipulated in the Quran and hadisth, as well as in the classical books, are very rich in the principles of justice, freedom, and human equality and moral teachings and enlightenment on the importance of holding human dignity and value in high esteem, and are all, in essence, very accommodative to the notion of emancipation.

Accordingly, what is needed now is how to socialize and disseminate Islamic teachings which advocate emancipation, without having to create apprehension and anxiety about the possible threat to the dominance of men and about the occurrence of moral decadence in the society. The concrete solution we offer is to embark on theologically grounded deconstruction on the Islamic teachings, especially on those which pertain to the relationship between men and women.

CLAIMING THE FUTURE FOR WOMEN RIGHTS

The campaigns and efforts to strive for women equality and self-reliance have been waged on: First, socializing and disseminating gender concept through various trainings, meetings on science, routine meetings on religious affairs, Islamic preaching, either held in mosques or other Islamic institutions. Second, carrying out training for decision and policy makers, Muslim prominent leaders, teachers of religion, and preachers.

Third, conducting educational program on human rights for organization activists, religion-based-non-governmental woman organizations, Fourth, stepping up the activities of study of books on religion, especially classical books on the religion of Islam, followed by the publication of the results of such studies in the form of magazines, books, school textbooks, training modules, and other reading materials. Fifth, embarking on critical reviews of various regulations and laws which discriminate women, and proposing revised concepts, such as providing counter legal draft for the Compilation of Islamic Laws, revised legal draft on Marriage, and revised legal draft on Health.

Sixth, preparing legal drafts, which duly accommodate the protection for women's rights, such as legal draft on Anti Violence, Trafficking in women and children, and legal draft on Civil Registration? Seventh, giving prominent attention to various public policies, on both central and local levels, for example, the policy on formalizing Islamic shariah in several regions, which cause women to suffer and to be in great inconveniences, such as the compulsion to put on head veil (*jilbab*), a ban to go out at night, and interdiction to leave home without legitimate male relatives or guardians.

It was while recording stories like this that staff at Indonesia's National Commission on Violence against Women, a branch of the country's Human Rights Commission, decided in 2007 that they needed to focus on religious leaders if they wanted to protect women. That insight led to intense brainstorming, studies and analysis, which with time has morphed into three books written by female scholars and religious leaders representing Islam, Catholicism and Protestantism.

Titled 'Breaking the Silence: Religions Listen to the Voice of Female Victims of Violence in the Name of Justice', the books in Bahasa Indonesia were launched in the capital Jakarta, late-April. They aim to break the monopoly held by men over interpretations of holy books and to challenge the hegemonic patriarchal culture upon which domestic violence is based. Komnas Perempuan has recorded 54,425 cases of violence against women in 2008, a 113 per cent increase from 2007.

Some 90 per cent of the cases were classified as "domestic violence", which includes "economic violence" - a category which included women being left economically vulnerable, financially neglected by their husbands or having their own economic opportunities stifled. It is believed that this number is only a tiny percentage of the real figure. A staffer of the independent Komnas Perempuan, who did not want to be identified, said that while the books are to be distributed free, it would take time before they make an impact, but "this is potentially a breakthrough".

Muslim-majority Indonesia is a deeply religious country that forbids atheism by law. Here Muslim ulamas, Christian pastors and Catholic priests are held in high esteem. "They (women victims of violence) often prefer to confide in ulama or pastor instead of the police," Neng Dara Affiah from the education department of Komnas Perampuan, told IPS. "But unfortunately, we have observed that religious leaders' understanding of domestic violence is biased in favour of men."

The manuscript for Muslims was written by a team affiliated to Muhammadiya, Indonesia's second largest Muslim organisation which has considerable political influence. With some 30 million members, it is mainly focused on social and educational activities. The head of the Social Council in the female wing of Muhammadiya, Susilahati, one of the authors, explained that the book project was important in the campaign to stop domestic violence as "it allows a discussion about how to accommodate the victims' needs and thoughts in a theological context."

Susilahati is also a commissioner at the Komisi Perlindungan Anak Indonesia (Indonesian Child Protection Commission) and the president of the Ikatan Pekerja Sosial Indonesia (Indonesian Social Worker's Union). Take for instance the Hadith that has time and again been used by ulamas that says, "If a man calls his wife to bed and she refuses, and he goes to sleep angry with her, the angels will curse her until morning."

For Susilahati, who like most Indonesians has only one name, this Hadith is a "classic case" of how people misinterpret religion to justify what is done to victims. The Muhammadiya writers have argued that the Hadith should not be taken literally. They quote a series of other Hadith to underline the prophet's fairness. One of these says, "A sublime man is the one who respects his wife and a contemptible man is the one who humiliates his wife."

"This is why this project is so important," Susilahati stressed. According to her, the problem of interpretation is not limited to Islam but "it also happens within other religions". The Hadith is from the oral tradition relating to the words and deeds of the prophet Muhammad. It is part of traditional Islamic jurisprudence and used to determine a Muslim way of life. Iswanti, who has started on a doctorate in theology and feminism and is one of the writers who scrutinised the Bible, was very forthcoming. "There is no doubt that some interpretations of religious texts weaken the position of women. They could even be used to legitimise violence against women," she said in a phone interview with IPS.

The new publications from Komnas Perempuan have published many real-life examples where interpretations of the Bible have been used to the detriment of women. Roughly 5 per cent of Indonesia's 240 million people are Protestant, and a further 3 per cent are Catholics. Domestic violence, for example, has at times been hushed up, or excused by literal interpretations of passages that say "wives must be submissive to their husbands like they are submissive to Christ".

"Besides offering a modern reading, we hope that this book will help change the paradigm of theology so that the Church can take a more proactive approach in helping women," Iswanti said. "When women go to church asking for help, statements like, 'be patient' or 'pray to God' are not enough," she asserted. "We hope the church can change the way it counsels women, so that they are no longer viewed as guilty." Iswanti is an activist with the Jakarta-based Mitra ImaDei, which organises domestic workers.

Komnas Perempuan knows that support from the male-dominated religious leadership is critical if their plea for gender equality is to be accepted by the ulama in small villages in central Java or by pastors in the remote highlands of Papua. Encouraging initial endorsements have come so far from Din Syamsudin, head of Muhammadiya, Andreas Yewangoe, head of the Indonesian Church Council (PGI) and Yosep Dedy Pradipto, head of the Indonesian Bishops Conference (KWI) who were present at the launch on April 22.

Newspapers reported that all the three agreed that it was time to reinterpret the Koran and the Bible to take women's rights into account. Din was quoted by The Jakarta Globe newspaper saying that he was really concerned about the condition of the status of women in Indonesia, and their subordination to men. "The interpretations (of religious texts) made by males lead to misunderstanding, and the strong patriarchal culture in the country puts the women as subordinates," he is quoted by the newspaper.

Andreas, leader of the Protestant Church, stated that all attempts to reinterpret the holy books should be based on equality and justice. The KWI's Yosep advised religious leaders and people to start seeing the situation from the victim's point of view if they are to fight violence against women. At the dimly lit Sudirman International Cafe, the literati have gathered to drink beer, smoke cigarettes and listen to a young woman talk about sex.

The scene wouldn't be notable in most cities, but this is Jakarta, capital of the world's most populous Muslim country. Ayu Utami, 35, a slender Javanese beauty with sharp features and an open smile, is launching her newest book, a collection of essays entitled "Sex, Sketches and Stories." Sporting a skintight top, Utami deftly fields questions on such topics as marriage, infidelity and sexual liberation. "People think of free sex as something done by people who aren't married, but actually free sex is something done by married people," says Utami to shouts of approval. "I love you!" yells one young woman, hoisting a beer.

Since the downfall of the autocratic President Suharto, Indonesia has undergone plenty of upheaval: three presidents, innumerable riots and demonstrations, bloody sectarian clashes between Muslims and Christians. Far less noticed has been the rise of provocative Indonesian literature, thanks largely to a group of bright, bold, attractive, media-savvy young women who are willing to take on the subject of sex.

Their growing body of work has been lumped under the label *sastra wangi*-literally, "fragrant literature"-a somewhat derogatory term that has nonetheless stuck and helped the movement catch on. "There is a newfound freedom now," says Richard Oh, owner of the QB World Book chain. "These writers aren't afraid to say anything. This is the first new trend in Indonesian literature for ages and ages."

Utami, a former journalist and a Roman Catholic who cites the Bible as an early inspiration, launched the movement with her first novel, "Saman," two weeks before Suharto's fall. Set during his oppressive regime, the novel raised eyebrows mainly for touching on both religious and sexual matters: the main character has an affair with a Catholic priest. Drawing skillfully on both Indonesian slang and literary allegory, "Saman" won the prestigious Jakarta Arts Council competition for new novels and quickly went on to sell 55,000 copies-a good run in Indonesia.

A succession of women writers quickly followed, each pushing the boundaries of the one who came before. In Dewi Lestari's wildly popular first novel, "Supernova," the main characters include a gay couple and a prostitute. Djenar Maesa Ayu published a book of prize-winning short stories, including one entitled "Nursing from Daddy," in which she expresses a young woman's rejection of the traditional place of women in society through the metaphor of her suckling her father's penis instead of her mother's breast.

And Dinar Rahayu, who wears the traditional Muslim *hijab* scarf in public, wrote about sadomasochism and transsexuality in her first book, "Ode to Leopold von Sacher Masoch." Soon after it was published, she resigned her position as a chemistry teacher at a progressive, privately run Muslim high school. But like most of her peers, she made it onto Indonesia's top-10 best-seller lists.

Some believe the sastra wangi writers are merely bringing to light the country's natural lustiness. "We Indonesians are a raunchy lot," says Julia Suryakusmana, academic, writer, publisher and self-proclaimed feminist. "We've got our own traditional culture that is very sexual. It's just that there is schizophrenia between historical reality and what is called 'Eastern' values." That schizophrenia reached new heights under Suharto's long rule, from 1966 to 1998.

After allowing an initial period of openness, in the early 1970s Suharto cracked down hard on all forms of critical and creative thinking. "For a period of about 25 years there was a lost generation in terms of Indonesian literature, when writers wrote more and more obliquely," says John McGlynn, director of publications at the Lontar Foundation, a nonprofit organization that translates Indonesian literature into English. "The refreshing thing-not just about the women writers but the whole generation of new writers-is they are reclaiming their voice."

So far, that voice is in no danger of being silenced. Indonesia's Muslim leaders, who have been waging strict campaigns against pornography and suggestive dance shows on TV, have left the sastra wangi set alone. That may have less to do with the message than the medium; since most Indonesians don't read, literature is not deemed as dangerous as other media. "The religious establishment doesn't pay attention to art and literature because the impact of literature is limited," says Nirwan Derwanto, former editor of the respected journal Kalam. "One of the greatest things about the sastra wangi movement is, it is bringing people to literature." The hordes of women clamoring for Utami to sign copies of "Sex, Sketches and Stories" are clear proof of that.

AYU UTAMI

Ayu Utami (born in November 21, 1968 in Bogor, West Java) is a female Indonesian writer. She has written novels, short-stories, and articles. *Saman (novel)* (1998) is widely considered her masterpiece. It was translated into English by Pamela Allen in 2005. Ayu Utami is a leading voice among the new generation of Indonesian artists and writers emerging after the fall of Suharto. Utami was born in Bogor and grew up in the Indonesian capital, Jakarta. She obtained her Bachelor degree from the University of Indonesia, where she studied Russian language and literature.

During her college years she had already begun publishing reports and essays in various newspapers. In 1990, she was selected as a finalist in Wajah Femina, a beauty pageant in Indonesia. However, she did not pursue a modeling career due to her dislike of cosmetics and make-up. She has been a journalist for various Indonesian magazines, including *Humor, Matra, Forum Keadilan,* and *D&R*. Shortly after Suharto banned three magazines in 1994 (*Tempo, Editor,* and *Detik*) during the New Order era, Ayu joined *Aliansi Jurnalis Independen* (Independent Journalist Alliance) in protesting the ban. She continued her journalistic work underground, which included the anonymous publication of a black book on corruption in the Suharto regime.

Utami's first novel, *Saman*, appeared in 1998, only a few weeks before the fall of Suharto, helping to signal the changing cultural and political landscape in Indonesia. The novel won the Jakarta Arts Council's first prize that year and caused a sensation, and controversy, among Indonesian artists and intellectuals. It was acclaimed by many reviews and was considered as a new milestone in Indonesian literature. *Saman* also won the Prince Claus Award from Prince Claus Fund. "Saman" has sold over 100,000 copies and been reprinted 34 times. The sequel to *Saman, Larung* was published in 2001.

Ayu Utami currently works for Radio 68H, an independent news radio station that is broadcast all over the country as well as a writer for the cultural journal *Kalam* and in Teater Utan Kayu in Jakarta. Her new play and book protesting anti-pornography legislation, *Pengadilan Susila (Susila's Trial)* appeared in 2008.

SAMAN

In *Saman,* Ayu Utami weaves together the twin stories of Indonesian feminist awakening and resistance to neo-colonial policies that devastated farmers and villagers during the Suharto era. The structure of the novel is complex, moving backwards and forwards in time from the 1990s to the 1980s and 1960s and among a variety of narrative points of view. A framing romance tale follows the story of Laila, a journalist who has fallen in love with Sihar, an already-married oil rig worker that she meets on assignment.

When she witnesses a tragic accident on the rig caused by the negligence of the oil company's supervisor, Laila becomes caught up in Sihar's quest for justice. This leads her to put Sihar in contact with Saman, a former priest she once loved as a youth and who now works as a resistance activist. The plot takes us back in time to follow Saman's journey from the seminary to prison to continuing struggle against state oppression. This central part of the novel provides a harrowing account of how the Indonesian state is an accomplice to mercantile fascism, as a palm oil producer is allowed to expropriate the land and village of poor rubber farmers in South Sumatra.

This is a compelling and distressing account of how the original Dutch colonial exploitation of Indonesia continued under the neo-colonial policies of Suharto's "New Order." In the end the novel returns to the lighter story of Laila and her female friends in the 1990s, who each represent different choices and possibilities for women in Indonesia. *Saman* provides an important critique of the New Order, which was overthrown by students and workers in 1998. Coming out from under the censorship of Suharto, Ayu Utami's novel is a daring expose of truths that could not be previously told. Its candid and celebratory treatment of new freedoms for women, including sexual freedom, was dramatic innovations when they appeared.

Utami treats social taboos in an open way, thereby breaking with Indonesian literature to date. She writes freely about love and sexuality and picks up the difficult relationship between Muslims and Christians as a central theme – as well as the hatred towards the Chinese minority.... Utami's prose is lively and modern, and as such reflects the richness of the Indonesian oral tradition. The author masterfully switches between various narrative perspectives, locations and time scales; links dream sequences and old myths with descriptions of the political and societal relations in Indonesia in the 1990's.

Barbara Hatley argues that "a key 'innovation' of the text *Saman* is its subversion of long-standing conventions of female representation and women's writing in Indonesia, and of the concepts of womanly nature and gender relations in which these conventions are grounded." Utami's novel violates the traditional expectations in Javenese and Muslim culture that women be accepting, domesticated, subordinate, and sexually innocent. The sexual boldness of its female protagonists and the frequent use of sexually explicit language in the novel go a long way toward explaining the uproar caused by the book's publication, something that readers from the West might find surprising.

WRITING AS NEGATING

On October 26, 2005 Ayu Utami participated in a panel discussion on the topic "Why I Write What I Write" at the Iowa City Public Library, sponsored by the University of Iowa's International Writing Program. Her opening sentence states: "The beginning period of my fiction writing was probably a sort of adolescent struggle to negate the father figure." This figure, as the novels demonstrate, includes a variety of patriarchal social structures and institutions, literary conventions, and regimes such as that of former dictator Suharto.

In terms of literature, Utami explains that "My first two novels *Saman* and *Larung* negated the convention of novel writing in Indonesia at that time, which was that a novel should have a linear and coherent plot. My novels do not have that. Both are stories told through different kinds of narration and by different characters. Each character has his or her way of telling stories.... The books have the rhythm of their content. Each book always starts with the introduction of the main character in a detailed description as if to seduce the readers, but then finishes abruptly."

Utami goes on to articulate how the specific plot elements of each novel inform the shape given to the narrative rhythm of the book, and defends her against criticisms that seemed not to appreciate her method. Her unconventional style, she says, was also "a reaction to the discipline of journalism" and the repressive rules it imposes. Thus she rebelled against the linearity of journalistic writing as well as against the "euphemism that prevailed in the Indonesian language" when it comes to sexual references. She concludes her remarks by giving a number of examples of how she deliberately used "negative sentences" in her novels-sentences whose use of forms of "not" or "no" create ambiguity.

The "negative sentence," she claims, is a more complex sentence than affirmative or positive sentences.... Negative sentences are always more playful than affirmative ones." As an example she cites this sentence from *Saman*: "When I was nine I was not a virgin." The following sentence clarifies, a bit: "People didn't consider a girl who didn't yet have breasts to be a virgin." Thus for Utami, "Writing as Negating" works from the level of politics and plot down to the level of syntax itself. Looking forward, she playfully ends by speculating that "If I'm successful in negating the father figure, my next work will be a step forward to an attempt at self-negation."

PENGADILAN SUSILA (SUSILA'S TRIAL)

In March 2008, Utami published *Pengadilan Susila* (*Susila's Trial*), based on the script of her theater play *Sidang Susila*, co-authored by veteran playwright Agus Noor. According to The Jakarta Post, "Ayu considers her new book a weapon to fight against the morality movement and regulations that violate women's rights." The theater piece and book grew out of Utami's involvement in protests against a proposed anti-pornography bill being discussed by the Indonesian House of Representatives.

In an article covering the play's production by Yogyakarta's noted theater troupe *Teater Gandrik*, actor Butet Kartaredjasa said the play exposed the camouflaged moral truths that the Constitution tries to enforce: "*Sidang Susila* hints at the dark shadows of an authoritarian regime that acts under the name of morality." A summary of the play goes like this:

Sidang Susila begins with the impact of the enforcement of the Law on Decency on the public. In the play, those believed to have violated decency are arrested by the authorities, including Susila, who is played by veteran actor Susilo Nugroho. The play then centers on Susila, who is put behind bars, powerless, by the state authorities. Susila is accused of "committing" pornography for bearing his large "breasts" in public, therefore violating the new law passed by the political elite. In fact, he is only a poor hawker of children's toys and has committed no wrong.

The arresting officer in the play ignores Susila's claims that he is in fact a man, and that his chest is enlarged due to a tumor. Susila is then incarcerated and tried. It is here that the rulers act arbitrarily. The official interrogation report is made by force and the court proceedings are directed to cater to the rulers' wishes.

SEXUALITY AND RELATIONSHIPS

Besides research in the literature, personal communication was undertaken with historians with expertise in Indonesian and Javanese history. With this combined approach gained a more holistic understanding of the history of sexuality and how values relating to sex have changed over time. The objective of this chapter came from my wondering about the origin of the notion of conservatism in regard to sexuality. Has it always been rooted in our cultural and social values? Or are there other forces either from religion or Westernisation that also have influenced our values towards sex?

From historical documents it is clear that in the past, Indonesian women had more power than men did over their sexual activity. Women initiated sexual intercourse and men sometimes underwent very painful penis surgery to insert tiny balls under their loose penis skin with the aim of pleasing women. This is in contradiction to contemporary Indonesian attitudes on sex. Even though premarital sexual activity is increasingly evident people do not openly talk about sex. Virginity is regarded as crucial for marriage and sex outside marriage is regarded as immoral. State regulation, the political environment, religious beliefs and traditional norms and values influence sexual activity.

Yet double standards exist, as shown by young men having sexual intercourse with prostitutes but wanting to find virgin wives. This chapter attempts to evaluate the source of conservative attitudes towards sexuality. It is quite difficult to study sexual activity using historical accounts owing to their scarcity and because literature dating from the tenth to the eighteenth centuries was written in Javanese. This poses difficulties for scholars who do not read and understand Javanese, and who rely on translations.

Nevertheless, sexual and other aspects of life can be studied through written literature. To trace the notion of conservatism towards sexuality, and to provide an overview of this matter, this chapter uses Javanese literature that has been translated into either Indonesian or English, as well as other documentation from the early part of this century such as Indonesian folklore, the Sumatran novels, the Pudjangga Baru Era novels, popular novels and traditional popular art.

This chapter will analyse about the notion of traditional Indonesia sexuality, the adaptation to the outside world and how Westernisation came to Indonesia, stories relating to sexuality from folklore and Indonesian literature, and the coming of Islam as a source of conservatism in sexuality.

Within political Islam it is often difficult to find evidence of direct influence by women on decision-making. In the past much of their influence seems to have been applied behind the scenes, but in recent times it has become much more overt. As a striking example we can take the influence exerted within Nahdlatul Ulama - the largest Islamic organization in Indonesia - by two generations of women in the family of Abdurrahman Wahid.

Within Nahdlatul Ulama (NU) it is acknowledged that Abdurrahman Wahid's late mother, Solichah A.Wahid Hasyim, had a strong influence on the organisation. She was a leader of the so called Muslimat NU and a member of parliament from 1960 to 1982. Interestingly, apart from her talent as an intermediary between disputing factions, she is also credited with having played a decisive role in getting the NU to take a firm stand against the Communist PKI ("Partai Komunis Indonesia") after the Communist 'coup' of 1965.

INCREASING INFLUENCE BY HIDING IT

Although leaders of Muslimat NU claimed that their organisation has had a tradition of avoiding conflict, at least one of their leaders was thus willing to advocate conflict as well as resolve it. However, she rarely allowed her influence to be seen in public – and perhaps it was the stronger for that reason. Abdurrahman Wahid's wife, Sinta Nuriyah, and his sister Aisyah Hamid Baidlowi belong to a younger generation and operate differently. Sinta Nuriyah makes no secret of her strong desire to implement feminist reforms within moderate Islamic circles.

She has campaigned successfully to review misogynist teachings in the texts used in pesantren, (the Islamic boarding schools in Indonesia). Like her mother, Aisyah has been a long-serving member of parliament for Golkar (Suharto's former party) and the head of Muslimat NU, within which she has supported liberal changes in relation to the position of women. She has argued for "more strategic positions" for women in the leadership of NU, because, as she puts it, "The fact is that the majority of NU members are women".

MEN INCREASINGLY SUPPORT ISLAMIC FEMINIST THINKING

In general not enough research has been done on what women do to influence political Islam from within. Books published by Muslimat NU or the Islamic PSII Wanita ("Partai Syarikat Islam Indonesia") nevertheless hint at covert conflicts between their groups and male leadership, often resolved in favour of the women. The impression gained is that women within NU and PSII had to wheedle or defy the male leadership to introduce changes in favour of women.

In organisations like Muslimat Nahdlatul 'Ulama (logo) women in recent years have increasingly been able to make themselves heard. It is indeed striking, in recent years, to witness the increasing eloquence of Islamic women and their readiness to debate gender issues. In alliance with sympathetic men within these organisations, women are helping to strengthen the support base for Islamic feminist thinking.

A recent example of a pluralist, progressive Islamic organisation in Indonesia is the formation of "Rahima", a centre for training and information about Islam and women's rights, an organization focusing on women's empowerment with an Islamic perspective. Its Board of Management features some of Indonesia's best-known Muslim intellectuals and activists, both male and female.

Criticism takes Scholarly Knowledge and Strength of Mind

An effort is now being made to counter radical propaganda on women, including the publication of popular and academic books propounding a liberal Islamic feminist point of view. While radical literature is often connected to the Middle East, the recent counter-propaganda is often published with help from Western funding sources. The task of influencing Islamic practices from within the Islamic movement is fraught with difficulty for women.

It takes considerable training in Islamic theology plus unusual strength of mind for a woman to stand up against well-established ulama (Islamic scholars) and argue the point on Islamic hadith (narrations about the life of the Prophet) or jurisprudence. The price paid for being taken seriously by Islamic leaders may be cutting oneself off from support in the non-Islamic world by accepting the premise of the universal Islamic claim to truth and arguing only within its parameters.

Trying to "Change the System from Within"

For such women, to admit the force of argument of feminists or "outsiders" may undermine their own argument based as it is on a view of the world in which secularism; feminism, the West and non-Islamic sources generally are frequently demonised as anti-Islamic. Thus small advances within an Islamic framework for the women's cause may be at the expense of understanding of and identification with women of different religious affiliation.

Such problems have beset Indonesian Muslims arguing about gender for at least a century. During the colonial period tensions already existed between Islam and "modern" notions of women, and those who propounded reforms within Islam laid themselves open to charges of encouraging licentious Western-style behaviour between the sexes.

After colonialism rifts opened between Islamic factions

But during the colonial period it was easier to smooth over the contradictions by reference to shared nationalist goals. Now the divide between radical and moderate Islamic views of women is much more difficult to bridge within political Islam. While undoubtedly many Islamic women continue to argue for reforms within the rarified discourse of Islamic theology (meaning: reserved for an elite group), some Islamic women are willing to defy radical Islam quite openly. An example is the stance of Suraiya Kamaruzzaman, the director of the women's organisation Flower Aceh.

After wearing a jilbab (i.e. headscarf) as a sign of her Islamic identity for many years, in 2001 she decided to leave it off in protest against a decision by the Acehnese local government to enforce the wearing of Islamic dress on women, in accordance with their reading of sharia law:

"I became so mad when I heard cases of women being chased and pelted with eggs and tomatoes for not wearing the jilbab," Kamaruzzaman says. "A woman on a bus to Takengon was so angry with a group of young men who harassed her for wearing a loose shawl that she threatened them with her sickle. I've concluded that the issue of women's dress can be used to domesticate women for many purposes. Any man, from school boy up to old man, now thinks that he is the morality police."

Quiet Revolution Concerning Status of Women

It is perhaps easier to see the influence of women if we look at some of the issues relating to how Islamic political activity has affected women. On all of these issues Indonesian women, both within and outside the Islamic community, participated in debates and, together with sympathetic men, produced reforms leading to further empowerment of women. In some cases it was a matter of persuasive, educational work to change attitudes, the kind of quiet revolution that occurred to turn around Islamic thinking on the education of girls and early marriage.

At least one dramatically progressive change, the admission of women as judges to Islamic courts, occurred with minimal controversy. On other matters there has been direct confrontation. Secularist women openly confronted Islamic organisations on issues like polygyny (one man marrying more than one woman), and they have been increasingly vocal in recent years on matters like the 1998 rapes case, the Megawati presidency debate, and violence against women.

Acceptance of Liberal Interpretations Ahead

Political Islam has had to take account of the opposition it encounters from within and outside its ranks. The more radical elements are defiant, rejecting such opposition as Western-influenced and anti-Islamic. Judging from the way in which thinking has shifted in favour of women's empowerment over the years, however, the more pragmatic elements must be aware that on some issues, like marital rape and sex education of teenagers, it is just a matter of time before they accept more liberal interpretations of scriptures.

The new requirement for parties to put forward a minimum of 30 per cent women candidates, if enforced, will impact on Islamic parties, in ways that are as yet unforeseeable. This is a good example of sustained lobbying by women across the political and religious board having an impact on political Islam.

Challenge to Islamic leaders

Finally, it is worth pointing out that, as in every Muslim society, Indonesian women often act or are treated in contravention to the teachings of Islam. Sometimes this is to their advantage, as for instance in customary law on inheritance in West Sumatra, where property is inherited through the female line. At other times, Muslim women quietly corrode religious teachings, exposing a gap between doctrine and lived reality. For instance, they seek abortions in large numbers.

This constitutes a challenge to Islamic leaders, who can either continue to hold the line or, as has so often happened, go back to the religious texts to reassess them in the light of changed circumstances. In Iran the Islamic regime has had major difficulties to withstand the resistance to its hardline policies by ordinary people, including women. Political Islam has to contend with the needs and wishes of ordinary people who often feel they cannot live according to scripturalist teachings.

Indonesia's religious life in the post-Suharto era has been marked by the emergence of extreme religious radicalism. The conflict between Muslims and Christians in Poso in the province of Sulawesi Tenggara, and in Maluku province exemplifies this phenomenon, as do the 2002 and 2005 Bali bombings. The rise of radical organizations such as Defenders Front for Islam (FPI), Jihadist Paramiliter (LJ), and Indonesian Mujahidin Council (MMI), confirms the new power of the conservatives in Indonesian politics.

Ten years ago in May, the late Indonesian President Suharto resigned. He had been the country's president for 32 years and stepped down in response to massive protests by university students who were frustrated by the economic crisis that Indonesia had been mired in since the previous year. Suharto's resignation led to political change from an authoritarian government to a democratic one without much political and social strife.

This shift toward democracy has had many positive impacts. For example, freedoms of association and expression have manifested themselves in the emergence of new political parties and social organizations. Even the Indonesian press benefited from the shift and is currently regarded as the most independent in Southeast Asia. But religious radicalism has concurrently gained a strong foothold among the country's Muslims, and can be gauged from the types of books that have become popular in Indonesia.

In the 1980s and 1990s, Indonesian Muslims were reading philosophical and liberal religious discourses by distinguished intellectuals such as Pakistani Fazlur Rahman, Egyptian Hassan Hanafi, and Algerian Muhammad Arkoun. Their humanist ideas complemented and enriched the modernist philosophies of such Indonesian intellectuals as Nurcholish Majdid, Harun Nasution, Munawwir Sadzali, Ahmad Wahib and others. Now, however, there is a demand for Islamic texts that tout religious radicalism.

Bookstores provide translations of extremist texts by popular intellectuals such as Palestinian Abdullah Azam. Also popular are books and essays from Indonesians who have fought in Afghanistan, mostly denouncing concepts like democracy and secularism, and demonstrating non-tolerant attitudes toward non-Muslims. As radical Muslims begin to gain prominence in religious discourse, there has been a tendency to used religious doctrines to undermine religious freedoms in the name of security.

As a consequence of a decentralization policy introduced by the central government in 2001, the regional administrations have issued several controversial rules that enforce certain practices, including an obligation for Muslim women to wear the hijab, or headscarf, and the prohibition of women from leaving their houses at night without being accompanied by a male relative. In general, their policies were inspired by the leaders of the Aceh province in western Indonesia, who were given authority to fully implement a strict version of shariah law, based on Islamic principles, under a special autonomy law.

So why has radicalism increased in the Indonesian reformation era? Australian political observer, Greg Fealy, blames the confrontational methods employed by liberal intellectuals in introducing religious discourse. For example, religious jurisprudential codes introduced by individuals who are associated with Paramadina – a foundation established by the late Nurcholish Madjid have permitted, among other things, inter-religious marriage, a sensitive issue in Islam. In response, radical Muslim groups denounced the groups as providing a distortion of Islamic teachings and encouraging apostasy.

Factors cited by radical Muslim activists to justify their violent methods include poverty, rampant corruption in domestic bureaucracy and legal system, the wars in Afghanistan and Iraq, and the ongoing Israeli-Palestinian conflict. Others look to historical roots to explain this trend, including separatist movements, such as Darul Islam in West Java and Permesta in South Sulawesi that aimed to create an Islamic state in Indonesia. With such complex and easily misunderstood root causes, it is difficult to identify straightforward solutions for reducing radicalism among Muslims.

However, certain steps would go a long way to ensure that the Indonesian public is not vulnerable to the anarchic activities adopted by radical groups. The current Indonesian government must focus on law enforcement to protect citizens from the consequences of violent actions by non-governmental factions. In addition, involving respected Islamic organizations, such as Nahdhatul Ulama and Muhammadiyah, in the active mediation of conflicts could help to rectify religious concerns with the broader public's rights and interests, build a non-violent forum for resolving disputes and dispel the myth that violent radical organizations are operating in the name of all Indonesian Muslims. These changes would go a long way in ensuring that the post-Suharto advances extend to all areas of life in the coming decade.

5

Emergence of Women Writers in Thailand

LITERATURE IN THAILAND

Literature in Thailand was traditionally heavily influenced by Indian culture. Thailand's national epic is a version of the Ramayana called the Ramakien. A number of versions of the epic were lost in the destruction of Ayutthaya in 1767. Three versions currently exist: one of these was prepared under the supervision (and partly written by) King Rama I. His son, Rama II, rewrote some parts for khon drama. The main differences from the original are an extended role for the monkey god Hanuman and the addition of a happy ending.

The most important poet in Thai literature was Sunthorn Phu, who is best known for his romantic adventure story Phra Aphai Mani and nine travel pieces called *Nirats*. Kings Rama V and Rama VI were also writers, mainly of non-fiction works as part of their programme to combine Western knowledge with traditional Thai culture.

20th century Thai writers have tended to produce light fiction rather than literature, but the Isan region has produced two notably sociocritical writers in Kamsing Srinok and Pira Sudham. Thailand has had a wealth of expatriate writers in the 20th century as well. The Bangkok Writers Group is currently publishing fiction by Indian author G.Y. Gopinath, the fabulist A.D. Thompson, as well as non-fiction by Gary Dale Cearley.

The earliest literature, that of the Sukhothai period (13th to mid-14th century), survives chiefly in stone inscriptions, which provide vivid accounts of contemporary life. The most famous of these is the Ramkhamhaeng inscription of 1292, in which King Ramkhamhaeng records the economic abundance of his kingdom and the benevolence of his rule.

Classical literature, written in verse dates from the Ayutthaya period (1351–1767) and it includes religious works such as *Maha chat* ("The Great Birth"), later rewritten as *Maha chat kham luang* ("The Royal Version of the Great Birth"), the Thai version of the *Vessantara jataka,* which recounts the story of the future Buddha's penultimate life on earth; *Lilit phra Lo* ("The Story of Prince Lo"), a tragic romance, widely regarded as one of the greatest of Thai poetic works, and *Lilit Yuan phai* ("The Defeat of the Yuan"), a historical work, celebrating Ayutthaya's defeat of the forces of the northern Lan Na kingdom.

The reign of King Narai (1656–88) is seen as a golden era, in which writers were welcomed at the royal court, and new verse forms were developed; some of the most highly regarded *nirat* poems- a genre characterized by the themes of journeying, separation, and love-longing- date from this period, including Si Prat's famous *Nirat khlong kamsuan* ("A Mournful Journey"), describing his journey into exile in Nakhon Sri Thammarat.

Much literature was lost in the sack of Ayutthaya by Hsinbyushin of Myanmar (Burma) in 1767. After the restoration of Thai sovereignty, and the establishment of a new capital at Bangkok, many law codes, religious works, and literary texts were rewritten. These include the *Ramakian,* a Thai version of the Indian *Ramayana,* which was composed during the reign of Rama I (1782–1809); *Khun Chang Khun Phaen,* an epic poem full of martial and amatory exploits, which took its title from the two main protagonists; and *Phra Aphaimani,* named after its hero. The second and third both date from the reign of Rama II (1809–24).

Translations of best-selling Western fiction by authors such as Marie Corelli, William Le Queux, Charles Garvice, H. Rider Haggard, Sax Rohmer, Anthony Hope, and Arthur Conan Doyle, began to appear at the beginning of the 20th century, but by the mid-1920s original Thai stories, often serialized in newspapers and magazines before their publication in a book, had become more popular. Most were romantic novels, typically involving a poor boy–rich girl (or rich boy–poor girl) theme, in which the plot was brought to a happy conclusion by a series of improbable coincidences.

The late 1920s heralded a golden decade in which a number of writers began to address social issues (such as polygamy, prostitution, social inequality, and social class) in a serious way. Works such as *Lakhon haeng chiwit* (1929; *The Circus of Life*) by M.C. Akatdamkoeng Raphiphat, *Songkhram chiwit* (1932; "The War of Life") and *Khang lang phap* (1937; *Behind the Painting and Other Stories*) by Siburapha (pen name of Kulap Saipradit), *Ying khon chua* (1937; *The Prostitute*) by K. Surangkhanang (Kanha Khiengsiri), and *Phudi* (1937; "The Gentry") by Dokmai Sot (Buppha Kunchon), have since come to be regarded as classics. Of these, the most famous is Siburapha's *Behind the Painting*, which by the turn of the 21st century had been reprinted almost 40 times, translated into Chinese and Japanese, and twice adapted for film.

Set partly in Japan, the story relates the doomed love affair between a young Thai student studying finance in Japan and an older, unhappily married Thai aristocrat. It differs from most fiction of the period in its attempt to deal honestly with emotions; more than 10 years after its appearance, an influential essay by P. Mu'angchomphu (Udom Sisuwan) suggested that, at a deeper level, the characters symbolize the eclipse of the old aristocracy by a new comprador capitalist class.

In the late 1940s many writers were influenced by Socialist Realism and for a brief period produced novels and short stories highlighting social injustice. Most were silenced or fell silent during the literary "dark age" of the 1950s and 1960s when freedom of speech was severely curtailed; in the later years only escapist fiction, called "stagnant water literature," survived.

One writer who proved an exception during this period was Lao Khamhom (Khamsing Srinawk), whose subtle stories about country folk, first published in a collection called *Fa bo kan* (1959; *The Politician and Other Stories*), often carry a more subversive message than is immediately apparent. Although his output was small, with most of his best work dating from the late 1950s to the early 1970s, Lao Khamhom's stature within the literary world continued to grow, and in 1992 he was awarded the prestigious title National Artist of Thailand.

By the late 1960s a new generation of writers was rediscovering Socialist Realism, known as "Literature for Life" in Thailand, and their work played a part in articulating the intellectual climate that led to the overthrow of the military government in 1973; however, such fiction, with its often simplistic treatment of issues, had little broad appeal and soon disappeared, hastened by the vicious military counter-revolution of 1976. This event caused many writers, intellectuals, and students to flee to the jungles to join the Communist Party of Thailand.

But fears of a new "dark age" proved unfounded when the coup leaders of 1976 were quickly replaced by a more liberal faction. In 1977 the writer, artist, and prolific editor Suchart Sawatsi set up the groundbreaking literary journal *Lok nangsu'* (1977–83; "Book World"), which, with its eclectic combination of articles, interviews, reviews, short stories, and poems, covering both the Thai and international literary world, provided a real and challenging focus for all who aspired to be a part of the literary community.

After the demise of *Lok nangsu'*, Suchart continued to play a major role in the Thai literary world, promoting short stories through his quarterly magazine, *Cho karaket* (1990–2000; "Screwpine Flower Garland"), and annual prizes and undertaking research on early 20th-century Thai literary history. The rapid economic and social changes that were beginning to sweep through Thai society by the mid-1980s offered writers new and challenging themes, while the introduction of literary prizes, accolades, and constant media attention also played a part in creating a vibrant literary scene.

Of the writers that emerged during this period, Chart Korbjitti (also spelled Chat Kobjitti) proved to be the most successful, both artistically and commercially. His skillfully structured short novel *Chon trork* (1980; "The End of the Road"), with its constant time shifts, chronicles the economic and moral descent of a decent working-class family, who no matter how hard they work are unable to withstand the relentless pressure of day-to-day living on the minimum daily wage; unlike "Literature for Life" writers, Chart forced readers to draw their own conclusions from the accumulation of detail rather than pointing the finger of blame at a sector of society.

The same uncompromisingly bleak vision is also apparent in his award-winning novel *Kham phiphaksa* (1982; *The Judgment*), in which a well-meaning rural school janitor is turned into a social outcast through the narrow-minded gossip and hypocrisy of the community in which he has grown up. By publishing his own works, Chart achieved a degree of financial independence that most writers in Thailand could only dream of. It is a measure of both his serious literary purpose, in wishing to reach an international audience, and his financial astuteness, that he published English translations of his novels.

Thai literature has historically been fostered by the kings, who themselves often produced outstanding literary works.

The earliest Thai literature is that of the Sukhothai period (13th to mid-14th century), survives chiefly in inscriptions, which provide vivid accounts of contemporary life. The first literary work must be the Stone Inscription of King Ramkhamhaeng.

The literature of the Ayutthaya Period covers many topics, including religious teachings and moral principles that are tools for governing the state, descriptions of scenery, the beauty of women, and expressions of love. Many literary works borrowed plots from other countries such as India and Indonesia (Java). Monarchs, other members of the royal family, and aristocrats wrote most of the works in this period.

Another important literary work in the Ayutthaya Period that functioned as a tool of the ruling class is Lilit Ongkan Chaeng Nam, by an anonymous poet. This lilit (mixed poetical composition) was chanted approximately every six months in an allegiance ceremony, on the occasion of a new king ascending to the throne, or when the king appointed new aristocrats. The ceremony consisted of giving a pledge of loyalty to the king and drinking sacred water from a vessel in which weapons were laid. The lilit chanted in this ceremony combined Buddhism with Hinduism.

In the early Rattanakosin Period there were many literary works that had a foreign influence. The Ramakian, the Thai version of the great Indian literary epic the Ramayana, was especially popular. It was composed in the form of a poem and was then turned into a drama. The recitation used the traditional mask play (khon) and had numerous episodes. Inao and Dalang used plots from Java. The Mon Chronicle was translated into Rachathirat. The Chinese historical tale of Sam Kok (The Three Kingdoms) was another example of these literary works. The literary works using plots from other countries indicate that the Thai royal court had numerous contacts and relationships with foreign countries and was trying hard to get to know the outside world.

After the reign of King Rama IV, Thai literature began to reflect the opening of more relations with the West. Nirat London (The Voyage to London) was composed by Mom Rachothai when he was appointed as an envoy to carry King Rama IV's letter to establish contact with Queen Victoria of England. King Rama V's Klai Ban was written in the form of a diary to record his trip to Europe in 1907.

From the end of King Rama V's reign to the reign of King Rama VII, Thai literature began to change from poetry to prose. Short stories and novels were written in a form that was influenced by the West. The first three Thai novels were Luk

Phu Chai, by Sri Burapha, Sattru Khong Chao Lon, by Dok Mai Sod, and Lakhon Haeng Chiwit, by Prince Akat Damkoeng.

In 1942, after Thailand had changed its form of government from an absolute monarchy to a democratic system, the atmosphere of the liberation of thought made authors step out of the narrow limits of stories that presented only the life of the ruling class. Now there were stories of farmers and fishermen and even a story of a prostitute - Ying Khon Chua, by Ko Surangkhanang. At the same time, some authors wrote of love and romance in their novels as well.

After World War II, Thai politics went into a dark age when Field Marshal Sarit Thanarat had political power (1958-1963) and restricted press freedom. There were orders to forbid the publication of certain literary works and to close many newspapers. Authors of social criticism were arrested and imprisoned. Therefore, literary works during this period were written as a form of social escape; love between a prince and a commoner and novels about the first wife and the mistress were typical themes.

During the 1970s, however there was a genre of literature called "the literature of life." This emerged from a political situation that restricted freedom of thought. Society had a dictator as a leader, so literary works searched for a better society, criticized the happenings in society and revealed inequality and the barren life in the countryside. Such works took the form of novels, short stories, and poems.

In the last three or four decades, there have been many outstanding authors in the Thai literary world. The names include Yakhop, the author of Phu Chana Sip Thit, a story of love, war and the Burmese King; M.R. Kukrit Pramoj, a former Prime Minister, the author of classic works like Si Phaen Din, which portrays the life in the Thai court through one woman who lived from the reign of King Rama V to the reign of King Rama VIII; and female authors including Krisana Asoksin, Wimon Siriphaibun, and Khunying Winita Dithiyon, who write of love and romance as reflected in present-day family and society.

Thai traditional literature is essentially religious. Most of the literature in the old days consisted of works on Buddhism and Hinduism directly or indirectly. Whatever culture the Thai people brought with them from their homeland in Southern China where they had been in contact with Chinese culture for centuries was adapted to its later conception of Buddhism, their adopted religion. Traces of their original culture may be found here and there in a disguised and weak form embedded in their literature. Most of the works of emotive literature were written in veerse in various patterns. Five prominent examples of such works may be cited briefly.

1. The Romance of Khun Chang Khun Phaen, an indigenous story of love and pathos, at time humourous, of a triangular love plot of one heroine with two lovers. The story, apart from its beautiful expressions, contains a mine of infomation on old beliefs and social customs of the Thai before the impact of Western culture. The story as is known has been traslated into English and French.
2. Ramakian (or Ramakirti in transliteration) is the story based on the famous Indian epic, Ramayana. It is unique, containing many episodes and details which are not to be found in the original epic, but showing traces of contact with certain versions of the Ramayana in India, Malaysia, Java and Cambodia. There is an English translation.
3. The Romance of Inao- This is a translation from the well-known storty of adventures of the national Javanese hero prince. It is written in a refined and perfect style of the Thai Language and meant for dramatic performance.
4. Sam Kok- This is a translation from San Kuo Chi, a Chinese historical romance of the Three Kingdoms. Unlike the three preceeding ones, it is written in prose with perfect expressions of style of the language.
5. Phra Aphaimani- This is a romantic tale written in verse by one of the most famous and popular poets of Thailand. It is an imaginary tale of love, intrigue and adventure, and reflects some ideas of the people towards the Europeans of the last century. There is an English translation in concise form by one Prem Chaya.

The employment of prose in Thai emotive literature along the lines of the Western style is of recent date due obviously to the influence of Western literature. Not too many years ago it wasn't uncommon for Thais critical of the social order to find them faced with the choice between exile and a life in prison. Writers were a particular target for many years and many Thai authors beloved today spent years in jail or died in exile, or both.

So Sethaputra, the renowned lexicographer, wrote his first dictionary while a political prisoner on Tarutao Island. Progressive thinker Chit Phumisak spent six years in prison only to be acquitted, and eventually shot to death in the Northeastern jungles at the age of 36. Kulap Saipradit is perhaps the most prominent example. Best known by his pen name Siburapha, also spelled Sriburapha, he was a writer and journalist by profession, composing his first novel before the age of 20.

He would go on to write more than fifteen novels in all, as well as several non-fiction books, a number of Thai translations of foreign literary works, and dozens of original short stories. All of his major works were republished with funding from UNESCO in celebration of the centenary anniversary of his birth in 2005. He is also the namesake of the Sriburapha Award, which recognizes excellence in journalism, writing, and the arts.

The writing style of Siburapha evolved over the course of his career as he became more involved in human rights activism, and the fight against social injustice in Thailand. In 1951, he set up the Peace Foundation of Thailand. The next year, during a trip to the Northeast of Thailand to distribute goods to the needy, he was one of many "agitators" arrested by the dictatorial government of Field Marshal Plaek Phibunsongkhram. Convicted of treason, he spent four years behind bars before being released in 1957.

In 1958, while Siburapha was in China attending a writers' conference, General Sarit overthrew the Thai government in one of the country's many military coups. Those in Siburapha's group who returned to Thailand were all arrested, so he elected to remain in China. He spent the last 16 years of his life there in exile. For those who prefer his earlier, safer romantic works, it is perhaps easy to dismiss Siburapha's later works as heavy-handed or lacking literary merit. But to do so is to miss the point. His later works are part of the first generation of the "Literature for Life" movement, which had a second wind in the social unrest of the late 60s and 70s.

And so I present the English translation of "Those Kind of People", a short story by Siburapha, first published in 1950 in the magazine (*Siam Samai*). It became popular again among student activists a quarter of a century later. Today I can't help but read it with my eyes open to how much it continues to reflect Thai society.

Though, things have improved considerably in particular with the introduction of affordable health care for the poor, the quality-of-life gap between the higher and lower strata of Thai society remains gaping wide.

"Those Kind of People" tells the story of a girl from an aristocratic family who disagrees with her parents' attitude towards the lives of the lower-class masses, and towards their own privilege. A piece of advice from the girl's father encapsulates the attitude well:

'You shouldn't go worrying too much about those kinds of people,' he said, referring to the people who lived outside Bangkok, the poor, and all those people who were not of the same class as Chao Khun himself. 'They've always lived like that. They're used to it, and they don't really need more than what they already have.'

Thai Literature has an extensive history and culture. Thai literature has always been influenced by Indian literature. The national epic of Thailand is Ramakien, which is a Thai adaptation of Indian Ramayana. All the kings of Chakri Dynasty have been eminent writers and poets. Thai literature greatly flourished under the patronage of these kings. King Rama I had himself written several love poems and edited some of the famous Jataka Tales.

There have been several remarkable developments in the Thai literature during the 19th and 20th centuries. In the 20th century, technological advancements and educational reforms have made literature more accessible to the Thai people. The literary works are no longer confined to the royal courts, monks and government officials. The style of writing in the modern literature has changed significantly. Writers have adopted a broader and realistic approach rather than limiting themselves with Buddhist philosophy, folklore and mythology. Changes in the political, military and economic scenario of the country have also influenced Thai literature.

Writers have started writing on varied concepts such as advocacy of social justice, virtues of democracy, and class discrimination. Works of writers such as K. Surangkhanang on prostitution reflected the changing trends in the 20th century. Post World War II, several literary works concentrated on the preservation of Thai culture from western influence. In the contemporary era, writers such as Vasan are addressing social and political issues. Issues such as environmental degradation, political corruption, and influence of western civilization on the native and rural Thai culture and erosion of Buddhist values in modern Thailand are being primarily targeted.

WOMEN IN THAI LITERATURE

Research evidence on women in Thailand is summarized, including demographic studies and considerations of women's status in the areas of economics, education, health, religion, culture, law, and politics. Also reviewed are women's development plans, a major focus of the 5th 5-Year Plan (1981-86). Fertility in Thailand is steadily declining, especially among educated women. Rural women in the labor force have a larger number of children ever born than those who do not work outside the home, whereas the reverse trend holds in urban areas.

Family planning practice has been increasing at a rate of 4.5% per year since 1975. 46.3% of women were in the labor force in 1979, with the majority in the agricultural sector. Despite advances in employment, Thai women face discrimination in promotional opportunities and income levels. Traditional mores tend to promote the belief that women are less competent than men. If women are to participate in the economic development process, social and economic barriers such as low education, job discrimination, and social prejudice must be addressed.

The women's development plan in the 5th 5-Year Plan targets 6 groups of women: agricultural workers, nonagricultural workers, government officials and public enterprise employees, minority groups, prostitures and women in the service sector, and female prisoners. It is recommended that the years of compulsory educaton be increased and that vocational training be further developed. Most studies on the status of Thai women have been based on scanty data or small populations. Systematic research that can be used for policy formulation is required, especially in the areas of problems of aged women, out-of-school adolescents, female migrant workers, regulations discriminating against women, and evaluation of women's development projects.

Thailand is one country in the world to boast of highest percentage of population as Buddhists, the government quotes 94% of the 62 millions as Buddhists, where as Myanmar comes second with 87% of its population is Buddhists. Buddhism is entertwined in many facets of Thai ways of life yet when one turns to look at women participation in Buddhism, one finds that it is off balance. With 62 millions populations, there are 300,000 monks and male novices, no women. But when the Buddha established Buddhism he trusted the responsibility of Buddhism on the four groups of Buddhists, bhikkhus (monks), bhikkhunis (nuns), laymen and laywomen.

While the history of education in Thailand has been a productive area of research for numerous authors, particularly in its relationship to nationalism and modernization, it remains only a partial history. For this history has primarily documented the evolution and "progress" of Thai men's education as if it could represent the experiences of Thai women as well. This is indeed not the case. In an exploratory examination of the mainstream historical literature, I found that emphasis was typically placed on the education of royal and elite men, especially in connection with the rise of the Thai bureaucracy and state centralization under the reign of King Chulalongkorn. Thus, in many instances, women remain an undeniable absence in Thai history.

In order to outline a tentative history of women's education to complement that of men, it was necessary to rely on sources from a number of disciplines, including education, history, anthropology, political science, economics, and population studies. A book entitled *A History of Thai Education*, published by the Thai Ministry of Education, proved to be the most sensitive to issues of gender in Thailand's educational history. That may be a result of the fact that the majority of committee members compiling the book were Thai women: nine out of a total thirteen. What follows is a preliminary attempt to map the evolution of formal education for women in Thai society in order to discover the possible relationship that education, in particular tertiary education, has had with the development of women's political activism in the contemporary period.

The significant gains made in tertiary education by women of various classes since the 1970's have indeed had an influence upon the heightened politicization of women and have had at least a partial role in the formation of numerous organizations and associations within civil society that have the potential, and in many cases the established goal, of instigating critical social change in the future.

As history tells us, the majority of Thai women have only had access to formal education for the past seventy years. Furthermore, it has been only in the past fifteen to twenty years that women's political organizing has emerged as a significant phenomenon. Yet, there are two clearly opposing viewpoints evidenced in the literature on education in Thailand regarding its liberatory potential.

Education is viewed by some authors as a disciplinary technology of nationalism that serves to mold bodies into docile manifestations of Thai national identity, while for others education is seen as a tool of empowerment and a means of resistance against larger structures of social and political authority. While both arguments are equally valid, and perhaps more provocative when held in tension, The latter position is more relevant to the case of Thai women in the context of their recent political efforts. Because much of the literature is centrist in focus (i.e., Bangkok), generalizations and comparisons about education in the provinces are more difficult to make. This opening section will be followed by a short discussion of both the oppressive and liberatory aspects of formal education in the Thai context. The contemporary situation of Thai women's political activism and organizing will then be examined, albeit briefly, in relation to the preceding discussion.

Historically, formal education has been the privilege of Thai men. During the pre-modern era, two kinds of instruction existed:

1. Royal institutional instruction for princes and sons of nobles (*rajpundits*) and
2. Religious and family instruction in the monastery and home.

Both elite and peasant men had the opportunity to study at the local *wat* (temple) as a necessary requisite for entering the *sangha* (monkhood), a rite of passage ritually performed by the majority of Thai men. At the *wat*, men learned the sacred languages of Pali and Sanskrit in order to read Buddhist texts and perform religious chants. They also gained expertise in fields such as astrology, medicine, poetry, and customary law. However, as women were barred from the monkhood by virtue of their sex, they were denied learning at the *wat* and, as a result, prohibited access to an enormous body of knowledge considered to be culturally and socially valuable. Women did have other bodies of knowledge relevant to their life worlds: for example, relating to the home and childrearing, the marketplace, the rice fields, and support of the *sangha*.

While these bodies of knowledge were important resources for women, they were not useful in providing them with the kinds of understanding necessary to participate in the larger social and political worlds of men. It is also important to consider class distinctions when discussing "women" in Thailand, as they are by no means a homogenous group. In this chapter "class" refers primarily to the distinction between elites (royalty and nobility) and commoners (peasants). Since Thailand is a society characterized by social relationships of hierarchy (superior-subordinate), such distinctions certainly require incorporation into the analysis. Further divisions could be made to include the merchant class (predominantly Chinese) and slaves (though slavery was gradually abolished during King Chulalongkorn's reign, 1868-1910).

However, because information on these latter two groups is less substantial, only brief references will be made to them. Because of its royalist nature, much of Thai history focuses on the Thai nobility and elite. For example, Prince Damrong Rajanubhab (1862-1943) wrote about the education of princes and princesses during the Ayuthaya period. According to him, boys and girls studied together under the auspices of a female teacher at the Royal Palace compound from the age of three to seven.

When children reached the age of seven, they were separated by gender, so that boys studied with male teachers while girls studied with female teachers. At 13, princes began to learn about Buddhism and other topics such as politics. Princesses, at the age of 11, studied morality and domestic subjects and were trained to become "refined ladies." It is clear that elite women *did* receive formal education in the palace, though subjects were gender specific. For example, women were taught what was considered to be culturally appropriate forms of manner and speech, as well as craft making and how to run a household.

On the other hand, peasant women, the vast majority of women in Thailand, had virtually no opportunity to learn to read unless a male family member took the time to teach them. Whether or not particular men chose to do so is open to speculation. Sir John Bowring describes the role of Thai women in the nineteenth century as follows:

> The education of Siamese women is little advanced. Many of them are good musicians, but their principal business is to attend to domestic affairs; they are frequently seen as men in charge of boats on the Meinam; they generally distribute alms to the bonzes, and attend the temples bringing their offerings of flowers and fruit. In the country they are busied with agricultural pursuits. They have seldom the art of plying the needle, as the Siamese garments almost invariably consist of a single piece of cloth.

By the end of the nineteenth century, Thailand had entered a period of nation building which had critical consequences for education. The Thai government began to acknowledge that *wat* schools and missionary schools (which had been in existence since 1848) were no longer sufficient to meet the needs of its growing and modernizing bureaucracy. In order to hold the colonial powers of Britain, France, the United States, and the Netherlands at bay, Thailand had to prove both its modernity and power. A passage published by the Ministry of Education succinctly sums up the feeling of this nationalizing period: "As the politics of reform in the reign of King Chulalongkorn evidently points out, 'New Siam' requires 'Modern elites', a new generation of a progressive group to counter-balance the reluctant old one."

At this time, three kinds of schools existed alongside traditional monastic *wat* schools: missionary schools, Chinese schools, and palace schools. In 1889, the Ministry of Education was established by King Chulalongkorn, organized around the previously existing Department of Public Instruction. This enactment wrested control of education from foreign missionaries and began to establish a state administered education system that could assist in nationalizing and disciplining the populace. Soon after, in 1892, King Chulalongkorn issued an edict resulting in the restructuring of the entire Thai bureaucracy and the founding of twelve ministries as components of the new government.

King Chulalongkorn commissioned Prince Wachirayan (supreme patriarch of the monks) to carry out his "Plan for the Organization of Provincial Education" in 1898. This plan invested traditional *wat* schools with a new function: to teach modern education curricula. A centralized and uniform educational system was created with standardized textbooks, syllabi, and language (Central Thai). Undoubtedly, this attempt at homogenizing the general public was a significant step in assimilating physically, culturally, and ideologically disparate groups and placing them under the twin disciplinary regimes of monarchy and nation.

These "hybrid" schools accepted only boys, as Prince Wachirayan decided to postpone addressing the education of girls until a later date. These boys' schools remained in operation until 1921. At that time state sponsored education became compulsory for both genders, and monks were replaced with teachers formally trained by the centralized education system. The Chinese and lesser nobility were given an opportunity for upward mobility with the founding of these new schools since they became available for attendance by different groups of men at the turn of the century. Commoner men were also increasingly recruited for ministry work and sent abroad for proper training.

In 1915, the government initiated another education plan attempted to give girls more educational opportunities. But prevailing cultural attitudes slowed such advancement for a number of reasons. First, the general public still believed that women should care for the home and family and that book learning was unsuitable for girls. Second, the majority of schools were located in provincial monasteries, and it was thought indecorous for women to attend school in these principally male religious spaces. Third, a shortage of teachers, especially in the provincial areas, made it even more difficult for peasant girls to receive formal education.

Charles Keyes mentions that "some women in pre-modern urban settings did become literate, but rural women were almost without exception, illiterate until after compulsory primary education was instituted." This occurred in 1921 when universal compulsory education, four years of primary schooling, was declared a legal requirement for both boys and girls of all classes. Between 1921 and 1925, the number of female students in Thailand rose from 7% to 38%. The period from the 1930's to the 1970's saw considerable expansion in the educational system, although there is a lack of specific information.

According to Keyes, by the 1930's the national school system was well ensconced in Thai villages, and as other evidence reveals, also in Bangkok. But the literature reveals little about education in Thailand from the 1930's to the 1960's. It would be interesting to see the differences between male and female educational attainment during this period, as women are likely to have made significant gains based on the data we do have from the 1960's forward. During the 1960's, government control further penetrated distant villages via newly constructed highways, visual and aural media (television and radio), and a growing bureaucracy administered from the center, Bangkok.

Rural areas saw thousands of primary schools built, and, by the 1970's, most children, boys and girls, completed the mandatory four years of education. A new wave of investment capital, coinciding with the Vietnam era, further infiltrated the countryside. Tertiary education began to gain importance in Thailand during the second decade of the twentieth century, resulting in far reaching effects on Thai society and the Thai populace, both men and women. The first tertiary institution in Thailand, Chulalongkorn University, was established in 1917.

Its primary purpose was to train individuals that had been educated in the new centralized school system to work for Thai government agencies. Initially, the privileges of attending university and being employed by the government were enjoyed only by men. Not until 1927 did Chulalongkorn University admit its first seven female students. Five years later, in 1932, three of them graduated with a B.A. in medicine.

This was the same year that the Thai monarchy, under the reign of King Prajadhipok, was superseded by a coup instituting parliamentary democracy. In 1932, Thai women were also granted the right to vote; only eleven years after compulsory education had been made law.

In evaluating this enactment, it is important to note that it was strategically crucial for the Thai government to educate Thai women not only to prove that Thais were "modern," capable members of the increasingly internationalized world of which they were a part, but also to discipline Thai women's minds and bodies into becoming model Thai citizens (*chat*). Since women had (and continue to have) important roles in socializing children, the state required assurance that mothers would appropriately shape these future generations, reproducing good Thai citizens and a model social order.

If women were not inculcated with the new paradigm of the Thai "geo-body," metaphorically expressed in the nation-monarchy-religion triad, they might pose a threat to state authority and the national image in the international context. Without education, women represented the "backwardness" of particular "traditional" aspects of Thai society. While the successors of King Chulalongkorn also wanted to maintain some aspects of "traditional" Thai culture, they also wanted Siam to be considered as modern and as advanced as other European powers. On one level, based upon their long term goals to prove their progressiveness, Thai leaders had little choice in granting women formal education in addition to other jural rights.

It is unclear from the literature whether there was either any grassroots activity among the peasants or pressure from the upper classes to commence education for women of any class. Because Thai historical literature has typically been royalist and nationalist in focus, as well as earnestly androcentric, it is often noticeably silent on the activities of the masses, particularly women. Thus, it is difficult to know whether there was any social activity challenging the state to provide more access to education. Likewise, it is not easy to gauge whether much group organizing among women occurred or not.

The first formally recognized voluntary organization in Thailand, it is reported, was established by a group of elite women in 1885. This was the Sapa Unalom Daeng, which has since become the Thai Red Cross. Darunee and Pandey cite a "brief emergence of 'new enthusiasm'" among highly educated middle class women prior to the overthrow in 1932. There was some discussion in women's magazines and newspapers concerning the desire to attain equal rights with men. But women's organizations do not seem to emerge until after the 1932 revolution. Nonetheless, although Darunee and Pandey state that some elite women's groups were established after the democratic era of 1932, they do not provide many examples.

Higher education continued to expand from the 1960's onward. With a growing emphasis on regional development within Thailand, the first regional university was opened in Chiang Mai in 1960. The Private College Act, which allowed for the foundation of private colleges and universities, was passed in 1969. In 1971, Ramkhamhaeng University, the first "open" university in Thailand, was founded. This meant that many more Thais, regardless of class position, could attain a university level education provided they could afford to purchase books and live in Bangkok. A statistical chart provided by Wyatt demonstrates that from 1937 to 1947 there was a 25.2% increase in women's literacy, a 20.9% increase by 1960, and a 13.8% increase by 1970, bringing women's literacy to 74.8%.

Not surprisingly, the period from the 1970's to the present has seen the greatest improvement in women's education as well as women's rights in general. Between 1961 and 1972, the number of Thai universities expanded from five to seventeen, and student enrollment increased from 15,000 to 100,000. Until 1972, tertiary education was still focused upon preparing individuals, primarily men, for civil service. But, after 1972, the civil service was saturated, and the need for bureaucrats declined, channeling Thais into other careers, especially in the rapidly developing export-oriented market economy. For the first time in history, a larger number of university students came from small towns of lower-middle class status.

This may partially have been a result of the time lag as primary schools gradually became firmly established in the rural countryside. As the number of rural peasant students increased in the university, the atmosphere began to change, and students increasingly met to discuss social and political issues. It was precisely at this time that left-wing literature and political organizations were banned by the government. Students began challenging the government curricula and questioning many assumptions about their society. The 1973 student foment culminated in an unprecedented revolution on October 14.

The new found optimism generated by the students and their success led to many changes in the university system as well as larger bureaucratic and jural structures. This included the production of a new constitution, passed in 1974, that guaranteed equality between men and women and legislated the revision of all discriminatory laws. However, just as the political sphere finally appeared to be opening up to a broader range of voices in Thailand, the spirit of democracy embodied in thousands of students protesting throughout the country was violently crushed by the right wing military on October 6, 1976-a day now enshrined in the memories of Thai people as *hok tula* (the sixth of October).

Many of the reforms were later reversed, but the universities remained a place where students could gather and discuss political issues, though perhaps more cautiously. The 1990 census indicated that the historical gender gap between men and women in educational attainment had finally closed at all levels. Particularly noteworthy is the fact that, since 1980, the number of women attaining a tertiary education has surpassed that of men.

This is but one of the consequences of the increase in compulsory education for both genders from four years to six in 1978 and six to nine years in 1994. The longer students remain in primary and secondary school, the more likely they are to continue on to higher education. Between 1970 and 1991, the number of tertiary educated people in the work force multiplied ten times giving rise to what is now generally recognized as a Thai "middle class." Knodel argues that this reversal in educational attainment on the part of women reflects differences in the socialization of gender roles in society, where boys and men are granted far more freedom and social mobility than women, and women are viewed as the loci of responsibility and stability. Women are assumed to be better disciplined and more focused on their studies and thus more likely to succeed.

This points to a number of underlying gender differentiated cultural attitudes that could perhaps be traced back through the pre-modern era, as some historical sources suggest. Various studies of male/female family remittances regularly demonstrate that women send more money home than men and Knodel cites the 1986 national survey as confirming this fact. In the end, the education of daughters may result in a better "pay off" for parents than the education of sons, argues Knodel, especially if the daughter remains single, as she will be more likely to send money home. Since the censuses report a clear trend toward later marriage by women, this may in fact be the case.

Furthermore, it is now generally assumed by the Thai populace, rural and urban, that higher education is a guarantee of better employment opportunities and, hence, upward social mobility. More current census data confirms the feminization of tertiary education in Thailand (both as students and teachers) and the prevalence of women in all tertiary institutions except vocational schools. Will the status of educational employment be lowered as a result of the field's feminization as appears to have been the case in the United States?

Are academic subjects in Thailand stereotypically dichotimized into male "hard" and female "soft" subjects? Contrary to popular assumptions, this does not appear to be the case in Thailand. More interesting the potential effects women's newly acquired education might have on Thai society in the future. In particular, might this new knowledge and awareness result in the increased politicization of women and the growth of voluntary associations and non-governmental organizations (NGOs)? I take up these issues in the remainder of the chapter.

As mentioned in the introduction, education is one of the most efficient disciplinary techniques of the nation-state. Through centralized curriculum development and teacher training administered from the capital, those in power can mold individuals into citizens of the new nation-state, constituting an "imagined community." Whether or not this happened in Thailand is not at issue here. Charles Keyes and Chayan Vaddhanaphuti, among others, make persuasive arguments in this regard.

Keyes states that the crucial role of national schools was "preparing villagers to accept a subordinate position in the centralized bureaucratic world of the Thai nation-state," while Chayan similarly argues that rural schools prepare "village children to be agents of production as well as members of their national community." Thus, in their liberal haste to interpret compulsory education as a human right and necessary path to upward mobility, some Western scholars and Thai activists may have underestimated the possibility that such education was *also* utilized to keep certain classes of Thai individuals in their place-"to accept existing social contradictions and inequalities" -: to maintain, as it were, the social hierarchy.

Keyes argues that the "spatial culture" of the school serves as a "model of the state" on a smaller scale, one to which villagers can relate in their everyday lives. It teaches peasants how to interact with government officials and prepares them for smooth entry into the burgeoning capitalist economy. As such, the Thai school may be best termed, in Foucault's words, a "technology of the body." Indeed, Chayan states categorically that national schools "produce docile, submissive and loyal citizens who accept the legitimacy of the social order." These bodies are the micro-targets of a national power that is pervasive and intense, as well as productive. In many instances, schoolteachers, already embodiments of national discourse, were the first central government officials to enter rural locations.

They brought with them new sources of knowledge and power that not only challenged local knowledge but identified state and "modern" knowledge as superior. Thus, the teacher has played and perhaps continues to play an important role in orienting villagers properly towards the state. However, this view suggests that teachers, as well as students, were, and are, completely passive tools of the state, empty vessels into which nationalist doctrine was poured and from which it was then reproduced. Such an interpretation removes any agency these teachers may have had and effaces any differences of opinion voiced by teachers or students to each other and to the wider community.

While national discourses and structures of power in the form of education may constrain individual agency, they may also be a source of creation and imagination. In fact, many times only a few key individuals are necessary to begin the questioning of dominant discourses and/or structures of power and to persuasively convey their doubts and challenges to a wider community. Education, I assert, may indeed provide those tools of challenge by showing people alternatives and expanding their conceptual and practical horizons. This raises a more critical question about school teachers. Women have virtually taken over the field of education in Thailand at all levels.

We might ask if this is because women are more easily inculcated with nationalist doctrine. For example, do women conform to nation-state expectations in a different and more comprehensive way than men? Does women's entry into the field of education represent an attempt by women to enter a previously male dominated and privileged position? If women enter the teaching profession merely to reproduce nationalist policies, images, and identities, are they not in fact contributing to their own subordination and discipline in a kind of "false consciousness"? On the other hand, what if teachers, male and female, are actually turning some of that same power of the state against itself through processes of subversion? What sorts of everyday resistance might be occurring at the micro level that are not so easily observed?

It would be interesting to examine some of the tactics teachers use inside and outside of the classroom in order to see if and how those tactics actually intervene and subvert nationalist ideologies in any way. Again, this raises more questions than I am prepared to address in this short essay. Nevertheless, in order to suggest some of the more positive potential possibilities of education. In other words, can education make women into able activists rather than merely compliant members of the nation-state? In addition to being a tool of nationalism, education may be conversely and yet simultaneously viewed as one of the most powerful tools for individual and community empowerment.

Researchers in various disciplines have identified a clear link between education, literacy, and women's social status: the higher one's educational and literacy level, the higher one's social status. Relatedly, Keyes draws on Bourdieu's concept of cultural or symbolic capital in his discussion of education and its links to status in rural Thai villages. Keyes states, "Literacy is always associated with a social division of knowledge that, in turn, contributes as much to the structuring of the realm of social relations as does the social division in the ownership of the means of production."

Due to his larger interest in class difference, Keyes pays less attention to the gendered nature of symbolic capital. However, he does note that women have a complementary symbolic capital related to the domestic arena, marketing, as well as in their supportive role of the *sangha:* a "separate but equal" type of argument. This of course sidesteps the possibility that such a division might operate to keep women in an inferior social position relative to men. Yet it does appear quite obvious that peasant and, perhaps, merchant women were excluded from attaining the symbolic capital of literacy and formal education until the mid twentieth century, several generations after peasant men.

Keyes, referring specifically to Southeast Asian villages, states that "one of the striking changes in social structure that has come about with the introduction of compulsory education has been that females as well as males have been given access to schooling" which has allowed women to "visualize a world very different from that known by their grandmothers." With more education, a higher level of literacy, and the exposure to new ideas and new worlds, women's horizons have been broadened and their interests piqued. Likewise, female school teachers provide new and different role models for village girls and point to possibilities beyond the home and village.

Suteera and Maytinee note that because women play key roles in educating and socializing children (particularly in school and the family unit), they are crucial "social change agents" and contributors to development in Thailand. They argue that, when women understand their equality with men and their important roles in society, they will pass these beliefs on to their children, thus altering "backward social values and traditions."

It has only been in the past twenty years that women outside of the elite class could be said to have attained the knowledge and symbolic capital necessary for entre into certain realms of civil society such as politics. It is thus not surprising to find that the emergence of women's voluntary associations and NGOs and the slow ingress of women into the formal political sphere has occurred only in the recent past. What *is* surprising is that significant changes have occurred so rapidly and in such a short period of time-the last fifteen to twenty years-and that women now play crucial and visible roles in welfare and political organizations agitating for change.

While it is perhaps common knowledge among scholars of Thailand that Thai women have long been relatively absent from formal politics, it is far less acknowledged that women currently play prominent roles in NGOs and other informal arenas of power and decision making. Consequently, I see these developments in women's formal and informal political activism as inextricably tied to the gains made in educational attainment over the past seventy years. I turn now to a few of these developments. Due to the exploratory nature of this chapter, the discussion is regrettably a cursory one. Nonetheless, I do believe it will provide another way to view recent changes in Thailand's civil society.

Suteera and Maytinee argue that the UN Decade for Women (1975-1985) was crucial in making women more visible in Thai society. Members of NGOs, many women's groups, and even the government participated in various events promoting the status of women. The 1980's and 90's have seen an explosion of NGOs, with three hundred and seventy-five NGOs formally registered in 1990. The enthusiasm among women's groups was most recently bolstered by the 1995 United Nations World Conference on Women and the preceding NGO forum in Beijing, China.

A number of Thai NGOs and smaller grass-roots organizations attended, along with several Thai academics. Thus, during a preliminary research trip in October 1996, many NGO members with whom I spoke were still reveling in the energy stirred up by the Beijing conference and subsequent events organized within Thailand. Some of the larger and more visible Thai women's NGOs include the Foundation for Women, Friends of Women, Gender Watch, EMPOWER, and the Gender Development and Research Institute.

These groups are progressive and emancipatory in that they are working towards structural change. Their activities include, but are not limited to, the following: developing media and educational resources for women's consciousness raising, monitoring images of women in all forms of public media, offering health services to prostitutes and the poor, teaching women new and practical skills, providing shelters for battered women, incorporating women's rights into the constitution, and providing conferences and programs for leadership training.

Other women's organizations which are more conservative in approach include the National Council of

Women in Thailand, the Girl Guides Association of Thailand, and the Association for the Promotion of the Status of Women. Additionally, smaller women's organizations and grass-roots groups, whose memberships range in size from one to thousands, exist throughout the country. These developments in social and political activism have occurred together with an increase in tertiary education for the Thai populace and the slow but steady entrance of women into formal politics. Over the past fifteen years, the number of men and women attending university has surged, with many Thais taking the opportunity to be educated abroad.

In fact, many of the leaders of women's NGOs are women with higher degrees (M.A.s and B.A.s), and often they are also of a higher class than the target population of their organizations' programs. Leaders typically have the resources-educational, financial, and social-to initiate organizations and activities and, frequently, the charismatic personality necessary to rally others to action. Meetings with NGO leaders and members in Thailand in October 1996 revealed both a highly educated NGO network and a few key individuals who were well-recognized and avidly admired. The importance of tertiary education cannot be underplayed.

Most of the younger women at the few organizations had become politicized during their university years, while several of the older women had actively participated in the 1970's student movement during their university years. Women's gains in formal politics have unfortunately been less pronounced than their gains in education, yet there have been some key developments. For example, in 1993, two female governors were appointed for the first time in the nation's history, and, in 1995, 15% of the nation's judges were women. The Constitution promulgated in February 1995 enshrined women's rights.

Although women's participation in the formal political arena remains extremely low relative to men, with approximately 4% of the decision-making positions at the national level filled by women and only 6% at the local level, women's participation in the informal arena as campaign organizers and supporters, NGO members, and voters has increased. According to Suteera, 300,000 more women than men voted in the 1992 election. She boldly asserts that "Thai women may be more updated and knowledgeable about politics than men."

The 1996 election saw a number of women running for office, although none were considered for the role of Prime Minister. Currently, the composition of the House is 5.6% female. Notably, the female Ministers of Parliament, when considered relative to men, consistently have a higher level of education than their male counterparts. The 1990's have seen a general societal acceptance of and perhaps even a growing dependence upon voluntary organizations to agitate for their interests.

Even Thai academics are discussing the significance NGOs have for future social change. That it took as long as it did for some of these groups to establish themselves is partially a result of the hostile environment the frequently authoritarian Thai government fostered toward any groups not towing the official party line, especially following the October 6 events. Yet, as I have endeavored to show here, these developments are also related to the advances made in women's educational opportunities during the past seventy years, from 1927 to 1997. As education has become increasingly accessible for both men and women of all classes, the boundaries of what is "possible" have expanded and blurred, opening doors to new opportunities and profound challenges.

Based upon this brief exploration into the history of education in Thailand, it appears quite clear that Thai women's activism, especially among non-elite women, did not appear until after education became not merely a right for women but firmly entrenched even in remote villages. The increase in women's activism seems closely tied to women's attainment of tertiary levels of education, both undergraduate and graduate. This is not surprising. However, the issues regarding education as both a tool of nationalism and a tool of empowerment are not so easily addressed.

As much as education can be interpreted as the handmaiden of nationalist discipline, it can also be understood as an empowering process that has the potential to politicize the populace. Whether or not women's education has had negative effects on their aspirations to political participation and improved status is still open to debate. The tensions between tradition and modernity are complex and function within multiple and shifting fields of power at the local, national, and international levels.

"Progress" and modernity, as has been well demonstrated in many nations of the world, can have detrimental as well as positive results, and, in this respect, differences of class, ethnicity, and region among women require further attention. As more Thai women attain higher degrees and knowledge of local and national problems and transnational issues that affect women differentially in all classes and societies, they may further contribute to the grass-roots activism occurring in Thailand and the larger Southeast Asian region.

Thailand is a place of contradictory phenomena with regard to sex. Despite Thailand's reputation in the western world as being a destination for 'sex tourists', the country has a rather modest sexual culture. In reality, sexual issues are hardly ever openly discussed in Thailand, especially among women. To be considered as morally good, Thai women are not supposed to have autonomous sexual desires, less so act upon them or act them out. Therefore, any woman writing about sex is considered to be controversial. This chapter explains the historical background of Thai erotic writing and discusses an awkward blend of unconventional and conservative attitudes to female sexuality in the work of Thida Bunnak, Rayong Wenurak, Suwannee Sukhontha and Sujinda Khantayalongkot.

This conflict of woman writers' attitudes towards sexuality could result from the fact that each of these writers was influenced by patriarchal Thai social values pertaining to 'good' and 'bad' women. Although attitudes towards female sexuality in Thai erotic writing by women writers have changed gradually as a result of parallel changes in Thai society and increased western influence on women's rights and gender equality having made the new generation of Thai women more independent and more confident in expressing their own sexuality, the conservative element still exist in their works.

The topic of sex is taboo in many societies, especially in those of the West, where it is linked to notions of danger, destructiveness and the darker powers that be. Here sex is a great sin, associated with the negative values of craving (*kilet*), passion (*tanha*) and lust (*rakha*), and precipitates the downfall of the individual, and hence society at large. Like many other societies in the world, Thai society is one of the places of contradictory attitudes with regard to sex. Contrary to Thailand's reputation in the western world as being a destination for 'sex' tourists, the country has a rather modest sexual culture. In reality, sexual issues are hardly ever openly discussed in Thailand, especially among women.

According to Harrison, to be considered as morally good, Thai women are not supposed to have personal sexual desires, less so act upon them or act them out. Talking or writing about sex is considered culturally and morally improper. This view of sexuality, as from this public discourse, is dubbed by Sutham Thammarongwit as 'a culture of silence'. Therefore, any woman not 'silence' about sex is considered to be controversial.

The emphasis on erotic writing by Thai female authors, the reasons for, and the difficulties that such authors encounter in producing their works and the tensions and ambivalences regarding sexuality which they express through their literary characters which results as the work of conflict with the awkward blend of conservative and controversial idea on sexuality. Given the patriarchal features of twentieth-century Thai society, women writers clearly approach the topic of sexuality differently from those of their male counterparts.

This feature is similarly evident in pre-modern Thai literature, in which classical works, the production of which was dominated by male authors, invariably included depictions of sexual intercourse or 'love-making scenes'. Erotic episodes in classical literature provided an opportunity for male writers to reveal their talents in depicting a taboo subject in the most aesthetically pleasing and metaphorical terms. The erotic scenes written by male writers tend to be more descriptive and extensive than the very few written by female poets such as Khun Suwan, the only pre-modern Thai female writer to discuss the issue of sexuality in her work.

According to Nai Tamra Na Meuangtai, a famous Thai intellectual, the original model of erotic writing is in the famous work of classical Thai literature called Lilit Pralor. There is no clear evidence about the author and the period of writing for this poem, however, the widely-accepted assumption is that a male writer wrote it in the mid 15th century. Nothing like this appears in any other older Thai literature. The story is about two princesses who have heard about the beauty of the young but married prince and fall in love with him without seeing him.

They then try to make him aware of them and get him to come to meet them by means of magic. After the prince hears about the beauty of the two princesses, he falls madly in love with them without seeing either. He then asks for permission from his mother and his wife to go to see them. Neither the wife nor the mother wants him to go because these princesses are the daughters of an enemy king. However, nobody can prevent the young prince and he travels a long way to meet the two princesses.

When they meet, there is a very detailed description of their love-making, which constitutes the erotic part of the story. At the end, the prince and princesses are all killed together on the orders of the princesses' grandmother and the two warring kingdoms finally become friends. The following quote is an example of love-making scene, which is the erotic part of the story. Wibha Kongkanan, a Professor of Thai literature in Thailand, once raised her own opinion that the author of Lilit Pralor is female. She suggested that the depiction of the mother's love is so real that no male writer would be able to imagine such feelings and the author pays much attention to describe the beauty of the prince but not the princesses.

In Wibha's opinion the author could only be a woman and a mother to be able to write something like this. However, Wibha's theory is not widely accepted by any academics, as the evidence to support is not sufficient. The prince and the two princesses embrace each other and lean down. They feed each other with their lips. It tastes like juice from heaven. Their arms are around each other, flesh is next to flesh. The young and bright faces are next to each other. Breasts next to breasts, stomach next to stomach. The lovers are enjoying the new taste of lust, losing themselves in their cravings.

The flower is opening its petal. The carpenter bee is nuzzling in the middle. They make noises together. (The prince said) "Bathing in the pond in heaven is not as good as in your pond. Your flesh pond is so smooth. It is very enjoyable in your pond. The fish is happy and jumps to touch the lotus. The bank of the precious pond is amazing. It is nice and clean. Even the hill of heaven cannot compare with it."

After Lilit Pralor, comes a traditional style of writing that includes erotic scenes or episodes. The poets have to use beautiful language, simile and metaphor to describe the love-making scenes, rather than straightforward language. The erotic scenes or Bot atsajan becomes one of the important elements in traditional Thai literature as is mentioned by a Thai literary critique, Pong Payajak: Aesthetics in Thai classical literature depend on the ability of the author in describing nature, the beauty of the characters and many other things.... including erotic scenes.

All of the great Thai classical literature then has erotic scenes, all written by male writers and widely accepted as canonical literary works. The following example of the love-making scene is taken from the famous Thai classic Kakee, written by Jao praya praklang Hon. Kakee is the very beautiful wife of King Prommathat. She is kidnapped by Khrut ('Garuda'), a supernatural half bird half-man creature living in a world different from that of human beings, vehicle or bearer of Vishnu.

Suddenly, there was a big downpour of rain. The sky was all dark, the thunder echoed to the biggest mountain in heaven, the mountain and forest were shaking and the water was wavy in the river. The fish was playing with the water and puffing up its body. The heaven blossom, after being hit by the big rain, was now starting to bloom. When the petals opened, beautiful scent came out. The magic carpenter bee hurried to dip him in and bathe every inch of his body. The two lovers were euphoric. Khrut forgot to go swimming. Kakee forgot the king. Khrut forgot to go out and play. Kakee forgot her husband's face (Kakee; Jao praya prakhlang Hon).

Erotic scene like the above example is found in most of the great Thai classical literature written by men. However, the phenomenon is different when it comes to woman writing about sex. Erotic Thai literature written by women writers is quite different from that written by men. They only have some sexual themes but the writer does not give the description in as much detail as the literature written by male writers.

This may be because female writers were too shy, or really innocent, or afraid of being condemned by society. An example of early Thai literature about sexuality written by a female comes in the reign of King Rama IV (1851-68). Khun Suwan was the first female writer who wrote about lesbians in the court. The story is called Mom Pet sawan and concerns a lesbian couple that is court ladies, who are found kissing each other under the blanket while the princess is asleep.

The couple was messing around with each other by the princess' feet. They thought nobody could see them. Therefore, they behaved according to their hearts. It was dark because there was no light. The couples were whispering in the dark by the princess's feet. They were busily engaged in outrageous intimacy under the blanket (Khun Suwan, 1968:78-79). The love-making between the two lovers is described modestly by the female poet, compared with the love-making scenes written by the male poets. However, the interesting thing about this story is Khun Suwan writes this story in an amusing tone; she makes it seem as if lesbian practice is accepted.

Khun Suwan's most famous work is called Pra Ma-leh-theh-thai ('Prince Ma-leh-theh-thai'). This story shows her fantastic skill with the Thai language by putting meaningful and meaningless words together, and the story turns out to be meaningful. What makes this story interesting is the way the hero and heroine are brought together. In Thai traditional writing the female and male characters are mated with God's help. God usually brings a male character to a female character's bedroom. But Khun Suwan makes God bring the female character from her bedroom to sleep with the male character in the jungle. This may be because Khun Suwan is a court lady.

Having spent most of her life in the court, the world outside the court must have been challenging for her. Therefore, she imagines being taken outside the court to meet a man. This was considered funny for people of her time and many liked to come and listen to Khun Suwan tell the story. However, Khun Suwan's imagination is analysed as female sexual fantasy by Kepner, as quoted: Phra Malethethai is a female fantasy of sexual adventure and escape from repression; the intervention of the god Indra absolves her of responsibility. The name of this heroine, "Talaeng-gaeng", can be literally translated as "the place where the prisoner is to be executed", by which Khun Suwan suggests that a woman's safe, chaste bedchamber is a prison (Kepner, 1996:10).

Although it was controversial for Khun Suwan to write about female sexual fantasy, she was not controversial enough to describe the love-making scene between Prince Malethethai and Princess Talaeng-gaeng explicitly. The erotic scene in this story remains as modest as the erotic scene in the previous example from her other work Mom Pet sawan.

The following extract is to exemplify the description of the erotic scene between Prince Malethethai and Princess Talaeng-gaeng. It was my great fortune that god has brought you to me," the prince said, and moved himself close to her. "Please do not be shy". The princess was embarrassed and tried to stop him from touching her. The two were engaged in foreplay with each other. They then had pleasure together (Khun Suwan, 1968:23).

Both of the extracts from Khun Suwan's works illustrate how female writers wrote about sex. Obviously, it was not as explicit as those written by male writers. This was not because of a lesser talent for writing. Actually, Khun Suwan was very talented. Another interesting story written by Khun Suwan was Unnarut roi reuang ('A hundred stories of Unnarut'). Khun Suwan composed the story by bringing well-known characters from many different Thai classical works together.

This could be equivalent to something like Hamlet falling in love with Juliet, but her father, Othello preferring her to marry with King Lear. Khun Suwan composed this story at a time when there was no education provided for women. She must have worked very hard to learn about all those different stories and remember them. Therefore, Unnarut roi reuang and Pra Ma-leh-theh-thai show Khun Suwan 3 All the names are characters from different stories written by Shakespeare is a genius. Writing descriptive love-making scenes should not have been too difficult for her literary skills to cope with.

The only reason for her to avoid writing it would be because she was a woman and Thai. Although Khun Suwan was a genius, Prince Damrongrachanupap, son of King Rama V, discredited her, claiming that she was mad. His opinion was accepted until the middle of the twentieth century when literary scholars took another look and found not insanity but true genius: Because sexual desire was considered to be a delicate subject and because Khun Suwan was determined to write about it anyway, she devised elaborate linguistic and stylistic strategies. It is possible that she encouraged the idea that she was insane to protect herself, for a work composed by a mad woman could be overlooked and her position at court preserved. The above quote confirms the difficulty a woman writer has to encounter if she wishes to write about sexuality. This difficulty does not exist in Thai woman classical writers only but women writers in the later or prose generation also has to be struggle for quite a period of time.

EARLY PROSE FICTION AND EROTICISM

As it has not been socially acceptable until relatively recently for a woman in Thailand to talk or write about sex, there have been no other works touching on sexual issues written by women until the mid twentieth century. At the close of the nineteenth century, the popularity of compositional style in Thailand has changed from poetry to prose and modern Thai prose fiction reveals a marked increase in the number of women authors writing on sexuality, though their numbers are still limited.

Kor Surangkhanang was the first female prose writer to touch upon the subject of sexuality in 1937 novel Ying khon chua, the tale of the life of a prostitute named Reun. However, this novel can in no way be argued to be sexually explicit, although it provoked a certain controversy among Thai audiences of its day because of the nature of its subject matter and the way in which its female authoress had researched her topic of concern. Following the early work of Kor Surangkhanang, Thida Bunnak represents the first female writer to explore topics of eroticism in her numerous novels and short stories, from the late 1940s to the mid 1960s.

A marked contrast in sexual attitudes appears to exist, however, between Thida's more explicit earlier texts and her considerably more conservative later works. While the female protagonist of her 1950 novel Roi pitsawat is highly controversial in both its attitude to female sexuality and to sexual practice, that of the short story Bap thee sam, published sixteen years later, is much more traditional in its approach sexual behaviour. In this piece Thida emphasises a sense of Buddhist belief and morality through the actions and thoughts of her main female character, Patsee.

It can therefore be argued that the older Thida gets the less erotic her works become. This could be because of her change in career to being an agony aunt as well as her role as a mother, both of which require her to behave or write in a more respectable way. The following extract illustrates Thida's controversy. "Do you think my kissing has improved?" And again she kissed him, pressing her lips up to his and darting her tongue back and forth, sweeping it around his mouth from left to right and twisting it round and round from top to the bottom of his mouth (Thida,1950:289).

Although the above quote only mentions kissing, it is a very detailed one. Being a woman in the 1950s to describe kissing explicitly is very controversial. However, the contrast character of Thida could be seen through the following quote from the Daily News whereas she acts as an agony aunt. There was a woman whom her husband was having an affair and she was hesitating about leaving him. She wrote to Thida seeking an advice. Please remain with him and use your wisdom and goodness. Then you will not have to live as a half dead person but you will live a complete life with your heart and his heart next to each other's.

Advising the wife to remain silent in the relationship while the husband is having an affair is rather a conservative idea and less to be expected to hear from such a controversial woman like Thida. Thida's works are universally marked by a conflict between controversy and conservativeness in both her female characters and in the subject-matter of her stories, so rendering her texts distinctly ambivalent in nature. Beneath an audacious exterior, Thida therefore actually proves herself to be a somewhat typical Thai woman who exhibits numerous conservative ideas.

However, based on the evidence of her biographer, Jetsada Na Bangluang, Thida's repeated failed love affairs may have had the effect of making her become more widely flirtatious and more relaxed in her attitude to sexuality. The conflict that appears to exist in Thida's writing extends to that of other fictional works by subsequent woman writers such as those of Suwannee Sukhontha and Rayong Wenurak. During the 1960s to the 1970s, Suwannee Sukhontha, the great female writer of the time, produced a lot of unique work. She is not primarily known as an erotic writer and her work is not categorised as erotic literature.

Nevertheless, Suwannee's works always contain sexual, and sometimes sensual, themes. Suwannee herself was controversial and independent woman, which is reflected in the independent and controversial female characters she creates in her fiction. She creates female characters that are like real people, or in the Thai saying, mee leuat mee neua ('have flesh and bloods'). Suwannee's male characters are a reflection of typical Thai men who always look down at non-virginal women, and on those who "misbehave" sexually. Like Thida Bunnak, Suwannee brings her life experience to use as raw material together with some Buddhist teaching. In contrast to Thida's work, Suwannee's use of language is more refined. This is her significant talent which brings her fame and recognition by Thai academics.

This is an example of Suwannee's style of writing a love making scene. He forgets everything when she is in his arms. The weather is getting colder. The rain has already stopped but the couple is full of passion. There is the sound of the waterfall jumping from the cliff... and hitting the rocks. The evening sun shines on the spray from the water and gives a shiny rainbow. The golden colour of the sun is also on the top of the trees. Her fair face seems to be a blur to him. Her hair is all over her neck, cheeks and sweated forehead. In such a dark place like this, she does not look as old as he used to see. She is hot all over her body. He never thought that she would be able to give him more than just an ordinary woman could give (Suwannee, 1997c:151-152).

Apart from writing the outdoor love making scene, many of Suwannee's female characters are controversial about their sexual attitude. For instance, Mae Rabiap, a married woman in Jamorn (1997a) is a vendor selling sweets at the school canteen but she earns extra money from sleeping with men. Her idea about this extra job is that she gains both money and enjoyment. This is considered to be a very controversial attitude. Contrary to these controversial ideas, Suwannee's writing concerns a lot about the widow's status in Thai society. Her female characters are always worried or have inferiority about being a widow which is seen as a 'used' woman in Thai society. The following extract is an example of Thai men's attitude towards a widow through Suwannee's perception. "Why don't you try to get her? It's good to get it for free. That way you can save the money from going to the prostitute." "A widow like Rot is nonsense. She is just dying to have a husband. Can't you tell from her eyes?" (Suwannee, 1997c:179). Suwannee's concern about being a 'used' woman and looked down by people especial men in Thai society is rather a conservative idea contrasting to her daring to write about 'outdoor' love making scene or a married woman enjoying sex with other men without feeling guilty. In the 1970s, the female writer who has produced few books of erotic literature is Rayong Wenurak.

Rayong can be noted as the first erotic writer to writes intentionally erotic fiction, in contrast to Thida Bunnak's style of composition, which was marked more by the depiction of sexualized relationships between men and women and than it was by the portrayal of any sexually explicit love-making scenes.

Rayong has shown her talent for descriptive language, used to make her fiction erotic, exemplified by her slow, smooth style in such short stories as Kradanga long song to enable the reader to imagine the erotic feel of her story. Rayong also makes use of the natural environment to help create the sense of a beautiful love scene in such stories as Khleun long fang. A similarity in style between the work of Rayong and Suwannee can therefore be noted. The following extract is an illustration of Rayong's autoeroticism.

The breasts under the water surface seem to be firm like the breasts of a sculpture, not the soft flesh of human being. The water helps my breasts look more beautiful than usual. They are quite beautiful, a lot more beautiful than seeing them without water and try to lift out of the water to waist level to see my real body, which is not at all as nice as when it is covered with water. So, I slide my body back into the water. The light mole is turning darker.

Rayong is controversial for writing to admire her own body which could also be interpreted as having a materbation. Despite the overt eroticism of Rayong's style of writing and choice of subject matter, she nevertheless sustains the sense of ambivalence towards female sexuality that is also displayed in the work of Thida Bunnak and Suwannee Sukhontha. In the case of Rayong, she reveals a surprisingly conservative view of woman's virginity, most of her work sharing the same theme of a woman who loses her virginity and consequently experiences feelings of internal conflict, either blaming herself as a 'bad' woman, or accepting herself because she is 'good' in every other way.

It could be true if we only value a woman for her virginity. In reality, it is only a thin membrane in a woman's body. Her beautiful heart, her kindness and her gratefulness must mean nothing then." "One more thing, does a woman who is not virgin have to be a bad woman? There are plenty of good women who are not virgins. What judgement do people use to measure a woman's good or bad deeds?

The awkward blend of unconventional and conservative attitudes to female sexuality that typify the work of Rayong Wenurak, Suwannee Sukhontha and Thida Bunnak may be argued to result from the fact that each of these writers are inescapably influenced by patriarchal Thai social values pertaining to 'good' and 'bad' women. Although these writers appear in some senses 'liberal' and liberated enough to free themselves from such values, they nevertheless remain uncertain in some areas of how they address the topic of female sexuality in their work. In marked contrast, this conflict of conservative and controversy in the work of women writers in their discussions of female sexuality hardly appear to persist into the 1990s.

The 1990s saw the emergence of the most controversial of Thai female erotic writers, Sujinda Khantayalongkot. Sujinda can be argued to be the most successful female erotic writer as her work has brought her considerable fame and notoriety as the best-selling Thai female erotic writer of her time. Sujinda uses her own experience as a 'heartbroken' woman (Pooying ok hak) as material for her compositions. This is the same phenomena as in Thida Bunnak, Suwannee Sukhontha and Rayong Wenurak's work that the writers use autobiographical material in their works. Both despite and because of the fact that her writings are extremely controversial as a result of their sexually explicit nature, Sujinda's work marks a major development in the creation of erotic fiction in Thai women's writing.

Each of the writers studied in this thesis prior to Sujinda are found to reveal contradictory characteristics in their works. In Thida Bunnak and Suwannee Sukhontha's works, the female characters in their novels and short stories misbehave sexually and are consequently often blamed by the author through a negative tone of writing. In contrast to the work of these three authors, Sujinda, however, creates female characters that are fully controversial in their attitudes to sexuality.

These female characters 'misbehave' according to traditional Thai norms and yet still feel good about them and are not blamed by the writer. They are the 'new breed' of Thai women as reflected in Sujinda's work. The following extract illustrates Sujinda's explicitness in writing about sex as well as the controversial 'new breed' woman's daring to criticise a man's sexual organ and performance. He inserts 'his' in as deep as possible. 'His' is not really big, not a great one, and she sometimes like it. Sometimes it can be very strong and make her wonder how it makes her come.

She does not like it too big. It is good that this time 'his' is quite all right. She can bear to give him co-operation, even though she is telling herself that it is so-so. She is not turned on, let him enjoy it by himself. There is minor conservative and conflict to be seen in Sujinda's work when one of her female narrator writes about her parents and confess her guilt for being a bad daughter and behave sexually 'wrong'. I'd like to say sorry to my mother and tell her that I have ruined her name. I have lived a dirty life. My sin has destroyed me from being her daughter... I would also like to tell my father that his favourite daughter has never behaved as a daughter of his. All the bad things I've done to destroy our family's reputation are indescribable. It's not about the good and the bad because these are only little things to me. The most important thing is the wound in my heart... the feeling of guilt.

Who am I angry with? Why did I take revenge on my father? Who do I want to tease? Why I did it to my mother? Who should I blame? Where can I confess all my sins? And who would listen to me? Sujinda's explicit description of love-making scenes in somewhat unrefined language, together with what is seen as sexual themes of low moral value in her work, has rendered it unpopular among Thai critics and academics as a result of which Sujinda has received a great deal of harsh criticism.

The extremely controversial nature of Sujinda's work shows the significant changes in the characters Sujinda creates in comparison with those of previous female erotic writers like Thida, Suwannee and Rayong. It is possible to argue that these changes have occurred as a result of parallel changes in Thai society, increased western influence on women's rights and gender equality having made the new generation of Thai women more independent, less concerned about losing their virginity before marriage and more confident in expressing their own sexuality. However, the existing of conservative issue in female writers writing about sexuality could be interpreted that these women try to liberate themselves from the oppression of patriarchal society but because the task is too difficult, it makes them fall back.

Although Sujinda's work lacks finesse and contains no didactic overtones, it can nevertheless be argued that she has made a significant contribution to the modern Thai literary world, especially to the field Thai erotic literature, by creating a strong base for women erotic writers in future generations. It was the early nineteenth century when the first Thai female writer, Khun Suwan wrote about sexual intercourse modestly. By the early twentieth century, it could be said that Thai female writers were not modest about writing about sex anymore. In addition, the bookshelves in bookstores in Thailand are now flooded with erotic fiction. Eroticism has existed in the Thai literary world since the 15th century, however, contributions to erotic literature were not made by women until the middle of the twentieth century, it being more acceptable for male writers to write about sex or to write erotically.

When women writers did begin to touch upon the subject of sexuality in their work they received no praise for their contributions, though they may have gained a wide (and temporary) following among readers.

Women writers initially had either to try to write about sex in a modest way or suffer from condemnation by society and internal conflicts if they did dare to do so. It results as a mixture of conservative and controversial issue of sexuality in their works. Although the changes in Thai society due to the influence of western ideas and ways of life make Thai women of the 1990s become more independent and feel free to produce extremely sexually explicit work, the conflict of conservatism and controversy still exist in their work.

6

Novels by Vietnamese Women

It is no secret that frequently there is a contrast, a certain dissonance, between the official version of a war, the sanitized record of noble endeavor sanctioned by the government that sent its sons and daughters to it and the much grittier, often more bitter, portrait revealed in the memoirs and novels of the participants who survived the turmoil. This is especially true, as we all know, of the Vietnam War, in which the confidence and affirmation of General William Westmoreland's memoir *A Soldier Reports* is debunked by other American narratives too numerous to name that depict disillusionment, drug use, racism, desertion, loss of moral compass, bloodlust, conflicts within ranks, soldiers cracking under stress, sexual assault, and a breakdown of discipline, just to name a few.

Though fewer in number, dissident voices questioned official versions of the American War in Vietnam have arisen across the Pacific as well. As a result, American readers now have the opportunity to balance the triumphant view provided by Van Tien Dung's *Our Great Spring Victory* (1977) with two 1995 English translations of North Vietnamese novels: Duong Thu Huong's *Novel Without a Name*, written in 1990, and Bao Ninh's 1994 novel *The Sorrow of War*. In each, our former enemy is given a very human face.

And though there are significant issues concerning national identity, the focus of this brief study, each work also contains, like its American counterparts, incidents of disillusionment, drug use, racism, desertion, and loss of moral compass, bloodlust, and conflicts within ranks, soldiers cracking under stress, sexual assault, and breakdowns of discipline. But before we turn to what the Irish Press referred to as "a tribute to the sheer spirit of the Vietnamese," we must consider why such dissident writers were allowed voice in the first place. Attached to Duong Thu Huong's satire of Communist rule in Vietnam, a novel appropriately titled *Paradise of the Blind* is "A Note About the Author" which states:

> In 1987, one year before this novel appeared, the Vietnamese Communist party called on writers and journalists to shake off the stiff, official Marxist style that had been imposed on them and encouraged them to reassert their traditional role as social critics. In this atmosphere of political openness and questioning, many Vietnamese writers and intellectuals responded with literary works, films, novels, and theatrical works that openly or implicitly criticized the excess of the party by satirizing bureaucracy, ideology, and official corruption. (*Paradise* 268)

The note further points out that Duong's earlier novels- *Beyond Illusions* (1987), *Fragments of Lost Life* (1989), and *Paradise of the Blind* (1988)- are works in which "Duong denounced, in simple, direct language, the dehumanization of her country" (*Paradise* 268-69). As an activist in the 1980s, this "fearless and charismatic orator" was according to the note, "driven by a deep need to bear witness to Vietnam's political and spiritual chaos".

All of this was too much for conservative Communist Party leaders in Vietnam- especially in light of the spread of democracy in Eastern Europe and the rise of democratic movements in China and Burma, far too close to home. Expulsion from the Party was followed on April 13, 1991 by arrest and imprisonment on several inflated charges, like "having smuggled 'secret documents' out of the country", which, one assumes, were manuscripts of her novels. She was released in November 1991, perhaps in part because human rights organizations, namely PEN and Amnesty International, identified her as a political prisoner. Some shackles still remain, however, for she is no longer published in Vietnam.

The circumstances behind Duong's struggles- arrest, imprisonment, and withdrawal of her novels from circulation in Vietnam together with the outrage of international organizations- may have made the publication of Bao Ninh's novel easier. But a more plausible reason may lie in the metafictional structure of the novel itself, which serves as an aesthetic protective device. Consider the last section of *The Sorrow of War*, where a naive redactor claims that he "simply played the role of the Rubik's cube player, arranging the order".

The censor may have anxiously swallowed the redactor's disclaimer on the last several pages. As though the prior two hundred plus pages- in which the only truly joyful times were pre-war- did not exist, the redactor rationalizes: "Our lives may not be very happy, and they might well be sinful. But now we are living the most beautiful life we could ever have hoped for, because it is a life of peace. Surely this was what the real author of this novel intended to say?" Calling the true author "the last true Bourgeois of the district, rebellious, extremist", the fictional redactor further strengthens the case for the censor to believe the redactor to be a reliable narrative voice of the novel, one with the appropriate politics.

In any case, both Duong and Bao have by their experiences earned the right to both create and criticize. The biographical facts printed on the dustjackets are brief, but telling. Duong, serving as a volunteer in a Communist Youth Brigade, spent seven years in the most heavily bombarded section of Vietnam, "living in tunnels and underground shelters alongside North Vietnamese troops." Of the original forty members of her unit, only three survived. Even more appalling casualties were suffered by Bao's unit. He is one of ten survivors of a brigade of 500 who entered combat in 1969. It is good to remember that for the North Vietnamese, there was no one year or thirteen month tour of duty; enlistment was for the duration.

To provide epic scope to their work, both authors create protagonists who serve ten year stints, from 1965 until victory in 1975, from the introduction of American ground forces until the fall of Saigon, from initial enthusiasm to gut-wrenching disillusionment. Like good epics, both novels provide a glimpse of happier earlier times before the American war as well as depict life outside the combat zone. Duong's *Novel Without a Name*, more traditional in structure than Bao's metafictional work, provides readers with an odyssey of sorts, Captain Quan's special mission to help a boyhood friend driven insane by the war.

Flashbacks, nostalgic conversations with old friends, bizarre meetings with eccentric characters, transparently symbolic dreams, and a visit home flesh out the journey. Bao's *The Sorrows of War*, wider in scope, is a combat veteran's attempt to fulfill what he believes to be a sacred duty, to depict the pain of war, and to do that the metafictional author Kien has to include the cruelties of peace, for him an additional ten year odyssey. Despite their differences in structure, there is a common link, aside from the horrors of jungle combat, between both novels- disillusionment with the war and ultimately with the political system that espoused it.

This unrelenting theme is echoed by several chords. The suffering of Vietnamese women brought on by the war is acknowledged and depicted, the timeless rhythm of Vietnamese civilian life is of greater worth than military glory, and criticism of Communist bureaucrats reinforces the fact that Vietnamese patriotism is indeed distinct from Communism. In both Duong and Bao, Marxism is an ideology dwarfed by the spirit of the Vietnamese people, perhaps a last vestige of western imperialism ready to crumble. While criticism of the current system is overt in *Novel Without a Name*, it is perhaps all the more telling because implicit in *The Sorrow of War*.

In Duong's *Novel Without a Name*, the suffering of women may, in part, be due to their very subordinate status, even marginalization, within Vietnamese society. Quan's remembrance of his childhood suggests as much: "In a mother's heart, there is no glory worth the life of a child, no ideal higher than the desire to give happiness. But this village was ruled by the authority of the father". According to Quan, his father, a Viet Minh veteran of the anti-French resistance, is "nothing but a brute, a cruel, hateful presence", whose pettiness, anger, and even vindictiveness caused, in Quan's opinion, his mother to die within eighteen months of his return.

His father, more of a warrior than a farmer, more of a Viet Minh than a father, nags Quan's younger brother to enlist; it is implied, to curry favor with the local Communist bureaucracy. Instead of studying to become a computer scientist, the young Quang soon becomes one of the honored dead. The death of Quan's mother when he was a mere seven years old has a lasting impact- for he dreams of her constantly, prays to his mother's soul to guide him when he is astray in the jungle, invokes the names of the mothers of soldiers he must discipline, even makes a special visit to return the belongings of a dead soldier that he finds by chance (in a maze-like valley) to the deceased's grieving mother.

Though Quan consistently remarks on the pain of Vietnamese women who lost their sons, he, like his father before him, cruelly mistreats a woman he once loved, his former fiancé, seduced by a local cadre. War is not easy on women in Bao's novel either, but the suffering he depicts is restricted to the young, where it is often violent, sexual in nature. In those intoxicating, blissful early days of the war, Kien's high school sweetheart Phuong accompanies him on a train only to be raped by Vietnamese laborers, then mistakenly abandoned by her boyfriend, and becomes so jaded by these cruelties that she assumes a life of prostitution and promiscuity that can only drive her and Kien apart on his return home.

Economic conditions after the war force the youngest sister of one Kien's friends into the same demeaning trade. By far the unluckiest female in *The Sorrow of War* is Hoa, a troop guide from the North, who during Tet of 1968 saves fifteen wounded North Vietnamese soldiers, first by shooting the dog of American trackers, then by "diverting the patrol from the trail which would have led directly to the sick and wounded troops, almost powerless to defend themselves against such a fit, well-armed force" (*Sorrow* 191). Her reward for such bravery is gang rape and, it is assumed, murder by an American patrol. When Kien questions the meaning of her death he inadvertently implies the role of many Vietnamese women in war "Was it that such sacrifices were now an everyday occurrence?" (*Sorrow* 192).

While there is no shortage of combat in *Novel Without a Name*, the rendering of the immemorial rhythms of Vietnamese life provides a more fully human face to the Vietnamese. Quan's earliest childhood memory, reiterated several times in the novel, deals with the birth of his brother. The agony of childbirth quickly gives way to a more affirmative interchange between mother and sons: "A final ray of sun lights her face; her eyes shine with tenderness. Her face is clear again. I grab the tiny red feet and rub them against my cheeks. 'Little brother. Little brother".

The sentimental portrait above is followed intermittently in the novel by a plethora of nostalgic vignettes, recounting harvest festivals, childhood pranks, schoolboy lessons, teenage insensitivities, adolescent love, and tea rituals in base camps, the chance meeting between male soldiers and female volunteers, and the memory of the sound of a flute recalling earlier pastoral times. Return to prewar peaceful existence is always a consummation devoutly to be wished: "Homecoming: the return to the native village. Showers of tenderness. The same dream haunted our days as soldiers. *Native Soil*. These two words expressed everything we had lived for, cherished, adored".

After costly combat operations, Quan poignantly daydreams of happier times and wishes for the possibility of future renewal in images of cyclical rebirth:

> Happy to have survived, I let my mind wander back to my village, let it follow the length of the dikes, through the fields. Wild ducks honked their way across the sky. I had gathered my lost fragments of life, had drank sic a bit of blue sky from the bottom of a cup.... Perhaps I could grow again like a strand of paddy spared the harvest, bent by hatred and storms but still able to flower, to bear fruit.

Even the glorious victory in Saigon on April 30, 1975 pales in contrast to a more perennial appeal- love of the Vietnamese countryside:

I see myself break away from the crowd. I grab onto red and gold lacquered posts, grope my way out a door, through ruined fields. Bits of fodder still lie about. In the distance the marshes glisten. A flock of storks paddles about in the silt, chasing tiny shrimp. I track them, silent as a shadow, my bare feet plunging into the grass, into the mud.

While the novel reminds us that the blood of Vietnamese soldiers nourishes the land, it is clear that the reverse is also true. The broader canvas of *The Sorrow of War* reminds us of other aspects of Vietnamese life, other immemorial rhythms. In fact, as a novel about writing a novel, much of the book immerses us in Vietnamese culture. We read of Vietnamese poets, artists, musicians as well as of Vietnamese folklore, folk sayings, and religious practices.

References to family altars, ghosts of the deceased, gift-giving at lunar festivals, the beauty of Hanoi in the springtime, and the naive innocence of adolescent romance reinforce Kien's assertions that "he knew it wasn't true that young Vietnamese loved war". Prewar experience is always idealized in the novel, for we hear that the past was "a never-ending story of loyalty, friendship, brotherhood, comradeship and honesty". However, even in a novel whose setting is primarily urban, one in which Kien reminisces and writes of those memories, we learn of the appeal of more traditional Vietnamese life-being in harmony with the land.

After the war, many North Vietnamese veterans returned to the Central Highlands to enjoy "healthy, outdoor, free living". Kien remembers a particularly idyllic moment years earlier when his unit came upon a South Vietnamese coffee plantation untouched as yet by the conflict. Kien and several of his soldiers shared coffee with the owners in an atmosphere described as one of "intimacy and warmth". Calling the incident a "special memory," Kien cites the owner's words at length:

We just live a simple life, growing coffee, sugarcane, and flowers, he began. Thanks to Heaven, thanks to the land and the trees and nature, and thanks to our own hands and energy and the money from our labor, we are self-sufficient. We don't need help from any government. If the president loses the fight, then let him be, even though you are Communists on the other side. You're human too. You want peace and a calm life, families of your own, isn't that right, gentlemen?

Knowing that severe fighting took place in the Highlands, Kien writes that the episode "was a symbol of paradise lost". Yet the virtues implicit in the owner's words-love of home soil, the necessity of hard work, the desire for independence, and the need for peace-seem, unless there be no truth whatsoever in Vietnamese fiction-to be enduring traits of the Vietnamese.

In both novels, Communism is overshadowed by Vietnamese patriotism, dwarfed by it, shamed by it. In Duong's *Novel Without a Name*, Quan dreams that he encounters a symbol of Vietnamese nationalism, a peasant soldier of centuries earlier who tells him: "We fought to defend the altar of the ancestors, the future of our country, we never fought for the cheers and applause of others". The novel clearly distinguishes between those who sacrifice and those who benefit from the misery of others, between those who protect the ancestral altars from those who merely seek applause.

Three vignettes come to mind. Consider, first, My Ly, a local Party secretary, a non-combatant, who speaks of certain victory because of the advantages of "the dialectical materialism of Marxist thought" while chewing roast duck, the food of another man. His transparent patriotism does not fool the prosperous farmer, Mr. Buu, who feeds him. "Never have the little despots conducted themselves so shamelessly," he says and continues:

Before, out of every ten of them you could find at least seven who were honest, civilized. Even during the worst intrigues, at least they feared public disgrace. Now the ones who hold the reins are all ignoramuses who never learned the most basic morals. They study their Marxism-Leninism, and then come and pillage our vegetable gardens and rice fields with Marx's blessing. In the name of class struggle, they seduce other men's women.

According to Mr. Buu, many a North Vietnamese general is little better than a whoremaster, perhaps suggesting a comical spin on the phrase, "our great spring victory":

> We country folk have gagged ourselves, our stomachs and our mouths, even our penises. But when it comes to the generals, they know how to take advantage of a situation. Wherever they go, whether it's north or south, they make sure they have plenty of women. In the old days they had concubines, now they call them mission comrades. It's still the same thing.

Those who betray family members to the state, Mr. Buu calls jackals. "Even their faces have changed," he notes. "Those aren't human faces anymore".

In her second case, Duong allows two members of the Communist hierarchy to speak for themselves. In a cruel parody of the Marxist slogan that "religion is the opium of the people", she depicts two prominent Communists, one a cynical college professor, who knows that Marxist Leninism is the true opiate, a mere replacement for more traditional religion: "So you think we're atheists? No way! We demolished the temples and emptied the pagodas so we could hang up portraits of Marx; enthrone a new divinity for the masses".

After drawing an analogy between recanting one's crimes against the state and church confession, the professor scoffs at the canonization of Karl Marx. "To canonize Marx they had to erase the real person," he states. His account of the philosophical inspiration behind his country's government is far from sanctified, for he calls Marx a "debauched little dwarf," who "hung out in brothels," was particularly fond of gypsy girls, and impregnated his own maid. When his conversation on the crowded train is reported, he vehemently outfaces the subordinate who accuses him only to boast to his colleague: "Well? Did you see that? A nation of imbeciles. They need a religion to guide them and whip to educate them". The distinction between these two fat-cat cadre and wounded North Vietnamese soldiers on the train could not be clearer.

Finally, in an orgy of looting that followed the fall of Saigon in 1975, Quan attempts to discipline his troops by pointing out what they had just destroyed was valuable American medical supplies that would have treated thousands of sick people and television sets that would have provided them entertainment. At that moment, Kha, one of the few soldiers to have survived the conflict as long as Quan, ten long years, notes: "But the ones who get to watch have nothing to do with the people.... The person, that's my mother, my father, your parents, the soldiers, none of them will ever get a crumb".

The soldier then explains a much earlier scam-purportedly a fundraiser to build a cemetery for Viet Minh killed in the anti-colonial resistance against the French- which only funneled money to the local cadre. "They put the people on an altar," Kha states, "and feed them incense and ashes. But the real food, that's always for them". While wanting to curse Kha, Quan also knows this soldier is correct in his assertions. The dissident voice of Bao Ninh is not usually found in such blatant setpieces, but rather by innuendo, implication, and tone. For instance, Kien notes that his scout unit is often spared "political indoctrination. Politics continuously. Politics in the morning, politics in the afternoon, politics again in the evening" (*Sorrow* 8). Hardline advice from political commissars goes unheeded when Kien believes his men would benefit from less discipline. The three don'ts, political slogans forbidding love, sex, and marriage that Kien learns in school, are undercut by Phuong, his rebellious girlfriend, who has more romantic ideas, "Let's go. Leave the straw heroes to their slogans". Even during victory celebration in Saigon, troops ridicule the admonitions they receive over the loudspeakers.

More telling in *The Sorrow of War* is the deadening conformity in North Vietnam which snuffs out the artistic sensibilities of those nearest to Kien. His father, upon dismissal from the Party for being a "suspicious malcontent, a rightist deviationist", one who was out of step with the times, unable to "accede to certain socialist ethics" soon became "senile and quite strange" only able to paint works which Kien labels "ferocious, diabolic" in nature.

His mother's second husband, a poet, "had gone into hiding to escape the anti-intellectual atmosphere of the state ideologies that came with Communism".

The effervescent, free-spirited youth of Kien's girlfriend, Phuong, cannot save her from her surroundings. "Her fine soul will be warped by the coarse style that's overtaking us," Phuong's mother confides to Kien; "she will be destroyed unless she's given preferential treatment for her artistry". In the novel, however, she is not given special consideration and her artistic spirit is destroyed.

Because of their rarity in *The Sorrow of War*, the few overtly dissident statements are all the more emphatic. By 1974, Kien, very much aware that his simple peasant fighters have very little say in the conduct of the war, listens to a fellow soldier explain his imminent desertion: "We have so many of those damned idiots up there in the North enjoying the profits of war, but it's the sons of peasants who have to leave home, leaving a helpless old mother sic to hardships". Later in 1977, just before a brawl between himself and another NVA veteran, Kien hears the former officer, now a street tough, analyze the consequences of the American War: "Victory, shit! The victory we got was for morons. Call that civilization and progress? Garbage!"

Even if war did not come to the idyllic safe haven mentioned above- the South Vietnamese coffee plantation- the consequences of the victory surely would, as one of Kien's soldier's notes:

That's the way to live! What a peaceful, happy oasis. My lecturers with all their Marxist theories will pour in and ruin all this if we win. I'm horrified to think of what will happen to that couple. They'll soon learn what the new political order means.

Both Bao and Duong assume what is virtually a Communist aristocracy, comfortable, corrupt, incompetent, driven more by greed and self-interest than either patriotism or nationalism. The ghost that Duong writes of, that symbol of Vietnamese nationalism always has tears in his eyes. *Novel Without a Name* and *The Sorrow of War* suggest it is with very good reason.

While the novels under discussion share with their American counterparts the by now familiar litany of the horrors of war- disillusionment, drug use, racism, desertion, loss of moral compass, bloodlust, conflicts within ranks, soldiers cracking under stress, sexual assault, and a breakdown of discipline- the North Vietnamese novels are distinct from most imaginative narrative written by Americans in their recognition and depiction of the suffering of Vietnamese women, their reverence for the immemorial rhythms of Vietnamese civilian life, and their unrelenting criticism of Marxist bureaucrats.

Sadly enough there is another frequent omission from American memoirs and novels of the Vietnam War, the plea, whether implicit or explicit, for reconciliation. Duong, with her international audience, pleads explicitly for reconciliation with Americans. Bao, still published in Vietnam, in depicting bravery and decency among South Vietnamese, implicitly pleads for reconciliation among his own people, whether from the North or South.

Though perspectives may differ, motivations for many an imaginative writer remain the same on both sides of the Pacific. Duong, I believe, speaks for all survivors of that conflict who put pen to paper- whether they label their experience the Vietnam War or the American War. "I never intended to write," she told a French journalist. "It just happened, because of the pain" (*Paradise* 270).

For many Americans, Southeast Asia and its inhabitants particularly, the Vietnamese and transnational ethnic groups such as the Hmong become visible only through the lens of the Vietnam War. At the same time, contemporary Vietnamese tend to see that war as only one of the many imperialist conflicts in which they have been engaged for the past millennium. And the Hmong, with traditional roots in agriculture and no national ties to speak of, hold an even longer view, seeing this war and subsequent migrations as part of an ancient four-thousand-year-old history of conflict and flight through the highlands of modern China, Vietnam, Laos, Thailand-and now to the United States.

Not surprisingly, gender roles in Southeast Asia and the United States have been profoundly shaped in both cultures by these traditions of invasion, resistance, and, often, flight. A complex, diasporic confluence of political history, militarism, immigration, and feminism emerged in the wake of the Vietnam War. To tease out these delicate global intersections, which continue to shape contemporary women's lives, in this chapter lets explore representations of Viet and Hmong women in Vietnamese publications and public spaces and compare them to representations of women in the writings of Vietnamese American and Hmong American women. To this end, I pair images of Viet women culled from two Vietnamese publications, Images of the Vietnamese Woman in the New Millennium (2002) and Female Labour Migration: Rural-Urban (2001), and from the Vietnamese Women's Museum housed in Hanoi with Lan Cao's negotiations of Vietnamese American womanhood in her novel, Monkey Bridge (1997).

As well, I examine representations of Hmong women at the Vietnam Museum of Ethnology in Hanoi, specifically a book of photographic essays by Hmong girls titled Through H'Mong Eyes (2003), and compare them to selections by Hmong American women writers and storytellers from the anthologies Bamboo among the Oaks: Contemporary Writing by Hmong Americans (2002) and Hmong Means Free: Life in Laos and America (1994). This chapter questions the ethical and practical ends of Western, Vietnamese, and Hmong considerations of Southeast Asian women's gender roles, especially when viewed through the sometimes totalizing grip of the Vietnam War-or the American War of Aggression, as it is called in the War Remnants Museum in Saigon.

To pursue such a comparative analysis, it is necessary to place American publications alongside Vietnamese texts that are often multi-authored sometimes with no clear sense of individual attribution. While the communal nature of these latter texts might reflect cultural traditions, the powerful state's role in shaping them also presents a challenge in reading Vietnamese publications as sources of contemporary reality.

In contrast, American texts of the sort I analyze here, produced in the relatively freer West, can be read as authentic, individual cris de coeur. Yet it is important to keep in mind that both types of publications are crafted in response to audience expectations and the unique demands of their respective publishing enterprises. The American texts are shaped by cultural traditions, gendered expectations, and economics. And even though the Vietnamese texts are products of the state, I read for moments that not only submit to but also strain against state orthodoxy.

It might also seem impolitic to pair the Vietnamese and the Hmong in this chapter, for they came to the United States under very different circumstances: the former, almost immediately after US troop withdrawal from Vietnam as officially acknowledged compatriots at war; the latter, somewhat later as unacknowledged fighters in covert Laotian operations. Many southern Vietnamese immigrants come from educated, urban backgrounds, while many Hmong emerge from a rural and oral culture. And yet the Vietnamese and the Hmong sometimes struggle to convey their distinct cultures and histories to Americans who do not distinguish between them and may see members of both groups as painful reminders of failed American military might-as Lan Cao puts it, "invisible and at the same time awfully conspicuous."

Nevertheless, both the Hmong and the Vietnamese came to the United States as a direct result of this conflict and are associated in cultural representations of modern Vietnam in the United States. Not surprisingly, their ethnic and class differences are rigidly maintained in contemporary Vietnamese public spaces, where America is predictably represented as the failed imperialist, Vietnam as the resistant victor. This war clearly has different ideological meanings within Southeast Asia than it does in the United States, meanings that profoundly affect gender roles.

Western feminists have also had to resist different but equally significant imperialist impulses. They have often and rightly been accused of cultural blindness as they have sought to analyze the plights of non-Western women in non-Western and Western countries by applying Western models. Amrita Basu summarizes this practice: "The vast literature on women's movements is characterized by three broad tendencies: it ignores women's movements in the Post-colonialworld, considers women's movements products of modernization or development, and assumes a sameness in the forms of women's oppression and women's movements cross-nationally."

These are all tendencies that have contributed to the insistence of some scholars and activists that women's progress in Southeast Asia was antithetical to the colonialist wars that ravaged the region during the twentieth century and remains impossible under socialist or emerging capitalist regimes. Ultimately, such reading practices promote the idea that Southeast Asian refugee women become more "liberated," more feminist, as they become more American. Inderpal Grewal and Caren Kaplan add that some women "live in the 'West' without being 'Western,'" fostering interstitial identities that are not "unitary"; however, the "postmodern celebration of hybridity often retains the 'us' and 'them' paradigm that stems from modernist modes of description and representation."

Grewal and Kaplan's work implicitly encourages us to probe further the specific contours of the relationship between the United States and Southeast Asia-and, subsequently, the relationship between the women who immigrated and those who stayed behind-because of the "losing" war waged in Southeast Asia. To decenter the West, I compare the gender roles represented in texts by Vietnamese American and Hmong

American women to those of Southeast Asian contemporaries, rather than measuring them directly against multicultural, Western ("American") traditions of womanhood. What do we do with the gender consciousness of women who have been exiled from the socalled third world to the first?

Of Vietnamese women whose former nation is proud of the third world's defeat of the first? How do these women's adaptations of Western and Eastern gender roles help to clarify a global understanding of women's roles and resistance to patriarchy? The oral narrative of one Hmong woman immigrant illustrates the particularities of such complicated subject positions. In "Ka Xiong's Life Story," as told to her son, Xiong writes to her children of their escape to Thailand from newly Communist Laos.

You were all still so small then. You were like little mice and piglets running alongside their mom. I loved you children so much then, and I love all of you so much now. You children meant and still mean everything to me. Sometimes, these days, when I see poor little children of other countries on television, it reminds me of how my own children were dressed in rags and were so very skinny due to the shortage of food and the difficulties we encountered along our way. This remark dramatizes the psychic mobility of women who reside between the so-called first and third worlds, whose children were once the "mice and piglets" struggling for survival, but who now see the rag-dressed, starving children of other mothers through the distance of television and time and relative plenty.

Those children are now of "other countries." I seek to map this space between nations that Southeast Asian and Southeast Asian American women inhabit together. For Hmong women, who have long eschewed national identities, this deconstructed, in-between space is especially crucial. Thus it is necessary to understand Vietnamese and Hmong women in Southeast Asia and America in a specific historical and diasporic context. The women represented in the texts I consider here are not just non-Western or ethnic American women-they are non-Western and ethnic American women at war and after-hostile enemies and fervent compatriots, heroic mothers and vulnerable daughters. However, while militaristic understandings of womanhood continue to occupy Vietnamese and Hmong writers in Southeast Asia, the present-day realities of dot moi, or the post-igSo crumbling of the Soviet Bloc and subsequent integration of Vietnam into the global free market economy, preys on their minds just as keenly.

The economic vacillations of post-war Vietnam and subsequent privatization of many social services, coupled with the maintenance of socialist control in many arenas of life, have had far-reaching effects on women's gender roles, simultaneously encouraging individual self- sufficiency while requiring national fealty. Yet another part of this specific context is the recent historical trajectory of American feminism. Those who have come to the United States as firstor first-and-a-half-generation (those who moved as children) immigrants have arrived here in the midst of or in the wake of the second wave of feminism and the cultural changes that have resulted. Thus while immigrants to the United States have always had to reconcile gender roles and expectations from their home countries with those of the United States, it seems we have witnessed and are witnessing a particular and interesting phenomenon in the texts of Southeast Asian American women.

Vietnamese American and Hmong American memoirs and fictions that treat gender roles and women's experiences in the United States typically highlight the more oppressive aspects of native gender relationships. Indeed, the emergence of the personalized forms of Southeast Asian American writing treated here, as opposed to the more formalized, state-sponsored works that depict the status of women in Southeast Asia, reinforces the notion that the "personal is political." Vietnamese and Hmong American literatures portray what Westerners would call "domestic abuse" and other cultural constraints that do not allow women to reach their full potentials.

One might argue that these new Americans' exposure to Western feminism and a so-called freer way of life has led them to see with new eyes the gendered worlds they have left behind-despite the immigrant communities' desire to maintain cultural traditions. But in saying this I might be accused of falling prey to precisely the sort of arrogance and cultural myopia that I encourage us to question and that informs many Americans' understandings of other non-Western cultures-particularly nations with which we are at war. Vietnamese and Hmong texts situate what they assert as women's "separate but equal" status within a broader military, national, and ethnic context and explain women's current troubles in terms of the difficult yet lucrative transition into a market-based economy, rather than as the failure of traditional gender systems or the long- term fallout of imperialist wars.

The war in Southeast Asia and its chaotic aftermath are understood as the triumphant proving ground of traditional values and women's importance to their national and ethnic communities. In this context, the deployment of "traditional" women's roles may be interpreted as the progressive retrieval of a repressed woman's culture, rather than as a sign of a retrograde society. Finally, it is important to remember that much Vietnamese American and Hmong American literature is written by first- and first-and-a-halfgeneration immigrants and tells of the women's experiences migrating to the United States-a narrative with a starting point inevitably situated in war. Thus stories by and about these women are more properly called refugee literature than immigrant literature, and this changes the relationship of these particular groups of recently arrived Americans to the national narrative and to American gender roles.

While those who remained in Southeast Asia contextualize the war with the United States in a larger narrative that includes any number of wars and experiences of exile, the stories of those who immigrated begin with the war with America-indeed, in many cases insist that we not forget their war service, for it is their loyalty to the United States forces that, in part, entitles them to Americanness. Still, much is lost in the move from East to West. Dwight Conquergood reminds us that "The Hmong word for refugee is neeg tawg rog, 'war-broken people,'" that "refugee" and "war" are integrally bound in the language, and that only war can drive the Hmong from their communities, threatening Hmong identity.

Min Zhou and Carl L. Bankston I contend that Vietnamese American narratives proceed from a similarly mobile and milltaristic identity politics: "The difficulties suffered in Vietnam and in the move from Vietnam to America have given adult Vietnamese a strong sense of their own identity," they suggest, confirming that the traumas of war and exile are seminal and defining experiences." Indeed, given the ubiquitous realities of our Post-colonial world rooted, as Constance S. Richards argues, in "contemporary global configurations" of "displacement, exile, and alien domination," one must keep in mind that we are all constituted through these modern phenomena in ways that require more precision of our reading strategies.

THROUGH VIETNAMESE EYES

The high position of women in Southeast Asian culture is shown to be distinctive by the authors of Images of the Vietnamese Woman in the New Millennium, published by the Center for Gender, Family, and Environment in Development in Hanoi. Basu has argued that "One way that women's movements have sought to challenge the notion that feminism derives from bourgeois or Western inspiration is by finding symbols of women's power within the precolonial context." While such formulations still suggest that indigenous feminist icons have been reclaimed to meet Western expectations, nevertheless warrior women and powerful mothers attain prominent roles in national narratives to this day.

Contemporary writers are careful to point out that women's high status is not founded on modern Western feminist principles of freedom and choice; rather, they show how traditional strengths are refined by the numerous, increasing, and modern responsibilities assigned to women. For example, like many contemporary thinkers, the authors of Images of the Vietnamese Woman begin by both critiquing and recouping traditional Confucianism, initially decrying the fact that "it denied the women's intelligence." Instead, they recast the four traditional virtues of "industry, appearance, speech, and behavior" to focus on the woman's role in a modern, industrialized world: women should, first, work hard; second, they should appear gracious, courteous, and intelligent to be a "female leader to solve successfully all affairs"; they should speak sweetly and patiently to "increase their powers of persuasion and the effectiveness of work"; and, finally, they should behave in a stereotypically feminine fashion to work for "the welfare of other people."

The "women warriors" who dominate contemporary renderings of Vietnamese women's history are depicted as sacrificing not just for the good of the individual or the family, but, more important, for the benefit of the culture. In the beginning of When Heaven and Earth Changed Places, Le Ly Hayslip explains that her father taught her "to sacrifice one's self for freedom... in the manner of our women warriors, including Miss Trung Nhi Trung Trac, who drowned herself rather than give in to foreign conquerors" when she and her sister triumphed over Chinese invaders in 40 A.D.

For many Vietnamese, "liberation" and "freedom" are terms that do not connote personal or sex-specific advancements, but rather national progress, although Western feminists, as Kathleen Barry phrases it, look still for the formation of an "independent women's movement" as a sign of progress. Alexander Soucy sees public images of warrior women, such as the dominant sculpture of Au Co, mother of the Vietnamese race, displayed at the Women's Museum, as promoting a "feminism in Vietnam, that, rather than challenging the hegemonic masculine structure, tends to become only a vehicle for carrying broader policy issues; it has become a Trojan horse of nationalism."

Yet his critique, too, measures the women's movement within Vietnam against an idealized notion of an autonomous feminism distinct from cultural and political constraint. Hayslip reminds us that the fundamental form of oppression in Vietnam is perceived as Western imperialism: "Vietnam was con rong chau tien-a sovereign nation which had been held in thrall by Western imperialists for over a century." Contemporary scholar Bui Thi Kim Quy does not argue for the primacy of women's or national liberation but, rather, for their interdependence: "liberating women is tantamount to liberating society as a whole." Thus Vietnamese publications reanimate traditional views of women within modern paradigms, or try to argue that those who have assumed that ancient Vietnamese culture was inherently oppressive for women have been wrong all along as they have been unable to see the ways that women's liberation is bound to the struggle for national autonomy.

In recent years, scholars have sought to reclaim the heroism of Vietnamese women during the war with the United States-a common tactic of liberal Western feminism as "lost" women are found and added to stories traditionally thought to be the sole domain of men. As well, war service is often proffered as a means for oppressed groups to earn fuller citizenship rights. Karen Gottschang Turner asserts that the reclamation of women's voices is meant to "empower them"-in other words, "help" them to see the value of their work. However, this work, too, has been recast within traditional Vietnamese paradigms; Sandra Taylor argues that the more contemporary "long-haired warriors" who fought during the war with the United States, though still subject to traditional notions of Confucian womanhood and filial piety, saw liberation fighting as a family tradition and a national one that went back to the triumph of the Trung sisters.

Though becoming more visible now through new scholarly work, the long-haired warriors were during the conflict the "invisible army" of "peasants by day, soldiers by night" who would booby-trap villages, hide Communist fighters, and communicate with guerillas in the jungle in the evenings while tending to children, the elderly, the home, and the economic needs of the family during the day. The supposedly private "productive labor" of the Mother (i.e., childbirth and childrearing) and the publicly meaningful "social labor" of the worker and nationalist warrior are mingled explicitly in the Vietnamese Women's Museum, where the first priority is to "portray the significance of the 'Mother' image in the Vietnamese frame of mind." secondarily, the exhibits represent the characteristics of Vietnamese women in the "course of national defense and construction as well as women's activities in the international arena."

One of the largest and most compelling exhibits in the museum is a tableau showing a Vietnamese woman in a hut speaking with hulking American soldiers while members of the "revolutionary cadre" nestle in a shelter below her home. While it might seem as if the woman is merely trying to defend her home, hide the revolutionaries, and get the Americans to leave, Tuyet et al. suggest that she may be working on the offensive, as well: "many enemy servicemen asked mothers to show them the way to side with the revolution or to assist them with returning home. One of the commanders of US-puppet troops admits: 'Mothers constitute a very effective weapon of attack in a political struggle. Their attack on the troops was the most dangerous.'"

Again and again, the museum materials and displays insist upon women's vital role in national construction and defense. However, just as the home is military theatre, domestic and military roles are naturally allied; as Tuyet et al. write, "the Mother myth is first of all the one of fighting foreign aggressors," Indeed, the "birth of the nation is closely connected with the mother's myth," thus intimately linking national identity, militaristic narratives, and reproductive capabilities. Western associations of peace with femininity and war-mongering with masculinity do not correspond with these gender roles. While these stories of war-era heroism surely highlight the significance of women's work during wartime, they also focus the triumphs and plight of contemporary women through the all- encompassing lenses of war and essentialized gender roles.

Though motherhood is almost fetishized in Vietnamese texts, becoming a "stay-at-home mom" as Americans understand the term in the context of modern capitalism is not an option for Vietnamese women, who are exhorted again and again to contribute to the national cause outside of the home. Even though Vietnam increasingly operates under free-market capitalism, the specific notion of distinct public and private realms does not seem to be a part of the Vietnamese tradition, though Western scholars continue to describe Vietnamese spaces in these terms. For example, Barry writes, "With economic development, women are able to move into the public economy and labor force, breaking their traditional confinement to the private sphere."

At the same time, Vietnamese writers chart their awareness of this paradigmatic slippage. Tuyet et al. state, according to the conception of almost all countries in the world, men are responsible for bringing about income to the family, while women are economically dependent on the male sex, stay at home to do housework to look after children and at the same time, try to get additional income for the family. In Vietnam, it is the tradition that women are also economically responsible and this remains unchanged.

Indeed, as the Vietnamese incorporate the free market with socialist impulses, Tuyet et al. suggest not only that individual women should be economically productive, but also that the family structure itself should be exploited for capitalist ends: "it is the positive aspect of the market economy to turn the family, which was in the past essentially considered a 'sentimental unit,' into an 'economic unit.'" Families have become even more important to the national economy since the emergence of dot moi. Vietnam is still largely an agrarian society, where 80 per cent of the population live and labor in rural settings; many urban families run small businesses or, increasingly, take on entrepreneurial ventures. Thus women's labor "outside" and next to the home has always been integral to the economy.

Indeed, the Constitution of the Socialist Republic of Vietnam, Articles No. 55 and 68, "define that working is a right and obligation of every citizen." Thus the model woman in

Tuyet et al.'s text runs an entrepreneurial household, but she works not just for the good of the family but, rather, for the whole community, using her profits to support charitable activities in her village. Barry also notes that the recognition of domestic chores as public domain activities "may actually contribute to the transformation, rather than the reinforcement, of gender identities." The private realm that some in the United States understand as an isolated, limiting space, does not correspond to the Vietnamese division of space and labor in the post-war era, where "the woman worker is the image of the new woman."

In Female Labour Migration: Rural-Urban, Ha Thi Phuong Tien and Ha Quang Ngoc outline the contours of "work/home" expectations for contemporary Vietnamese women who migrate from farming areas to urban centers. Tien and Ngoc emphasize again and again that the economic well-being of the entire family rests on women's shoulders; agricultural activities only take up the energies of the family for five to six months per year." Indeed, Tien and Ngoc argue explicitly that women are more suited to the task of working outside and away from their rural homes than men. As they write, "despite of the fact that the wage of women was often fewer than men, they sent back to family as much as men did, because they saved better and recognized their obligation and responsibility for family much more."

One young porter interviewed by these authors asserts that she, rather than her husband, works in the city because "I am a woman. I can drink pipe water if I am thirst and eat rice with salt even I can stand with hungry, hardship, but man cannot." Elsewhere, the authors assert that men spend their money on cigarettes, coffee, alcohol, and gambling. Thus men are as likely to stay at home, taking care of the children and minding the farmwork as women are in contemporary Vietnam, especially if it is perceived that women will be able to bring home more money-it is an economic decision as much as a gendered one. Le Thi argues that women do "everything," taking care of the labor at home and outside, while the husband "is the one to play the role of decision-maker and of manager of production and family activities."" Thus, one could infer that gender roles as Westerners understand them, to some extent, are reversed.

Women are the hardcore laborers, while men "manage" the household. Men are unable to manage their bodily desires, while women are eminently in control. The money these women earn sustains whole communities as it is used to take care of relatives, support their children's schooling, build houses, invest in new ventures, and pay debts. And yet they endure toxic work sites, sexual harassment, inadequate living conditions, and extortion from local mafia; the familiar and self-destructive rhetoric of female self-sacrifice resonates through these descriptions, as well.

The authors of Vietnamese texts about women insist that women produce on what they call "an equal footing with men." Indeed, "the idea of equality, participation in the electorate, and an independence movement on terms of shared sacrifice" initially drew women to support Ho Chi Minh and the communist movement as early as the 19305 in Vietnam. Literacy, equal pay for equal work, maternity leaves, and spousal choice were also integral elements of these ideology-familiar demands, not surprisingly, since Ho Chi Minh had been educated in the West. However, though some changes have occurred (e.g., polygamy has been outlawed), the promises made by the communists have not all been fulfilled, in part, because, while the government maintains control in many areas of private life, it has not created an economic safety net to provide for the basic needs of all citizens.

Given the multiple demands made on Vietnamese women during war and after, it should come as no surprise that women's contemporary complaints arise around what Western feminists would call "second shift" issues, or as they are framed in Vietnam, the "'double burden' of work in society and work at home." The woman must "work in the rice fields, in society, in the office and factory. She takes care of the children and holds the secondary job." Most scholars recognize, as Tuyet et al. write, that "in the process of economic restructuring women are much more affected than men," though they maintain that women are able to quickly adapt themselves to new circumstances. The female migrants and other urban dwellers increasingly take on jobs in the "unofficial economic sector" that provide no social, health, or long-term economic benefits.

The definition of "gender equality" deployed in Vietnam, then, entails the "gender-based labour division," creating a separate but equal logic that can be at odds with itself. Tuyet et al. argue that traditional relations between wives and husbands have changed; according to a 1994 study 96.5 per cent of wives devote themselves to sick husbands, while 78.7 per cent of husbands will wholeheartedly care for sick wives, proving "today men and women have equal rights: mutual respect, concern and care for each other."

Yet the authors find no contradiction in the numerical discrepancy cited here, nor in going on to describe the distinct roles of men and women within the family structure, for example, the disproportionate amount of housework taken on by women. In Vietnamese state-produced publications such as Images of Vietnamese Women, Female Migrant Labour, or the Vietnamese Women's Museum Brochure, both differences in rights, which are supposedly ameliorated politically, and those of biology, which are immutable though celebrated, are acknowledged, and the dilemma for contemporary women is how to be all things at once.

Though these representations clearly have their limitations, a more attentive reading of their imagery suggests the ways that a Vietnamese history of war and imperialism, as well as a present state oscillating between socialism and capitalism, both encourage and sabotage women's ambitions in contemporary Vietnam.

THROUGH VIETNAMESE AMERICAN EYES

Rather than producing state-sanctioned, historical documents of the sort found in Vietnam, first- and first-and-a-half-generation Vietnamese American women have developed a new series of autobiographical novels to tell their stories. Yet both genres seek to articulate a distinct ideology of womanhood rooted in historical tradition and present-day exigencies. Recent United States publications include Le Thi Diem Thuy's The Gangster We Are All Looking For (2003) and Dao Strom's Grass Roof, Tin Roof (2003), among others. For the purposes of this chapter I will focus on Lan Cao's Monkey Bridge.

While there are many important differences among these autobiographical novels, for all, the protagonists' childhood memories of their young lives in their native country are interwoven with the tall tales of adults, which together constitute the women's connections to Vietnam and their negotiations of contemporary gender roles in the United States. As Cao reveals in an interview, her shifting between past and present, Vietnam and the United States, her mother and daughter protagonists, and, I would add, Vietnamese and Vietnamese American notions of womanhood in Monkey Bridge is "natural" because "as an immigrant what happens is that when you look at an event or an object even in the present world, very often you view it the way you view it now as well as the way you view it in a different cultural context... through two different cultural lenses almost simultaneously without even necessarily noticing it."

Cao points out that this simultaneity is now signified by an ampersand rather than a hyphen-Vietnamese & American versus Vietnamese-American-not only representing a dual rather than a melded ethnic-national identity, but also gesturing toward the particular "double burdens" of gender and ethnicity, cultural responsibility and individual desire, war and refuge, that occupy many women refugees. In Monkey Bridge, a Vietnamese American teenager, Mai, attempts to unravel the mysteries of her family's history in Vietnam, which are most obviously embodied in her inscrutable mother, Thanh, who has also fled to the United States. As Mai notes repeatedly, Thanh's napalm scarred and stroke-ravaged "body had become a battlefield, she a war wound."

Thus when Mai feels "the tug of my mother through my body," she means not only her biological mother, but also her war-torn motherland and its notions of motherhood, heroism, and sacrifice. However, the seminal and traumatic war experience is also embedded in Mai, who wants desperately to escape memories of war-torn Vietnam. In the opening scene of the novel, Mai is visiting her mother in an American hospital after her stroke.

There Mai endures flashbacks of her work in a Saigon hospital during the war, focusing on the explosion in an operating room that killed and injured many staff members: "Who could have known before the man was cut up that an unexploded grenade, fired from a launcher-not a dead bullet-had lodged in the hollowness of his stomach?" This man and his dangerous load can be read metaphorically as representing how war becomes literally entwined into the beings of survivors like Mai, a "subverted interior" an "implant in (her) brain" as she calls it, that leads her to see and know things in multiple ways.

Mai and her mother embrace television's The Bionic Woman as a transnational symbol of heroic womanhood, "a little bit of Shaolin kung fu mixed with American hardware, American know-how." The Bionic Woman's "bionic ears" are compared explicitly to Thanh's ears, the length of which were believed to provide her with longevity and good luck. Indeed, Thanh claims in her diary that her ears heroically hear and then reanimate the lives of generations of young women whose inability to produce virginal blood on their wedding nights was announced by an earless roasted pig paraded through their villages-a ritual that led to their and their family's ruins and even deaths: "Inside my ears were the rage and revenge of every girl from every generation before whose return with a shameful and earless pig had destroyed her family's lives my mother had now gloriously resurrected" the mother reveals in her secret diary.

Cao has spoken of the Vietnamese martial arts novels that inspire Vietnamese girls today and influence such scenes. While American fairytales with their evil stepmothers and

Prince Charmings promote a "kind of envy and competition among girls and women" these Vietnamese novels often feature handsome, skilled male protagonists, but "the main female is always his equal or better and always self- sufficient and knows how to do martial arts just as well as her male counterpart." Thus Mais desire to leave home and study at Mount Holyoke is, as she explains to her mother, the "equivalent of a martial artist leaving her village to study kung fu at the Shaolin Temple."

While in her interview Cao concedes that Vietnamese culture is traditional, restraining women in many ways, she also reminds us that women "are not seen as needing male rescue... the idea of one's identity deriving completely from the husband or the father, I do not see it." This comment indicates, as Michele Janette also argues, that Cao is keenly aware of the Orientalist ways Western feminists might view Vietnamese gender roles, as well as the woman warrior tradition still dominant in Vietnam. The woman warrior tradition is an integral part of Mai's story as well, particularly that of the "sword-wielding Trung sister, the greatest of all Vietnamese warriors." The fact that Mai imaginatively inhabits the life of this Trung sister three times in the novel indicates that despite her seemingly successful integration to America, she continues to see her life in battle terms.

However, she clarifies that the Vietnamese traditions she invokes are not those developed by an "empire-building country" but derive rather from "a history of defending, not crossing boundaries"- not the United States, but Vietnam. Thus, when she shows up at Mount Holyoke for the "dreaded college interview," she draws strength from the "brilliant battlefield maneuvers" of the Trungs." The art of war the sisters develop is one where the woman warrior does not "oppose an adversary head-on" but rather steps aside, pulling the enemy (in the folktale, a tiger) "forward, deeper in the direction of its own motion."

While some scholars read this "all-out guerilla warfare, the poor person's weapon," as uneasily representing Vietcong tactics within the context of the novel, one might read it at the same time as a gendered strategy. The ability to "turn even an armed force one hundred times our strength into a terrorized one" is the strategy of the physically weak but strategically superior force-the strategy of women who might deliberately make the enemy "see a weak front" but who have "strengths-columns of reserves" from which to draw upon. Again, given the cultural context in which Mai operates, one could argue that she is manipulating American stereotypes about meek Asian women, ironically, by drawing upon traditional Vietnamese women's roles.

This warrior strategy is not deployed literally in the novel; rather Mai, her mother, and the other women in the refugee community transform the ancient tactics of martial arts into rhetorical and even economic strategies meant to help them not only survive, but thrive, in a culture which would underestimate them because of racist and gendered stereotypes and situate them in disturbing militaristic narratives.

At her college interview Mai chooses not to confront head-on the "preconceived notions" of the interviewer about Vietnam but rather to rhetorically weave "drunken-monkey style" and master the "art of evasion and distraction." Janette labels this strategy a "guerilla irony" that makes Vietnamese experience "indigestible" to American readers." Thus when the interviewer asks curiously what it was like in Vietnam, Mai describes the weather-clearly not the sort of sensational or tragic detail the interviewer was soliciting. As Mai claims later, "stereotypes aren't my enemy, as long as we tinker with them in a way that strikes an American chord," suggesting that she turns the rhetorical weight and heft of stereotypes to her advantage.

And just as the Trung sisters trained an army of women to fight together, to He in wait, and to stalk, the older women immigrants who dominate the refugee community work together to set up a "hui, a community pot of money designed to give those who would otherwise be unqualified for bank loans immediate access to a lump sum of cash." This strategy is in keeping with Vietnamese notions of female economic ambition coupled with communal tendencies. Later on, Thanh writes that her daughter is "under an illusion of freedom. Unless you create your own circumstances, make your own luck, determine your own fate, forge your own path through uncharted territory, you're not free in her eyes."

Despite the fact that the hui members discover "their favorite English word was 'entrepreneur'," notions of American individualism and capitalism do not suffice; Thanh believes in the pull of the past and the power of the community. Indeed, her entrepreneurial venture is directly derived from her Vietnamese past (she will produce "authentic" Vietnamese pickles for local restaurants) and from the pain encoded therein: "anyone with the right know-how and patience could massage the bittersweetness of nostalgia into hard cash." Just as contemporary Vietnamese pragmatically market war culture through venues such the nightclub "Apocalypse Now," the embalmed giant tortoise supposedly gunned down by United States forces in Hanoi, the Hanoi Hilton, the Museum of the War of American Aggression, and the Cu Chi tunnels, replete with wax figure soldiers, Mai's mother is willing to traffic in sensual memories of Vietnam-which are attached to war for Americans and Vietnamese refugees alike.

As the novel unfolds further, Cao comments on traditional Vietnamese "gender equality" and the Mother myth from a distance. As Mai is about to leave home for college, she begins to understand her mother's life in Vietnam. Thanh leaves a diary account of her marriage that draws on the language of battle and exile to make sense of women's gendered positions. As she prepares to move to her new husband's family's home at the age of fifteen, she claims that her marriage has been a love match; however, Thanh didn't realize at the time that she had lost a silent yet decisive battle: "there had been no singular calamity that conspired to vanquish me, no remarkable catastrophe that would warrant a battlefield badge or a medal."

Like other Vietnamese women, she lives in a sort of perpetual exile, even in her own country, as she is driven from her parents' home and into the home of her new in-laws. "This, of course, was the beginning of my emigration, years before my second one, to the United States" Thanh writes, explaining that she is a "special kind of exile... in her own country."(TM) Married Vietnamese women are already immigrants, a diasporic population within the home country. The traditional expectations of her husband "may not be much different from wars and other acts more stark and obvious in their capacity for violence," she realizes. Cao focuses not on physical violence within this relationship but rather on an intellectual and emotional distancing and abuse that causes a psychological disaffection similar to that suffered by some refugees and colonized peoples.

And it is through the tropes of war and exile that Thanh can connect her gendered experience as a Vietnamese woman to the immigrant experience of her increasingly Americanized daughter: she writes of her in-laws' properties, "a house, even another's house, a kitchen, a country store, each of these things could be made to have its own hidden beauty. That, I suppose must be what my daughter has learned to see in this new country we have suddenly found ourselves in, a beauty that she finds palpable but which seems to be beyond my reach. The mother's exile is situated geographically in the domestic realm (a house, a kitchen), while the daughter is located in the vast expanse of a "new country." However, they are both forced to identify the "beauty" of their adopted surroundings and to fit themselves to its contours.

Thanh's body becomes a living symbol of the fragmentation of war and exile; her stroke makes her appear to her daughter "altogether undone like bits of glass reglued." However, later we learn that the old burn scars that mark her face are not the result of a domestic cooking fire, as Mai had always been told but rather are "seared by a fire dropped into the free-fire zone from a plane." Thus the wounds supposedly suffered in the name of domesticity are both superseded by and politicized as the wounds of war. Cao eventually makes this connection between war and Motherhood explicit. In the end of the novel, Thanh commits suicide, and in doing so reclaims the role of the traditional Mother, but here for individualistic ends, to save her daughter from bad family karma.

As Cao states in an interview, "the epitome of female virtue would be a woman who, even though she is very strong and could be alone and does not need male protection, nonetheless decides to sacrifice herself completely for her husband and the children.

Thanh is, then, a self- sacrificing hero within the domestic realm, protecting her family line. However, the passage describing Thanh's suicide is followed immediately by a description of the Buddhist monks who immolated themselves to protest the war, an act of "supreme devotion"; this juxtaposition gives the Mother's suicide political and social significance beyond the family. Thus Cao negotiates an Americanized, a traditional Vietnamese, and even a socialized view of the Mother in her text. Indeed, motherhood-and subsequently war becomes transnational categories, "the same in every language," according to Cao.

"The true division in this world, I believe, is not the division founded on tribe, nationality, or religion, but the division between those of us who are mothers and those who aren't," Thanh concludes, denying the male/female dualism integral to Western feminist paradigms and instead announcing alternative duality- mothers versus nonmothers. Cao replaces one dualism-"tribe, nationality, or religion" versus outsiders-with another that is even more central to some feminisms in its essentialism-mother versus nonmother. Ultimately her novel does not eschew the Mother power of Vietnamese tradition but rather transforms and extends it, in this case, to the first-and-a-half generation of refugees who become not literal but figurative mothers to their parents, creating a "transmaternalism" of sorts.

Largely because of Thanh's lack of facility with English, Mai becomes her translator and protector in the new country, using her English skills and her growing knowledge of American culture to do her mother's bidding. This often requires deception on Mai's part, in keeping with the strategies of the Trung sisters, and elicits her embarrassment. But she recognizes that she has no other choice as she "scoops her mother out of harm's way and gives her sanctuary." And though she is ultimately unable to "save" her mother, Mai can use her defensive techniques to try and provide her with the safe space the perpetual exile has never had.

While Vietnamese women claim the label of perpetual exile, the Hmong as a whole are a deeply diasporic culture, for they have never truly had a "homeland." Ines M. Miyares demonstrates in her study of Hmong immigrants that the strong cultural identity of the Hmong developed precisely because of their existence as a migratory people who have during the last four thousand years "dispersed throughout southern China, northern Vietnam, northern Thailand, northern Myanmar, northern Laos, and since the fall of the Royal Lao government in 1975, in Australia, France, Canada, Argentina, and the United States."

To maintain their traditional ways, despite lacking a common geographic space or national identity, the Hmong tended to live in relatively isolated mountain communities in Southeast Asia, where they organized themselves in patriarchal clans and farmed rice, corn, and poppies. Most scholars believe that they had no written language until the 19505 and relied on oral narratives, material artifacts, and animist beliefs to convey cultural traditions. Some scholars assert that the word "Hmong" translates roughly as "free." Given the ideological importance of "freedom" to Americans generally, and feminists in particular, it is not surprising that this translation of "Hmong" has remained attractive for many in the United States.

Regardless of its direct meaning, the search for-or maintenance of, depending on one's point of view-cultural autonomy is clearly as significant for the Hmong as it is for the Vietnamese. Indeed, it is this passion for freedom that led the Hmong to work with the Americans during the Vietnam War, joining forces with the American CIA to wage a covert war against the North Vietnamese, who the Hmong feared would take over the Southeast Asian peninsula and once again disrupt their lives. Despite widespread belief among the Hmong that the CIA promised them an '"autonomous kingdom'" if they should suffer defeat, in 1969 the US government concluded that the United States was under no obligation to help the Hmong, Subsequently, when Laos fell to the Pathet Lao and the North Vietnamese after American troop withdrawal, "100,000 Hmong perished and an equal number fled across the Mekong."

Since the Pathet Lao murdered or marginalized the Hmong who remained in Laos, making their traditional mountain lives impossible, contemporary representations of Hmong women in Southeast Asia often derive from groups residing in Vietnam or Thailand, either in the traditional rural communities that have survived or in the refugee camps set up for the persecuted Hmong after the Communist takeover. Given this context of war, flight, and contact with Western culture, contemporary representations of Hmong women in Southeast Asia draw upon traditional Hmong notions of female subservience and domesticity and new notions of freedom claimed for the lives of modern women.

For example, while ethnic Viet women are represented in the Women's Museum in Hanoi as engaging in the public world of national defense and politics, ethnic Hmong women appear only on the floor that features the traditional handicraft products of various tribal cultures. In this way, they are made marginal to national narratives and a historical, as their handicrafts are shown to be unchanging and irrelevant to contemporary concerns. However, when one understands the history and subsequent recorded culture of the Hmong, as well as the contemporary roles of Hmong women in the capitalist economy, these handicrafts come to have significant meanings.

Discussions of women's needlework in the postwar era in particular draw on the past and the future roles of Hmong women, as well as their exploitation of militaristic narratives. For example, Jane Hamilton-Merritt claims that the ancient Hmong did have a written language despite claims to the contrary, but that it was outlawed by the Chinese under penalty of death. It was women, she asserts, who cleverly kept their alphabet alive by including its letters in intricate, hieroglyphic-like patterns passed on generation after generation from mother to daughter to adorn tribal dress. During the years of fleeing and disruption, however, the Hmong lost the ability to use their written language. Many twentieth- century Hmong women who still painstakingly embroider or batik ancient symbols and ideographs of historical events, are not able to read or write the language which their needles preserved.

This claim gives additional historical resonance to the handicrafts still done by Hmong girls and women. Not only marginalized in Southeast Asia, but often trivialized in the United States, despite recent efforts to garner appreciation for such women's work (e.g., quilting), the handiwork of Hmong women has been instrumental in maintaining cultural traditions and, in an oral culture, likely transmitting traces of a repressed written language- usually thought to be the purview of the patriarchy. Indeed, as Dwight Conquer good continues, there was "no tradition of graphic representational art" in Hmong textiles before war in Southeast Asia.

Influenced by life in Thai refugee camps and contact with the West, Hmong women have devised new modes of signification- altering traditional forms for Western tastes and developing embroidered story cloths that illustrate traditional Hmong tales and more recent war and exodus stories." Indeed, story cloths that detail escapes on foot out of Laos and across the Mekong river to Thailand are the most prized by Western collectors and the museums that have begun to display Hmong handicrafts in the United States. This needlework is produced primarily out of financial necessity, demonstrating the ways that Hmong women have managed to accommodate traditional work to the needs of their families in the new economies they negotiate American buyers symbolically "consume" conventional narratives of the "tragic" war in Southeast Asia, notions of the Hmong as a historical and unchanging craft workers, and Hmong women in particular as bound to tradition.

In the recent book Through H'Mong Eyes, published by the Vietnam Museum of Ethnology, the Hmong girls who narrate the photographic text also situate Hmong women in a contemporary, economic context. Provided with cameras by a program called Photo voice, Hmong girls who live near the tourist destination of Sa Pa, Vietnam, documented their lives in word and image for the book. In this way, we see girls and young women who are engaged in the traditional domestic work of childrearing, cloth dying, and embroidery.

Yet we also glimpse a new economy where girls are integral to the financial well- being of their families, much as other nationalistic Vietnamese texts extol the importance of Viet women to the national economy. One girl writes of the traditional gender roles in Hmong families that "each daughter in-law in a family owns a barrel of indigo, because daughters in-law have to dye and make clothes for their husbands' parents and brothers.... No boys know how to make indigo and hemp. That is the job of mothers and daughters." Thus the cloth-making work is neatly relegated to women in conventional ways and women provide domestic labor for their husband's families upon marriage.

The meanings and value of this traditional work have also been transformed. Another twelve-year-old claims important and lucrative public work for women as well: "first I came to town with my mother, and she taught me how to sell Hmong handicrafts," she writes. "I like selling. If I stayed at home, we wouldn't have any money and food to eat. Now I am the only one who goes selling in the family and I give my parents all the money I make." Thus working with the tourists in the village excuses girls from domestic chores and gives them a powerful place in the family structure.

Another girl writes that she would like to go to school so that she "will be able to go working in a hotel" and thus make a bigger financial contribution to her family."' Yet another ten-year-old proclaims she would like to have three girls and two boys when she has children; "I like having girls more," she explains, "because girls can work and earn money to help parents. Boys are very shy, they only stay at home." Here she inverts traditional Western and Hmong stereotypes of boys' assumed worth and earning potential versus girls' homebound status.

Though these Hmong girls live within the national borders of Vietnam, they do, of course, have a vexed relationship to Vietnamese national identity and ideology. And so the more individualistic and even rebellious claims made in this book could be seen as part of a distinctive ethnic tradition as well as evidence of an emerging national economy. A sixteen-year-old married girl writes that even though her husband's family is well-off, she still wants to "work to save some money, so that she can buy whatever she wants."

This audacious claim also resonates with notions of Western individualism. However, this project was endowed by the Toyota Foundation and supported by the ethnology museum, which is funded by the French government. One could argue that this artifact of tourism is designed to appeal to Westerners eager for depictions of outspoken and independent girls. Indeed, there is an interesting confluence between the representations of Hmong women's work in the Vietnam Women's Museum, the book on young Hmong women, and understandings of Hmong women's work in the United States, for all focus on traditional handiworks, women's increasingly enterprising roles in Hmong culture, and the economics of ethnic arts. As Conquergood insightfully observes, "Perhaps more than any other feature of Hmong culture, the textile artworks have been accessible and attractive" to Westerners and Americans in particular; apparently, they showcase both women's "private" domestic work and their entrepreneurial spirits.

Because cultural identity is the defining feature of Hmongness, rather than geographic or national association, and because "kinship ties define culture and priorities," traditional women's gender roles in the Hmong American community are freighted with extraordinary importance. For women (and men) to resist Hmong kinship roles and the "oppressions" they entail is for this migratory Hmong culture to disappear. However, one might also argue that the emergence of Hmong American womanhood is not only the result of Western feminism's unmooring of traditional Hmong womanhood but also is a new and innovative extension of adaptive and yet persistent Hmong traditions.

As NaIy Yang writes in her poem, "Spirit Trails,""My pltg will always wander, / though many may try to tie it down. I... I And the shaman's cloth, / made to bind, / falls not upon my legacy." Yang rewrites traditional belief systems that argue for the bound nature of the female soul, much as Cao rewrites the Trung sisters into modern warriors. Nancy Donnelly agrees that Hmong culture may not be as aggressively gender-divided as traditional readings would suggest, writing that "the seeds of gender equality are present in Hmong folk tales and in the concept that both men and women need each other to achieve maturity"-a version of the "separate but equal" philosophy evident in Vietnamese texts.

Recent Hmong immigrants to the United States are not as sanguine about life in Southeast Asia as the girls in Through H'Mong Eyes, nor as optimistic about the plight of Hmong American women. Many of the women whose stories Sucheng Chan transcribes in her collection of oral narratives, Hmong Means Free: Life in Laos and America, are empowered, the book suggests, by age and distance to tell much darker stories of Hmong life on both continents. The unique features of new Hmong American written narratives also shape their content.

As Mai Neng Moua, editor of Bamboo among the Oaks: Contemporary Writing by Hmong Americans, the first landmark anthology of Hmong American writing in the United States, contends, Hmong texts are "emerging" forms that bridge the oral and material traditions of Hmong culture and the imperatives of Western literacy. Moua explains that in traditional Hmong culture there "was no separation between what was art and what was culture," so that daily activities such as storytelling, cloth-making, metal-working, and even the construction of traditional homes all communicated emotions in ways that extended beyond "plain language." Thus transcriptions of oral narratives and the material cultures they seek to convey are central to this new Hmong American literature.

In Bamboo among the Oaks, we find a number of Hmong American women writers who are quite critical of gender relations in the ethnic community, both in Southeast Asia and in America. In "A Good Hmong Woman," True Hang transcribes the abuses suffered by her mother in Southeast Asia at the hands of her sadistic in-laws. Indeed, according to Hmong custom, "marrying is called 'becoming a daughter-in-law' (ua nyab)" and young Hmong brides entered the homes of their husband's family with few rights. Like Cao's mother, Thanh, Hang's mother recounts feeling like an exile in her new home. Hang's mother-in-law berates her, refuses to eat the food she prepares, ignores her, and even encourages the son and husband to beat and kill his young wife. Hang thinks "I am their daughter-in- law. They married me, and I came to live with them. Why don't they know how to use my strength?"

Notice the use of pronouns here: the girl has not married just her husband but his whole family, "they," connoting a communal subjectivity opposed to notions of individualism. As well, she understands that her "strength" is of most value to the family, though in this case they see it as a threat rather than a valuable commodity and it elicits their abuse. These abusive practices are carried to America. For example, in the poem "broken," by Pa Xiong, the author depicts crippling domestic abuse:

I watched him hurt her verbalizing and emotionalizing scars into her childhood and her womanhood... I watched her receive three years of his fists three years of blue and purple around her neck and in her heart I watched.

Xiong's reference to the "purple heart" could also be a subtle nod to militaristic modes of understanding domestic life; it is the women who deserve recognition for their sacrificial service in family battles. However, what Westerners call domestic abuse is a recurrent theme in writing by Hmong American women, as well is in interview transcripts-the dominant mode of communication for illiterate first-generation women. Indeed, in the introduction to her collection of interviews with Hmong women, Chan speaks to the difficulty of accounting openly for Hmong women's experiences in the United States.

Her cadre of Hmong students assigned to carry out interview projects with family members found they could get more candid responses when they left women tape recorders, because the men who attended the interviews would often interrupt the women, and the women felt inhibited from speaking freely about painful topics.

Donnelly posits that domestic violence and divorce rates escalated in Hmong American households after settlement in the United States because men felt they were losing their basis of command in the household-thus spousal domestic abuse was exacerbated rather than ameliorated by immigration to this "freer" society.

A popular joke among both men and women claims, '"When we get on the plane to go back to Laos, the first thing we will do is beat up the women!'" Donnelly explains that this joke registers Hmong men's frustrating unemployability, "the sudden economic value placed on women's work and the men's fear of losing power in their families. The state could circumscribe the authority of a man even within his own household, for instance by forbidding him to beat his wife." Physical violence against women often accompanies extreme cultural transformations.

A Western feminist might be tempted to read this confessional literature as the product of a more open society and Western feminism's influence on Hmong worldviews. As Chan observes, echoing the views of many other scholars, "Given the greater freedom as well as greater protection that women in the United States enjoy, it is not surprising that several available studies indicate Hmong women are adjusting more eagerly than Hmong men to life in America."

One cannot deny that such claims are true in many respects. Young Hmong women of the first-and-a-half or "Rising Sun" generation are beginning to postpone marriage and childbearing beyond their teen years, to attain higher education, and even to live outside the family home. And protecting women from physical assault is clearly a priority. But this focus on "liberation" in the United States, the assertions that women like it better here than at home, is a bit troubling, for it does not acknowledge what has been lost in the transition, nor the fact that life had been chaotic in war-torn Southeast Asia for years before immigration to the United States, making the immigration route and cultural transition more complicated and even violent than it might have been otherwise.

For example, in "Vue Yang's Life Story as told to her daughter," Maijue Xiong, transcribed in Chan's edition, 48-year-old Vang says:

I feel that there are good and bad things about America. The good part is we don't have to sweat over a piece of land to produce food for every meal. The bad part is, even though I am told that the United States is a land of freedom, I feel no freedom at all. Freedom, to me, is being able to farm our own land, raise our cattle, and own our own homes without obligation to anyone.

Vang does not accept capitalistic notions of "freedom," though she does long for communal ownership of land-or more properly, proprietorship-and a sense of self-sufficiency that resonates with American notions of rugged individualism. But not any land will do; she misses her family in Laos desperately and expresses a corporeal connection to the homeland: "Day after day, I long to return to my country. My heart is not here in America" she claims.

Mayli Vang, in her poem entitled "We Women of the Hmong Culture," writes

We women of the Hmong culture may now clean the plates of what the men have left... They call this a privilege, to be seated at the table of those who were seated before.... Yet some she-witched women "possessed by this newfound knowledge of excessive freedom" are weary of participating in such patriarchal rituals of the old motherland.

While Hmong girls in Vietnam write confidently of new gendered economic roles, Hmong American girls are witness to Old World oppressions. However, notice in this passage that freedom is "excessive"-not a word with positive connotations; the fact that the women are "she-witched" and "possessed" by the new knowledge suggests that there is something magical and perhaps even evil to some about women who now resist their native culture almost against their own wills. While the mealtime rituals are "patriarchal," the native land is the "mother," connoting a tension between Southeast Asian maternalism and Western feminism that Hmong American women must negotiate.

Interestingly, "motherhood" does not seem to be fetishized in Hmong culture to the same extent that it is in Vietnamese lore or Western cultures. Miyares claims that while "the family is elastic in character,""clan membership is permanent," and the clan's structures and hierarchies supersede those of the nuclear family. Thus while Hmong women's value in the traditional economy was based on their fecundity and their labor potential, the extended family is much more important than the nuclear family in organizing domestic relation.

Bibliography

Adburgham, Alison. *Women in Print. Writing Women and Women's Magazines from Restoration to the Accession of Victoria.* London: Allen & Unwin, 1972.

Arnold, Ethel M. *Literature for Ladies, 1830-1930.* Manhattan: K.S.A.C. Press, 1930.

Barrell, Joan. *The Business of Women's Magazines.* 2nd ed. London: Kogan Page, 1988.

Beetham, Margaret. *Victorian Women's Magazines : An Anthology.* Manchester: Manchester University Press, 2001.

Boston Women's Health Book Collective. *Our Bodies Ourselves.* New York: Simon & Schuster, 1976.

Braithwaite, Brian. *The Business of Women's Magazines: The Agonies and the Ecstasies.* London: Associated Business Press, 1979.

Braithwaite, Brian. *Women's Magazines: The First 300 Years.* London: Peter Owen, 1995.

Brody, Michal, ed. *Are We There Yet? A Continuing History of Lavender Woman.* Iowa City; Aunt Lute Company, 1985.

Burman, Barbara, ed. *The Culture of Sewing: Gender, Consumption and Homedressmaking (Dress, Body, Culture).* Oxford: Berg, 1999.

Coakley, Mary Lewis. *1907-Sex, Sisterhood, and Self-Delusion: What Happened to Women's Magazines?* New Rochelle: Arlington House, c. 1979.

Dancyger, Irene. *A World of Women. An Illustrated History of Women's Magazines.* Dublin: Gill and Macmillian, 1978.

Danky, James P., ed. *Women's Periodicals and Newspapers from the 18th Century to 1981: A Union List of the Holdings of Madison, Wisconsin Libraries.* Boston: GK Hall, 1982.

Doughan, David, and Denise Sanchez. *Feminist Periodicals, 1855-1984: An Annotated Critical Bibliography of British, Irish, Commonwealth and International Titles.* Brighton: Harvester, 1987.

Eskridge, Melissa J. *How the Psychology of Women Is Presented in Women's Magazines,* 1986.

Ferguson, Marjorie. *Forever Feminine: Women's Magazines and the Cult of Femininity.* London: Heinemann, 1983.

Friedan, Betty. *The Feminine Mystique.* New York: Dell Publishing Co., Inc., 1963.

Gough-Yates, Ann. *Understanding Women's Magazines: Publishing, Markets and Readership.* London: Routledge, 2003.

Grimstad, Kirsten and Susan Rennie, eds. *The New Woman's Survival Catalog.* New York: Berkley Publishing Corporation, 1973.

Hermes, Joke. *Reading Women's Magazines: An Analysis of Everyday Media Use.* Cambridge: Polity Press, 1995.

Hoffmann, Phyllis P. *Women's Magazines.* 1983.

Incantalupo, Patricia. *The Portrayal of Women in Sport Advertising in Two Women's Fitness Magazines,* 1992.

Johnson, Judy M, ed. *Spot Illustrations from Women's Magazines of the Teens and Twenties: 828 Cuts of Women, Family, Home, Garden, Etc.* New York: Dover Publications, 1989.

Mann, Robert S. "Women and the Newspaper." *The University of Missouri Bulletin,* no. 2640.

Millum, Trevor. *Images of Woman: Advertising in Women's Magazines.* London: Chatto & Windus, 1975.

Ramet, Adèle. *Creating a Twist in the Tale: How to Write Winning Short Stories for Women's Magazines.* Plymouth: How To Books, 1996.

Shevelow, Kathryn. *Women and Print Culture: The Construction of Femininity in the Early Periodical.* London: Routledge, 1989.

Sievers, Sharon L. *Flowers in Salt: The Beginnings of Feminist Consciousness in Modern Japan.* Stanford: Stanford University Press, 1983.

Waller, Jane, and Michael Vaughan-Rees. *Women in Wartime; the Role of Women's Magazines 1939-1945.* London: Macdonald Optima, 1987.

White, Cynthia L. "Growth between the Wars: 1920-1938." In *Women's Magazines 1693-1968.* London: Michael Joseph Ltd, 1970.

White, Cynthia L. *Women's Magazines 1693-1968.* London: Michael Joseph Ltd, 1970.

Winship, Janice. *Advertising in Women's Magazines, 1956-74.* Birmingham: Centre for Contemporary Cultural Studies, University of Birmingham, 1980.

Winship, Janice. *Inside Women's Magazines.* New York: Pandora, 1987.

Yackey, Lena Millicent. *Contributions of Women's Magazines to Homemaking Problems on Food.* New York, 1930.

Index

A

American Eyes, 254.
American Influence, 118, 150.
American Interlude, 114.
Ayu Utami, 168, 170, 171, 173.

B

Blurring the Boundaries, 40.
Bold Touch, 41.
Broad Subject Categories, 48, 50.

C

Classical Literature, 111, 112, 186, 216, 239, 253.
Collaboration Patterns, 52.
Colonial Tradition, 147.
Colonialism, 60, 108, 139, 163, 193.
Contemporary Roles, 119, 263.
Cross-Border Dialogue, 89.

D

Disjunctions and Intersections, 64.
Domestic Structures, 155, 156.

E

Early Prose Fiction, 221.
Easily Maligned, 40.
Emergence of Women, 185.
Eroticism, 31, 35, 36, 37, 221, 225, 228.

F

Feminine Imagination, 82.
Feminist Agency, 57, 62, 89, 90, 91, 92, 114, 115, 116, 117.
Feminist Critique, 1, 14.
Filipino Women, 107, 118, 123, 124, 125, 126, 127, 128, 129, 132, 133, 134, 136.
Filipino Women in Art, 123.
Filipino Women Novelists, 107.

H

Hispanic Philippines, 118.

I

Ideological Themes, 130, 131, 132, 134.
Indonesian Women, 153, 175, 179, 180.

Influences and Interventions, 121.
Islamic Factions, 179.
Islamic Feminist Thinking, 177.
Islamic Leaders, 178, 180, 181.
Islamic Teachings, 162, 163, 164, 183.

J

Japanese Intervention, 115.

L

Language and Education, 109.
Language Use, 2, 8.
Liberal Interpretations, 180.

M

Malay Identity, 6, 13.
Malay Islamic Literature, 12, 14, 16.
Malay Literature, 1, 2, 4, 5, 6, 7, 8, 9, 10, 13, 14, 15, 16, 19, 20, 21, 22, 23, 24, 25, 26, 38, 44.
Marriage and Relationships, 120.
Martial Law Years, 115, 151.
Migrant Literature, 116, 117.
Modern Literature, 112, 195.
Modern Malay Literature, 1, 5, 7, 8, 9, 13, 15, 19, 20, 21, 22.
Modern-day Challenges, 116.
Moral Values, 134, 135.

P

Pengadilan Susila, 171, 174.
Political Correctness, 1, 2, 4, 5, 8, 9, 16, 17.
Politics and the Nation, 132.
Power and Silence, 100.
Pre-Colonial Times, 126, 133, 145.
Publications Generated, 46, 50, 52.

Q

Quiet Revolution, 179, 180.

R

Radical Novel Challenges, 38.
Recognition and Support, 116, 117.
Revolution against Spain, 113.

S

Scholarly Knowledge, 178.
Sexual Discourse, 1, 9, 16.
Sexuality and Relationships, 175.
Singaporean Women, 57, 60, 62, 68, 82, 90, 92, 100.
Spanish Colonization, 113.
Spirit-World, 134.
Status of Women, 167, 179, 212, 211, 245.
Strength of Mind, 178.

T

Thai Literature, 185, 189, 190, 194, 195, 215, 216, 217, 218.

The Contemporary Period, 151, 154, 197.

Through Vietnamese Eyes, 247.

Traditional Malay Letters, 25, 26, 27, 28, 32, 36.

Tribal clan Setting, 120.

U

Urban Setting, 119.

V

Vietnamese Women, 229, 232, 233, 234, 240, 244, 249, 250, 251, 252, 253, 254, 260, 262.

W

Western Literature, 24, 26, 31, 32, 193.

Women Novelists, 1, 107.

Women Reinterpret Progress, 70.

Women Rights, 164.

Writing as Negating, 173, 174.